Silent Sisters

Also by Jenny Tomlin

Behind Closed Doors

JENNY TOMLIN AND
KIM CHALLINOR

Silent Sisters

*The true story of two sisters who
shared a nightmare and survived*

HODDER

A CIP catalogue record for this title is available from the British Library

ISBN 978 0 340 89885 7
ISBN 0 340 89885 2

Typeset in Sabon by Hewer Text UK Ltd, Edinburgh
Printed and bound by Mackays of Chatham Ltd, Chatham, Kent

Hodder Headline's policy is to use papers that are natural, renewable
and recyclable products and made from wood grown in sustainable
forests. The logging and manufacturing processes are expected to
conform to the environmental regulations of the country of origin.

Hodder & Stoughton Ltd
A division of Hodder Headline
338 Euston Road
London NW1 3BH

This book is dedicated to
Martine and the Hungry Years! xxx

Acknowledgements

Jenny

It's not often I get the chance to express love and thanks publicly, and my first thoughts are of my amazing family.

Martine, you are so wise and have given me advice and help all the way. My love for you is for ever and always. You have been there from the start and are the only one who really understands it all. You are an amazing, beautiful person, and I would be lost without you. You truly are the wind beneath my wings!

LJ. My special boy. You are everything I could ever want from a son. I love you so very much and you bring me so much joy. If only others had your wonderful big heart.

Alan, you are the reason for everything. My heart and soul are with you for ever. We know what we have together, and no one will ever change that. I love you.

Jonathan. Well done.

Kim, you nutty, crazy friend and sister. We are as one! You can't get rid of me.

To the Battys, Carrine, Howard and especially little man Lewis, thank you for letting me share your lives in this book. To Graham and Daniel in Switzerland, thank you.

To Jaine Brent, my manager and friend. Well, what can I say? We're here again and I am so glad you're here to share it all with me. Let's continue the dream!

To John McCutcheon. Hope you are happy. We had some great years.

To all my wonderful and amazing friends, you all know who you are.

Antony, my friend and confidant, you are always at the end of the phone for me. I love you dearly. Please live for you!

Jackie, my old mucker, Sylvia in Torquay and all my new wonderful friends in France. Love you all, especially Sam and all at La Famille, and Wayne and Dawn, and Isabelle.

To all those that are watching over Martine whilst I start my new life in France, thank you. Love you Gorgeous George and Karaoke Kim! Rachel and Sara and Macky.

Mum, Carole and Laurence, wherever you are, I hope you are OK.

Pam, hope you and yours are all well.

To my wonderful publishing house for allowing

me to continue my story and to Caro Handley for helping me to put it all together. To Rhian and Laura and all the support staff who work behind the scenes.

To the lovely Bridie and family. You are a wonderful woman and we love you dearly. To Sandra and Yasmin, miss and love you, too. Good luck in all you do.

As always, thank you to all who have supported me in what I love doing. Writing!

Finally, Chris, I love you still, and Auntie, you are immortal and your love and kindness are the qualities I try to teach my own. You will stay with us for ever.

Kim

When Jenny and I sat on the window-sill in our bedroom at Monteagle Court, aged nine and seven, we wished for a better life or just a *chance* of a life.

We made it. It was a long hard struggle, lots of heartache and pain, but along the way we learned to laugh. We never gave in. Every time we got knocked down, we bounced back stronger and wiser.

Jenny, remember the saying you sent me? 'I'm smiling because you are my sister, I'm laughing because there's nothing you can do about it.' It's true but there is nothing I would want you to do, I'm proud to be your little sister.

This book was not achieved without the love, friendship and companionship of all those nearest and dearest to me and in particular Carrine, Daniel and Martine, and for this I thank you from the bottom of my heart.

My love for my other family members is just as strong. Howard, Alan and LJ, I love you dearly. And my love is unconditional for the two newest men in my life: my grandsons Michael, aged seven, and sweet innocent little Lewis Howard Batty, aged three. You both make Grandma so proud! My wonderful friends Chris, Paul, Yaz, Sophia and Leanne, who have been there for me when my relationships started, blossomed and then faded, thanks for everything, especially the shoulders.

Not forgetting the lovers in my life: Graham, Eddie, Stuart and Gary, without you life would have been a trifle boring and I might never have discovered my true friends.

Virgine – *Merci beaucoup*!

And finally I don't think I'd be here telling our story without the love, strength and courage of Auntie, an amazing, wonderful woman. I am privileged to have been influenced by you.

Contents

Introduction

Jenny

As I am writing this, I am pinching myself. Being able to tell the story of my childhood and to see it in print and then go to number one in the bestseller lists has all seemed a bit unreal.

When I wrote *Behind Closed Doors* a year ago I wanted to tell the story of a family suffering terrible abuse, and I focused on myself and my sister Kim and brother Laurence. The story ended when I was sixteen and Kim was fourteen. I have been overwhelmed and humbled at times, but thrilled also when asked what happened to us all next. Now I have been given the opportunity to continue with the story, and this time Kim is joining me as co-author. *Silent Sisters* carries on where I left off, and tells the tale of the two deprived and abused children Kim and I were, and how we grew, learned, loved, suffered both terrible knocks and wonderful moments and ultimately became the strong, independent women that we now are.

We've been painfully honest about both the good and the bad. I went from an abusive father to an abusive, violent partner, and for Kim it was terrible seeing what had happened to our mother, and to us as children, happening to me all over again. But through it all our solidarity as sisters never wavered, and we came through in the end and found real happiness.

Some of what happened to us makes harrowing reading. But it also shows the hope and survival of the human spirit, and that no matter how tough things are, it is possible not only to survive but to conquer!

I

Leaving the House of Horror

Jenny

He was in the room, touching me, grabbing my hair and forcing himself on me. I could smell his odour and could feel his rough hands grabbing me under the blanket. As he peered down at me, beads of sweat were all over his face and his mouth was soaked with spittle. Droplets fell on to my face and I grimaced. His hands moved from my groin to pin down my small shoulders and his heavy body fell on to mine.

My arms flailed out to try and stop him, but I had no chance against this man. He covered my mouth with his and his tongue forced my lips apart. I began to gag, but he ignored me, intent on pleasuring himself. He slowly moved one hand away and undid his trousers. His other hand moved to my neck and his grip tightened, I could hardly breathe. He looked down at me with a sickly grin on his face.

'Now you're really gonna git it, girlie, it'll hurt more if you don't relax.' I knew this was really it.

He had never managed to penetrate me with his penis before. Panic set in and I started to scream and try to force him off me. I began to punch and kick as hard as I could.

Suddenly, I felt warm soft breath on my neck. John held me tightly and whispered slowly, 'It's OK, Jen, he's not here. You've been dreaming again.' I started to cry and he pulled me close.

'It'll never go away, John, he'll always haunt my dreams.' John tightened his grip. He didn't know what to say.

As he rocked me gently in his arms, I thought of my little sister Kim. She was at home with our younger brother and sister, Chris and Carole, and they continued to experience the mental abuse that Dad dished out. I knew he would never touch Kim sexually again, but she was still there, trapped in the hellhole that was 3 Monteagle Court, the filthy, run-down maisonette in Hoxton where we'd grown up. I tried to get her out and away from Dad whenever I could. I would often go round there to pick her up, or she would come round to my place and stay the night. John and I never minded her tagging along; we both worried about her. Just fifteen, she was terribly thin, her face had erupted in sores, and she was deathly pale. Her appetite was non-existent and she would often sit and just stare into space, not speaking a word. Many an evening, we would just sit, listening to music, both of us silent. When I tried to talk to her the words just wouldn't come out. Neither of us could talk about the past, we were both so fragile from the experiences of our childhood.

It was still very early in the morning and I knew I would never get back to sleep. I got up and went to run a bath, hoping that the hot water would cleanse my body and mind of all thoughts of my father.

Throughout our lives we'd suffered at his hands. His cruelty, beating, humiliation and sexual abuse had been part of our daily lives as far back as we could remember.

Our older brother, Laurence, had left home to live with our beloved Auntie, and I'd followed soon after. Now Kim, Carole and Chris were left to fend off Dad's abuse. And Mum? We'd long ago learned that Mum wasn't going to help us. Terrified of Dad, cowed into submission, she got the worst beatings of all and turned a blind eye to what was happening to her children in order to survive.

The only respite we ever had was when we went to stay with Auntie – actually our great-aunt – the only person who ever showed us love and kindness. When Auntie died in 1972, soon after my sixteenth birthday, it had affected us all very deeply. For Kim, who'd been fourteen and had worshipped Auntie, coming to terms with her loss was taking a long time.

Then there was the court case which had come only a few months later. Dad had been arrested and taken to court for sexually abusing Carole, who was just nine at the time. Kim was the one who'd caught him and reported him, and she and I were both due to testify against him. We waited months for our chance to tell the world what a monster he was. Then at the last minute the case fell apart and Dad walked out, a smug grin on his face, free to carry on abusing, tormenting and battering his family.

I could still see Kim's little face, tearful with disbelief as we walked away from the court, neither of us quite able to fathom what had happened. An acquittal was the last thing we expected and it had hit Kim harder than the rest of us. In the months that Dad had been remanded in custody, things had changed at home. Kim had cleaned and scrubbed away the filth of years, and for the first time there seemed to be a chance of some happiness. Even Mum had cheered up and found herself a new boyfriend. But Dad's release had put paid to all that.

The bath was growing cold. I wrapped myself in a dressing-gown and went through to the kitchen, where John was making coffee. He looked up and smiled. 'Hi beautiful, feel better?' I walked over to put my arms around him and as my face snuggled into his neck I could smell his warm skin and a hint of aftershave and I felt so safe.

John Falconer was six years older than me and was a trainee structural engineer. We'd been together for over two years and he'd been there for me no matter what. He had been my first and only boyfriend, and his patience and sensitivity had helped me to survive the nightmare of Dad's abuse – although he was unaware of the extent of it. As a young girl I'd been afraid that sex would always seem dirty and frightening, but with John I learned that making love with someone special could be very different.

John was kind, loving and dependable – everything I had ever wanted – yet at the same time there was a feeling of emptiness inside me that I couldn't tell him about. I couldn't understand it myself, and despite loving him so much, this feeling kept creeping back. It was a feeling that told me to run away, to go somewhere different and to escape. I couldn't explain it, not to myself and certainly not to John. I said nothing, smiled and kissed him as I went to get ready for work.

I had always worked and I was proud of myself. I'd left school at fifteen and got a job in Marks and Spencer's, along with one of my best friends from school, Sherri. We'd been so pleased with ourselves, in our smart blue uniforms with our silver till key chains and our photo passes dangling from them. Before Auntie became ill she had taken to popping into the store where I worked just to watch me. But after a few months I'd wanted to move on to something more challenging, and after spells in a couple of other jobs I'd landed on my feet as an assistant consultant in a well-known employment agency. My boss, Sue, had met me when I worked as a temp for another agency and when she got the job as manageress at Alfred Marks she'd taken me with her. I'd been determined to prove her faith in me was justified. I worked hard and found I was good at dealing with customers. The agency was in the Strand, in the West End of London, and it gave me a buzz every time I walked from the bus stop to work past all the glamorous theatres and restaurants.

I had a long journey to work each day, but I didn't mind. I'd been lucky to find a good flat with two lovely flatmates from Torquay called Jenny and Sylvia. Jenny was the quiet one, but Sylvia was outgoing and bubbly. She loved John and the three of us had a great relationship. Both the girls were excited to be in London. We spent lots of time together, shopping or going out for drinks, and we often talked about our childhood, though I never said very much. Their upbringing sounded so wonderful, the last thing I wanted was to tell them the truth about mine, so I just pretended that it wasn't great, but not terrible either. We were three young girls out to have a good time and enjoy life, and I kept my demons to myself.

Our flat was in Grantbridge Street, tucked behind Camden Passage market in Islington. It was in a row of renovated Victorian houses, a good place to live and very trendy. The antiques market on a Saturday always attracted the crowds, and people would cram into the local pub, the Camden Head. I worked several evenings a week behind the bar there and when I introduced Sylvia to the landlord he took her on too. We were both blonde and buxom and he was only too pleased.

It suited me to work evenings, as John was busy studying for his qualifications and it gave me a social life and the opportunity to earn extra money.

One night Sherri turned up in the pub. She wanted to talk to me and I managed to slip away early. We went back to the flat, where Sherri told me she had split from her long-term boyfriend, Patrick, and was thinking of leaving London and looking for adventure somewhere else. She told me about job opportunities in holiday camps, and by the end of the conversation I was ready to go with her. It seemed like the escape I was looking for. There was just one problem: John.

That night I lay in bed thinking about all that Sherri had said. I don't believe I really knew what I wanted or needed. I just felt this terrible urge inside to be free and to run away from everything. I truly believed that if I ran, I could leave it all behind me. In a new place no one would ever know the truth about me or my family. By the time morning came, the idea had become a drug, and I just had to keep taking it.

I went to work as usual, and sat on the tube contemplating what my next steps would be. It was 1974, the time of the three-day week – when government and union disputes led to the rationing of fuel and electricity – and we had candles scattered around the office. The Strand was strewn with rubbish and it seemed as if London had virtually come to a halt. The IRA was launching major attacks on the city. It was a scary time, but life was too exciting for me to worry very much.

I loved my job and it was going to be hard to leave. I spoke to Sue and she was her usual sweet self. She accepted my resignation and said I could go at the end of the week. In the meantime Sherri had sent off our application forms to Butlins and they'd replied to say jobs were waiting for us at their Barry Island camp in South Wales. Within a few days a new girl had been found to take my place in the flat, and I had even been round to speak to Kim and explain where I was going and why. I felt bad leaving her and the little ones. Thankfully, Kim had met a boyfriend, Graham, who seemed like a good person, and she was beginning to spend a lot of time at his place. Laurence would keep an eye on her too. As for Carole and Chris, who were now ten and nine, there wasn't a lot any of us older ones could do for them. Hard as it was to accept, they were stuck with Mum and Dad, just as we had been, until they were old enough to leave.

Sherri and I were due to go in a week and I still hadn't told John. I knew I had to face it. That evening I was trimming his long hair for him, as he sat at the kitchen table. I stood behind him with the scissors, took a deep breath and told him of my plans. I tried to explain that although I loved him I needed to have this adventure. But John couldn't understand why I wanted to go. He was angry and hurt, and my heart ached for him. I loved him, and had no intention of hurting him, but I knew I had to leave and break away.

The next week was terrible. John followed me everywhere, and would turn up at my workplace and at the flat, begging me to change my mind. He spoke to Kim and my flatmates, trying to get to grips with what was happening, but no one could help him.

I hated myself. I barely slept and I lost a lot of weight. I questioned myself the whole time. But I was young and selfish, and the world was mine for the taking. And deep inside I truly believed that no matter what I did, John would be there when I returned.

When the day came for us to leave, Sherri and I got on the train at Paddington, clutching a suitcase each and feeling petrified. For most of the journey to Wales I stared out of the window, watching with a mounting sense of excitement as we passed green fields, woodlands and small towns.

I wondered what Auntie would have thought. Would she have been proud that her Jinnybelle was off to explore the world? She'd certainly have made me promise to clean behind my ears, say my prayers and write every week. I smiled as I thought of her small, bustling figure, red hair piled up in a dough-nut on her head, fussing over her three treasures, as she called Laurence, me and Kim. She was our mother's aunt and, without children of her own, had doted on Mum and then on us. Our visits to her clean, warm, welcoming little flat had provided our only escape from the horrors of life at Monteagle Court. How I wished she was still around, with her loving, sound advice. Was I doing the right thing? Would I regret leaving John? Or was this going to be the adventure of a lifetime?

Kim

When Jenny left home and moved into the flat I was pleased for her. She deserved it, and I was glad she'd found such a nice place to live and a good job too. But being left behind at Monteagle Court was very hard. Life there had been even worse – if that were possible – since the court case.

Whilst Dad had been in prison things had begun to look up. I had scrubbed the house, got food in and cleaned up the two little ones. Mum had befriended an Irish couple, Jimmy and Mary. Mary was severely disabled, and one day Mum came home and announced that she had a job as her cleaner and home help. This was the woman who had never once cleaned our house in all the years we'd been there – I doubted she even knew the meaning of the term 'elbow grease'.

She took me to meet Jimmy and Mary at their home, which was on a council estate in Dalston. The house was very clean and tidy, with nice little ornaments and photos dotted around – very different from our neglected flat with its tobacco-stained walls and dirt everywhere. I remember this overweight lady who had several fingers missing and who wore her wedding ring around her neck. She couldn't walk and sat propped up on cushions and pillows in an armchair that had seen better days. Many of her teeth were missing and her Irish accent was so heavy that I found it difficult to understand her. Jimmy was a large man with a huge bulbous nose and tiny red protruding veins all over his face. Mum's background was also Irish, and she, Jimmy and Mary talked a lot about Ireland.

Mum had endured so many years trapped in our house and terrified of Dad that I was pleased she'd made friends. After some weeks, though, I began to suspect there was more to the friendship. Jimmy would turn up at our house and give Mum money, and if he saw me he'd say, 'Give your uncle Jimmy a kiss hello' and he'd reward me with two pounds. I would sometimes walk into a room and see him and Mum part from each other quickly, as though they'd been kissing, and I heard them talk of going to Ireland together.

Although Jimmy wasn't a good-looking or a clever man, I thought he and Mum were well suited. I half hoped he would take us away from everything and leave Dad behind to rot in jail where he belonged. But unbeknown to me Mum had continued to visit Dad in prison. She had told him of her new 'rich' friend, and they had made plans to swindle as much money out of him as they could.

Dad must have known that Mum was sleeping with Jimmy for the money, but that wouldn't have bothered him. When we were kids, men had often come round and disappeared into the bedroom for a 'chat' with Mum. It was a long time before we understood that she was prostituting herself for money. I'd like to have believed this was to put food on our table, but sadly it was primarily to pay for Dad in his addiction to cigarettes and expensive treats.

One day Jimmy arrived at our flat to tell us that Mary had died. He didn't appear sad or distraught; I think he saw his way open to a new relationship with Mum. He was a good man trying to help a family out of a bad situation, and I know Mum enjoyed the attention he gave her. But Dad's hold over Mum was to prove their downfall.

In the weeks leading up to the court case – which I knew nothing about – I had been sent away to Bognor on a council-run holiday for underprivileged kids. The bus we travelled in was packed with children of different ages and being fourteen, I was one of the oldest; the only common denominator was poverty. The smaller children cried and didn't even have hankies or tissues; they just wiped their tears on to their sleeves. I tried to cheer them up by playing 'I Spy' and singing silly songs that Auntie had taught me.

We were told there would be funfairs at Bognor, as well as a swimming-pool and games. We certainly had fun, and not just in the camp. We were all given pocket money and allowed to explore the Bognor sea front but we had to be back by the curfew time of eight each evening.

At the end of each week the holiday camp held a teenage disco which was also open to local families. At the first disco I was asked to dance by a ginger-haired lad of about the same age as me. I kept saying no, but he persisted and eventually I agreed. His nickname was Carrots and over the next few days we became friends. I was flattered that he gave me lots of attention and grateful that he knew nothing about my family. It made me feel so good to know that with him I could be anybody I wanted and make up the family he would never meet.

When the others I had arrived with went back to London I was kept at the camp. I was there for three weeks in the end. It was only later that I understood they were keeping me there until the day of the court case. With no warning, I was woken early one morning by one of the carers, who said I was returning home. I threw everything into my holdall and ran round saying my goodbyes. On the journey back to London I was told we were going to the courts. I wasn't aware of it, but one of my escorts that day was a woman police officer who attempted to talk me through the procedure and explain what was expected of me. Her words were lost on me, because as soon as I realised where I was going and that I was going to see my father I went into my own little world. I could hear her talking, but I couldn't absorb her words at all.

My thoughts were with Auntie. She always gave sound advice and I missed her so much. I would have given anything to have her sitting with me holding my hand. I prayed to her, asking her to help me if she could. As we neared London I felt my heart begin to beat faster. My palms were sweaty and I stared out of the car window. This was it. Once I had believed that I had caused all this trouble and that the guilt was mine. Now my chance was coming to tell everyone what my father really was and that the guilt really belonged to him and him alone. I was certain they would believe me, because it was true. My mind was going over and over the day, several months earlier, when I had confronted a nightmare.

I had been off somewhere with my friend Stacey and we'd decided to go out that evening, so I nipped back home to get changed. The flat was silent, and at first I thought no one was in. I took the stairs two at a time and as I reached the top step Carole appeared from the doorway of Dad's darkened room. He was behind her, tucking his shirt into his trousers, his hair all messed up. I froze as I took in the sight before me. Were my worst fears now confirmed? After all, I had once been his victim, it used to be me coming out of the room with him. I'd been so glad when I grew old enough to stop him. But suddenly the realisation hit me: he hadn't stopped abusing, he had simply changed his victim.

The sight of Carole brought the memories flooding back, along with the fear and pain that I had once felt. My anger was not only for Carole, it was for all the times Jenny or I had walked out of that room sad, scared, hurt and alone.

I felt so guilty that Carole was going through the same nightmare Jenny and I had suffered, and that I hadn't seen this coming and had left her alone with him. Why hadn't I realised he would pick on her next? How stupid I had been.

I screamed at the top of my voice, demanding to know what he'd been doing. He attempted to say 'nothing' and Carole began crying. I screamed at her to tell me what he'd done. She couldn't look at me; even at her young age was she feeling the shame that he'd inflicted on all of us? She bowed her head and continued to cry.

I remember being in such a rage, spittle was coming out of my mouth and veins must have been near to bursting in my neck. I screamed at the top of my voice through tears of fury, 'I'll get you for this, you fucking cunt, you're not going to hurt anyone again, ever.' I never swore like that, I hated it with a passion, but on that occasion nothing less could have expressed the horror I felt.

Now in the car the policewoman was still talking to me about what would happen, and suddenly I looked down and realised I was still wearing the trousers the other kids had written and drawn all over when we left the camp. It was a tradition that when you left everyone wrote their numbers and addresses on your trousers so that you could keep in touch. Auntie had been a stickler for neatness and would never have let me go to court looking so scruffy. I began to feel ashamed of how I looked and told the policewoman, but she said it didn't matter what I looked like so long as I told the truth, which of course I intended to do.

I had already told the truth over and over again.

After I had confronted Dad about Carole, I ran from the house and kept running. I remember getting breathless and collapsing on a grass verge by some flats, feeling sick, angry, ashamed and guilty. I sat there for a while and thought about what I needed to do to make it stop once and for all. With Auntie gone and no one else to turn to, I came to the conclusion that the police were my only option. I went back to Stacey's, told her briefly what had happened and asked if she would come to phone the police with me. We walked to the end of the road where there was a phone box and called the local police station. I blurted out my story and started to cry, while the person on the other end kept telling me to calm down. Then I was put through to someone else who asked where I was and said they were sending a car for me.

Two hours later they had Dad in custody, Carole in the next room and Mum creating merry hell at the front counter demanding to see her beloved husband. Carole and I were taken to see a doctor and examined. They could find no evidence of sexual abuse on me. Dad had stopped abusing me a year or two earlier, when I was twelve, and despite forcing me to take part in oral sex and molesting me time after time, he had never had penetrative sex with me. It had been the same with Jenny. I just prayed that a similar fate, or worse, had not now befallen Carole.

The car pulled into an underground car park. We'd arrived. When we got upstairs I saw Jenny and John waiting for me. Jenny held out her arms to me and John hugged both of us.

Laurence was there and so was Mum, who was chatting to some woman. She looked old and haggard, much older than she'd seemed three weeks earlier. She saw me and came over. There was no welcome hug from her, she just said coldly, 'Hopefully by tonight yer father will be back home, so stop pissing about and get it over with.'

Could this really be our mother? Jenny and I had sometimes hoped we had been mixed up at birth and given to the wrong parents, or adopted, and that our real parents would one day come to claim us and take us home. After all, if we were this woman's children surely she'd at least try to protect us from our abuser. Instead she was looking forward to welcoming him home.

Jimmy was there too, sitting on a bench, with Carole beside him swinging her legs. Did he really still think Mum would go off with him? Or had he accepted that he was just a stop-gap and some extra cash for her?

I heard my name being called, and the police-woman who had escorted me from Bognor held my hand and led me into the courtroom. Dad was sitting in the dock and he gave me one of his sickly grins. The judge and some of the others had silly wigs and it all felt a bit like a dream.

A man asked me to say my name and I replied 'Kim Ponting.' 'Is that your full name?' he replied, and I said, 'Kimberley Denise Ponting.' I was whispering. I had never liked being called Kimberley, Dad always used it when he was in a bad mood, although because of his speech impediment – he was born tongue-tied and couldn't speak clearly – it sounded more like Timberley when he said it.

The mere thought of him calling me Timberley conjured up the memories yet again. On weekends he would bellow from his bed, 'Jeanette, Timberley, come in here and see me now.' We would glance at each other and walk with bowed heads into what felt like the lion's den – the darkened room where the curtains were permanently drawn, forbidding the sunlight, and which stank of dirty linen, sweat and semen. He would summon us to sit on his knees and we'd have to sing 'King of the Castle'. When we got to the last line, 'We all fall down', he would open his legs so that we fell on to his groin area, which clearly turned him on. Or he would lie naked in bed with me and Jenny either side and ask us to lick his erect penis. 'Lick it like an ice cream that's melting. Go on, it tastes nice,' he'd say. I can still remember the smell and the time when, as I went to do as I was told, I retched and then ran from the room saying, 'I don't like it, it don't taste like ice cream.'

After I'd given my name nothing seemed to happen. I stood and watched as suited men sitting behind large wooden tables covered in files peered at me over their glasses and whispered to one another while shuffling through their papers.

Then one of them got up and walked towards me. He smiled. 'Hello, Kimberley, can you tell us what games you and Carole like to play?'

'Balls,' I replied. With that there was a great deal of talking, and eventually the judge banged a hammer on the table and called two of the men to see him. They spoke for a while and then the same man came back and said I could go. I tried to say, 'Don't you want to know what he did to us? You haven't asked me what he did to us,' but he wasn't listening, and I began to cry.

As I was led out of the court I saw Dad grinning and shouted at him, 'Tell them what you did, tell them how you hurt us.' I was taken back to where Laurence, Jenny and John were waiting, and I told them what had been said. John smiled and hugged me. 'Maybe you should have said "Two balls up the wall"' he said. It was only much later that I realised they must have thought I was swearing at them.

I sobbed. I wanted to tell them everything. That's why I thought we were there. But no one wanted to listen to us. After a long wait a woman came and spoke to Mum, who turned to us and said, 'Good news, yer father will be home tomorrow.'

It seemed the case had collapsed. They had decided that I was an unreliable witness as I hated Dad and could have made it all up. Carole was too young to testify, and Jenny's evidence was considered irrelevant as she had left home before the incident with Carole. And our mother was exempt from testifying against her husband. Once again the scales of justice weighed heavily against us.

I sobbed as I left the courtroom. I had wanted to tell them everything, I thought that was why we were there. I felt let down yet again. No one wanted to listen to us – as always they took the adults' versions over ours. I was so upset for Jenny and Carole too. We'd all suffered at his hands in the same way.

Jenny cried too when she heard what had happened. Laurence was white-faced and silent. I refused to go home with Mum, Jimmy and Carole, and the others took me to the pub with them. We sat silently round a table, too shocked, betrayed and angry to talk. What would we have to do to be heard?

We all knew that by the next evening Dad would be home, and with him the fear and misery. Chris and Carole would be beaten and abused and there was nothing we could do to help them. How could the authorities allow us to go back home, knowing that we were all at risk?

That night I stayed with John and Jenny. But the next day I had to go back to Monteagle Court. And I knew Dad wouldn't forget that it was me who put him away.

From the day he came home I did my utmost to stay out of the house. School was not an option. I was only fifteen, and I should have been there, but everyone knew about my family and the court case, and I wasn't about to be humiliated by people my own age. So I walked around the streets or went to friends' houses. I was lonely and unhappy and I missed Auntie more than I could say.

The flat soon became a filthy tip again; there was no way I could keep it clean once Dad was back. Jimmy continued to come round, and Dad simply acted as if he wasn't there. Mum and Jimmy would often canoodle in the kitchen, and after he left Dad would ask, 'How much did you get?' He didn't see anything wrong with selling his own wife.

I couldn't wait to get out. I remember hearing about the death of a young girl, run over and killed on Kingsland Road, and asking myself why God had taken her and left him here. Life just didn't seem fair.

As often as I could at weekends I went to stay with Jenny in her flat, or else with Laurence. He had got a good job as a trainee accountant, and his great friend Alf had found him a rented room in the house where he lived in Greenwood Road, Dalston.

Alf, who was older than Laurence, had been a lodger in our flat for a while, when we were kids. He'd fallen for Mum and had begged her to come away with him, but she wouldn't, of course. Alf had always been very kind to us kids, and when he moved on he'd kept in touch with Laurence, becoming a bit of a father figure to him and teaching him to play the guitar. Laurence had a little car he loved tinkering with – though he had yet to pass his test – and Alf would help him with it.

On Friday and Saturday evenings Laurence and Alf would go to a pub in nearby Newington Green called the Weaver's Arms, where a band called the Kingfishers often played. I was still only fifteen but I looked older, so they often took me along with them and there was always a buzz and an air of great fun. The band used to call people from the audience to sing or play with them and Alf was a regular on stage, always receiving rapturous applause.

In the Weaver's we got to know a group of six lads who were often there. I was a bit in awe of them, as they were a few years older than I was and they seemed so confident and easy together.

One evening one of them, Danny, went up on stage and sang three Buddy Holly songs. I knew the songs word for word because we'd played them at

Auntie's. Before she died, Laurence, Jenny and I had nursed her in her flat for weeks and we'd often passed the time by playing the handful of records we had, on her old 78rpm record-player. Auntie had loved Buddy Holly, along with Tom Jones, Elvis and Cliff Richard, who she called 'a nice clean boy'.

After Danny's Buddy Holly rendition the lads broke into Don McLean's 'American Pie' and we joined in. This was another from the family collection that I knew all the way through, and when the rest of them dried up suddenly all I could hear was my own voice, guiding them through the words. Afterwards I couldn't believe I'd done it, but it won me a few cheers and a couple of drinks, and from that night on I was accepted as one of the gang at the pub.

One of the lads, Graham, always made me feel special. He was quiet and serious, with a dry sense of humour and I thought he was lovely. He didn't know I was still only fifteen – he assumed I was eighteen – and I wasn't about to tell him the truth. This was a world away from Monteagle Court, I had earned respect and was treated like an adult and I wasn't about to throw all that away.

Graham had long curly hair and a moustache and he wore brightly coloured waistcoats – his everyday one was maroon and he was never seen without it. He and his friends did everything together, and soon Graham and I were treated by the others as an item, though we never did more than hold hands.

One Friday night, some months after we'd met, Graham and his flatmates were throwing a party after the pub closed. As everyone drifted home or off to bed at the end of the evening, Graham took my hand and led me gently into his bedroom, where we lay on top of the bed and cuddled. I hadn't felt so protected and loved since Auntie used to cuddle me when I was a small girl. We fell asleep, but later that night we woke and got under the covers and began to gently explore one another's bodies. I was very nervous but it felt right. The only sexual experience I'd had until now was the abuse, but with Graham it was so different. It didn't feel wrong or dirty. That night we made love for the first time and I felt I had become a woman.

By the time Jenny went off on her travels I was spending most weekends with Graham. He shared a house with three other lads and they all treated me like one of the gang. After the misery and awfulness of life at Monteagle Court, I loved every minute of the time I had with Graham and his friends. They were kind, funny, accepting and very, very normal. The horror I'd grown up with was beyond what any of them could have imagined, and I wanted to keep it that way.

I knew I would miss Jenny terribly. She was my best friend as well as my sister, and I hoped she wouldn't stay away too long. But I was growing up too, and making a life for myself, and I was determined it was going to be very different from the life I'd known before.

2

First Loves

Jenny

Sherri and I walked through the huge gates of the holiday park in Barry Island, lugging our suitcases with us. It was raining heavily, but the weather didn't dampen our spirits. This was the start of our adventure. On the journey to Wales, thoughts of John had still been uppermost in my mind. I had loved him so much, but once I'd made the decision to leave, there had been no going back. John had been my world, the man who had been there through everything with me, and I felt I had betrayed him. I felt guilty and I desperately wanted not to hurt him, but the urge to do what was right for me outweighed my remorse.

I had never really been given the opportunity to be myself. To go out into the world as an adult and try to survive. This was a huge step, and I needed to take it to become my own person.

When I look back now, I'm amused that Barry Island seemed so far removed from what I was used to. But it was. And once we got there I couldn't wait to see the place and start work.

At the employees' signing-in centre Sherri and I were told that we'd both be working as waitresses and that our first shift would begin at six the next morning. We were directed to the employees' quarters, which were far removed from the cheery holiday-makers' chalets we'd seen on our way in. While the chalets were basic but pleasant and comfortable, we were on the first floor of a rather run-down, ugly building. The rain continued to pour down, and by the time we got to our room we were both soaked to the skin. Inside there were two beds, an old wardrobe and a sink. The shared toilets were at the end of the balcony and the showers were a few blocks away.

By this time I was feeling rather unwell, so I dumped my suitcase on the floor and fell on to the bed. An hour or two later I had a raging temperature and it was clear that I was very ill. Sherri did her best to look after me, piling blankets from her own bed on top of mine and reassuring me that I'd soon be better. But I was shivering uncontrollably, and I knew I wouldn't make the six a.m. call to serve breakfast.

The next morning Sherri got up and made her way over to the restaurant, leaving me delirious with fever. I don't remember anything about the next three days. I slipped in and out of consciousness as Sherri came and went, hovering anxiously over me. Eventually she told the camp authorities and a doctor was called. By this time Sherri was panic-stricken; they had decided to terminate my contract unless I was well enough to start work the next day.

The doctor diagnosed pleurisy. He told me I must rest for several more days and that if I didn't I'd end up in hospital. Sherri and I were in despair. I had to pull myself out of this and get to work. The doctor had prescribed very strong antibiotics and I started the course immediately. Sherri set the clock throughout the night so that I wouldn't miss a dose. The next morning I woke free of fever but very weak. But there was no time to take it easy: I had to be at the restaurant at six a.m., or I would have to leave the camp.

We arrived a little ahead of time. I hadn't eaten for days, so I was tottering along on cotton wool legs, with Sherri practically propping me up. She had told me it was incredibly hard work, but I was still unprepared for what was expected of me. I was shown my allocated section of the restaurant where there were at least forty settings which had been laid by the night staff. I barely had time to get my bearings before the holiday-makers started to arrive.

As they ate their cereal I brought them tea and coffee, after which I had to clear the bowls and then serve each person a cooked breakfast. I had to carry these from the kitchen on a rack with six tiers, each one holding a metal tray with a breakfast on it. The metal rack was red-hot and I had only a small cloth to hold it with. I ran backwards and forwards, virtually throwing the egg and bacon on to the tables before racing back for the next lot. By the time I was half-way through, sweat was streaming down my face. Most of the campers were lovely and patient, thank goodness, as I fumbled and muddled my way through. But one or two were rude and aggressive, and by the time they'd finished shouting at me I was close to tears.

By ten my shift had finished and I was free for two hours before I had to be back to serve lunch. I walked slowly back to our small room and collapsed on the bed, exhausted.

Somehow I got through the next few days. We were given our meals, and though the food wasn't wonderful I was young and strong, and once I was eating again my health returned.

We worked a long day. Four hours for the breakfast shift, two for the lunch shift and then another four to serve teas. Trying to serve meals, while clearing dozens of others away was a bit like a scene from a Carry On film. We waitresses skidded across the floor, arms full of plates – either full or dirty – while holiday-makers beckoned us to get them food and drinks from one end of the dining hall and the kitchen staff urged us to get a move on from the other.

At the back of the dining hall were sections for the dirty crockery and cutlery. A poor young man would stand at each section and take the onslaught of the slops and dirty plates hurled in his direction by the waitresses. It was a disgusting job, but someone had to do it, and the lad in my section, Steve, was lovely. He managed to crack non-stop jokes and keep me laughing, despite the horrors of our job. I would rush down with the dirty dishes and Steve would be standing there in his not-so-white jacket and silly hat, food spattered all over him, and he'd flash me a smile and say, 'I'm dressed for dinner, babe.'

Our precious time off, what little of it there was, we spent with the other staff. We weren't allowed to mix with the campers, so it was a 'them and us' scenario. And of course we couldn't use the camp's facilities – the pool and the entertainment areas were out of bounds – so we hung around our rooms or went for walks outside the camp. Some of the campers were friendly and from time to time they offered to buy us drinks at the bars, but the rules were strict and reluctantly we had to decline.

Occasionally the management organised a social event for the staff, which was a welcome respite from our all work and no play routine. One day they announced a beauty pageant for female staff

members. We were told that we all had to take
part, whether we wanted to or not. I knew that,
with her stunning good looks, Sherri would win
hands down – and she did. I got into the final
twelve and was very pleased with myself, and I was
delighted for Sherri, who was crowned and pre-
sented with a large bouquet of flowers and a cheque
for 25 pounds. To us it was a small fortune.

The girl who'd come second – a supervisor at the
camp – was a nasty piece of work and we'd always
steered clear of her. She was not happy, and neither
were her disgruntled supporters. But we thought no
more of it until the next morning when we were
called in to the manager's office and told, out of the
blue and with no previous warning, that our work
was not good enough and we were both to be
dismissed. Sherri was stripped of her title and told
to give the money back. It came as no surprise that
the supervisor was given the title.

An hour later we'd packed our bags and were
outside the gates of the camp, where we stood
looking at one another and wondering what on
earth we'd do. We didn't want to go home yet, and
in any case we didn't have enough money.

During our time in the camp Sherri had become
friends with two lads who were working there,
Paul and Brian. They happened to be leaving at
the same time as us, and as we stood outside the
gates they appeared. They told us they were

moving on to find work elsewhere and invited us to join them.

We agreed to make our way south towards Devon and Cornwall. From the start Paul and Brian took charge. We had very little money, but they seemed to have plenty – it was only later that we realised they had none either and were just brilliant at conning their way along. We travelled by train, first class, stopping along the way to stay in really nice bed and breakfast hotels. Sherri and I had no idea how they paid, or that most of the time they didn't – we just enjoyed the trip. There was no romance between us, we were just platonic friends, but we enjoyed having company and travelling in style.

As Sherri and I enjoyed ourselves staying in beautiful bedrooms in smart hotels I often thought of Kim. These places, with their immaculate rooms and crisp clean beds, were such a long way from the dirt, smells and stained sheets of our childhood, and I wished she was with me to enjoy it.

We reached St Ives in Cornwall in late July. The weather was glorious and the place was heaving with tourists. There were few vacancies and we found ourselves staying in a rather dingy guesthouse. The owners were a rather miserable elderly couple who clearly didn't enjoy their work. The rooms were dark and drab, but we all agreed it would only be for one night and that the following morning we would move on. Sherri and I found it all rather exciting, and went to bed full of plans for our next destination.

The next morning we went down to breakfast expecting to meet Paul and Brian, but they hadn't surfaced yet. As we sat waiting to be served the owner appeared. He told us Paul and Brian had left earlier that morning, telling him that they had no money to pay and neither did we. We were to get our things and get out.

We went down to the town and sat on the harbour wall. We'd been abandoned by our friends, who'd clearly decided they'd had enough of travelling as a foursome; we'd had no breakfast; we had no money, and we weren't sure what to do next.

Lost and alone, thoughts of John and how safe I had been with him filled my head. How stupid I had been to leave him and all that was safe and loving behind me. I was starting to regret what I had done. Living the free spirit life and trusting others had left me hungry and scared.

Eventually we decided there was nothing for it but to find work, and we lugged our bags over to the local Jobcentre, where a young man interviewed us. He had two vacancies at a hotel in the next bay, he told us. One was for a kitchen helper, the other for a waitress. Both were live-in jobs.

The interviews were arranged for the next day, but we still had the problem of finding somewhere to stay that night. We had no money at all, and faced with the prospect of sleeping on the beach we decided to ask the young man for help. He was kind and understanding. He lent us money in return for a promissory note and we went off in search of a bed and breakfast guesthouse. After trudging round the town we found somewhere with a vacancy, dropped our bags there and set off to spend the small amount of money we had left on fish and chips. We hadn't eaten all day, and to this day Sherri and I agree that it was the best fish supper we ever ate.

In the morning, we decided to hitchhike to the next bay in time for our interviews. Being young we were happy to flutter our eyelashes at motorists and we had no trouble getting a ride. When we arrived we were interviewed by the couple who ran the hotel and given the jobs, starting straight away. I was to be the kitchen helper and Sherri the waitress. Mine was definitely the raw end of the deal. There were no dishwashers then and every pot and pan had to be scrubbed. And after spending half the day with my hands turning red and raw in hot water I had to go up and spend the other half making beds.

Also working at the hotel was a lovely girl called Debbie. We hit it off straight away. I'd never met a girl like Debbie; she was a bit of a hippy and had lots of friends who lived on a nearby caravan site.

She took me with her to visit them and I was fascinated by their free and easy lifestyle. After a couple of weeks Sherri decided she'd had enough and wanted to go home. She'd saved for her train fare back to London and asked me if I wanted to come with her. Tempted as I was, I decided to carry on, no matter what was thrown at me. I had Debbie to keep me company and I didn't feel ready to give up the adventure and go back.

Kim

Shortly before Jenny went away I began to feel a little odd, and then I missed a period. But it didn't dawn on me that something was up until I missed another and then another. I was so in love with Graham that I didn't want anything to spoil what we had, so I ignored what was happening until I finally had to admit to myself that pregnancy was a strong possibility.

I needed Jenny. But she was far away and, with no one else to turn to, I asked Mum to come with me to the doctor. Looking back it seems like a strange choice to make, but in the end, despite all her faults, she was still my mother and I was fifteen and scared and needed someone with me.

The GP confirmed my fears: I was five months pregnant. I felt happy and afraid at the same time. I wanted a baby and I loved Graham. But how would he feel about it? I waited until we met for the weekend, and on the Sunday afternoon I blurted out the truth about my age, my family and the pregnancy, all in one long sentence.

When I'd finished he looked shocked, then he cuddled me and said, 'I suppose we ought to go to Coventry and tell my family we're getting married.' He told me he had always wanted to marry me; we would just bring it forward. I wanted to throw my arms around him and kiss him, but that wasn't Graham's style, so I kept my emotions in check. He could see how happy I was. He made me feel safe, loved and protected, and I loved him more than ever.

A few days later Graham came to meet my parents and ask for their permission to marry me. I had just turned sixteen, so as long as they gave consent, we could go ahead.

I had already told him a bit about my family. Now, on the way there, I did my best to prepare him. He kept reassuring me that everything would be fine and I shouldn't worry, but of course I did. Despite my warnings he had no idea of the dirt and chaos in our flat, not to mention the unpredictable welcome. What if Dad refused permission for me to marry, or threw Graham out? It would be just like him to want to ruin my happiness.

Within five minutes of entering the flat, Graham had read the situation and he handled Mum and

Dad perfectly. He had Mum eating out of his hand, and Dad actually sat up from his usual slumped position and turned the TV down to listen to what Graham said. Graham was polite, but he didn't ask permission, he simply told them that he was marrying their daughter. For once in his life Dad tried to play the decent father, but his charade didn't wash with Graham, who knew he was a lazy, domineering bully who cared nothing for his children and who certainly wouldn't pay a penny towards the wedding.

By the time we left everything was agreed and the wedding date had been fixed. I was relieved that it was over. I'd been secretly afraid that after meeting my parents Graham might feel differently about me. But when we left he hugged me and it was clear that nothing had changed. The only comment he made was: 'It's not the sort of place I'd want my children to be brought up in.'

I had told him about the poverty and lack of love and affection in my childhood. He knew we often went hungry, and he knew that Dad regularly beat Mum and hit us kids too. But I had never mentioned the sexual abuse. How could I tell him? I was ashamed of what had happened to us. I couldn't even talk about it to Jenny, who'd been through it too. It was just too hard to put any of it into words. I kept it locked silently inside, the secret we sisters shared and would never speak of.

After the meeting with Mum and Dad we went to see Graham's parents in Coventry. They were a lovely, normal couple, warm and friendly and happy to welcome me into the family. His sister and three brothers were just as friendly.

On 24 August 1974 we were married in Hackney Town Hall. It was a typical Seventies wedding; I wore a long blue dress with a ruche bodice and a white floppy hat and Graham wore a brown suit. All the lads in his crowd were there, as well as plenty of other friends and both families. It was one of those occasions where I couldn't exclude Mum and Dad; if I had done I was sure that other people, especially Graham, would work out why. It sickened me that I had to invite them and introduce Dad as my father while he preened and paraded about. I refused to let him give me away though – that would have been too much – and instead I begged Laurence to do it. He didn't want to, because it would bring him into contact with Dad again, but in the end he agreed, to make my day special.

After the ceremony we held a reception in a room above a pub in Liverpool Street. It was lovely, a really special day and my only sadness was that Jenny couldn't make it back.

We started married life in a flat Graham had found for us above a greengrocer's shop, opposite the Weaver's Arms, the pub where we'd met. It was a lovely airy flat, with high ceilings and period features. I couldn't have been happier. I had escaped Monteagle Court at last and I had a home of my own. I wanted it to be everything that my childhood home wasn't – clean, warm and comfortable, with food in the larder and a welcoming atmosphere.

I settled into family life and thrived on it. Graham worked hard to support us, and in the evenings the two of us went out for a drink or curled up together in front of the TV. We didn't have a lot of money to spare, and I'd spend hours in street markets and charity shops looking for bargains so that our baby would have everything it needed.

On 22 September, soon after Graham, his friend Mick and I returned from their football practice, my labour started. I had no idea what to expect, I felt sick and the strength of the pains terrified me. Mick drove us to the hospital, St Bartholomew's in Smithfield, where I was wheeled straight off to the labour ward. Our daughter was born just four hours later, weighing seven and a half pounds. Graham was there, holding my hand, and when she was put into his arms he wept with joy.

I had always liked the name Carrie but didn't want an abbreviated name, so I chose Carrine. Her second name was Jeanette, after Jenny, my sister and closest friend.

A couple of days after the birth we took our

daughter home. I'd always helped to look after Chris and Carole, so I was used to nappy-changing and feeding. But being a mum and having a child of my own felt so different. I promised myself I would never let anything bad happen to her. It made it even harder to understand how Mum had failed to protect us from Dad for all those years.

I couldn't have waited a moment longer to escape from Monteagle Court, but I still visited because I worried about Carole and Chris. Dad was beating Mum as much as ever, and she often greeted me with black eyes or broken glasses and a lame excuse about falling. I couldn't help feeling pity for her, but having gone through life trying to protect her instead of being protected by her, I knew that she would never walk away from Dad or stop making excuses for him, and there wasn't much any of us could do.

Soon after Carrine was born I wrote to Jenny, telling her she was an aunt. I was so pleased when she wrote to say she was on her way back. Letters never really seemed to take the place of our long chats, and I had so much to share with her. I wondered what she would make of my new life. I needed Jenny; she was my friend and my silent partner of the past, the only person in the world who had been through the same horrors that I had and who would truly appreciate how much my new life meant to me.

Graham agreed that Jenny would be welcome to stay with us – we would never have allowed her to go back to the squalor of Monteagle Court. I counted the days till she came back.

Jenny

Kim had told me she was pregnant in a letter. I'd been stunned, but thrilled for her because I knew she was happy about it and would make a wonderful mum, despite her youth.

I had been devastated to miss her wedding, but at the time when I heard the news that she was getting married I was homeless and penniless and there was no way I could afford to get back to London.

Then a letter arrived in October to say she was now the proud mother of a baby daughter, and I knew I had to go back. I'd been away for five months and was longing to see everyone and to meet my niece. I handed in my notice, said goodbye to Debbie, promising to stay in touch, and boarded the train for London.

I was so grateful to Kim and Graham for their offer of a place to stay. Kim told me their flat was difficult to find, so she arranged to meet me at Monteagle Court.

As I walked down the road leading to the block of flats, a familiar feeling swept over me. I was a little girl again, returning from the shops, tired, hungry and scared that when I got inside there would be another beating – or worse – from Dad. I had run away from all of this. The last thing I wanted now was to bring it all back. Had it been a mistake to agree to meet Kim here? Was I strong enough to face it? I felt both anger and regret. My father had caused me to run away, in search of peace – and that had meant leaving those I truly loved.

As I stood outside the familiar dirty blue door, I took a step backwards and my eyes were drawn to my parents' bedroom window. It took me back to the days when my father would summon me and I would be made to join in his sick and perverted games. I felt the hatred well up inside me all over again. Hatred for a man who hurt and humiliated me, and who showed no remorse.

Taking a deep breath, I suppressed those feelings and I reminded myself that all that was past now. I knocked on the door and waited. Carole answered and called out to Kim, who appeared, carrying Carrine. We held on to each other for ages, both of us in tears. We had missed each other so much. I was desperate to hold Carrine, and as we let go of each other, I took her gently from Kim. She was beautiful, with downy blonde hair and huge blue eyes.

I didn't want to stay any longer at my parents' flat than was necessary. I went in to say a quick hello, anxious to be off. Carole and Chris looked malnourished, pale and dirty, just as Laurence, Kim and I had done a few years earlier. The smelly Pontings, other kids had called us. We'd been the lowest of the low, bottom of the pecking order in a neighbourhood where everyone was poor and underprivileged; the kids no one else would play with.

I hugged each one of them in turn and kissed the tops of their heads, before going through to the kitchen to see my mother.

Nothing had changed. The dirt and filth was all too obvious, and my mother was washing a few dishes at the sink – the tell-tale sign of a beating from my father. She always busied herself when they had fought. She turned to me. 'Oh, 'ello Jen,' she muttered, trying to hide her bruised face.

'What was his excuse this time, Mum?' I said, exasperated. No reply. I could hear the television going full volume in the living-room. He was obviously there, sitting in his usual chair, smoking and drinking tea.

Curiosity got the better of me and I went through. As I opened the door the stench of stale tobacco and body odour was overwhelming.

He turned to look at me. 'So yer back, are yer?'

I nodded. 'I've come to meet up with Kim and the baby.'

He didn't bother responding. He'd returned to the television. I went back to the kitchen, got my purse from my bag and called Carole and Chris out into the passage. I gave them a pound each and made them promise not to tell Mum and Dad.

I left with Kim and as we walked up the road to the bus stop, grateful to get away, I knew we were both thinking about Carole and Chris.

The entrance to Kim and Graham's flat was via the back, through a maze of alleys and gardens behind the block of shops. I'd never have found the place alone. For security reasons, there was only one gate key. Kim rang the bell and Graham opened the window and threw down the key. When we finally got upstairs I was amazed by how big it was. The high ceilings had all their original features, the lamps gave off a lovely soft glow and a fire was roaring in the grate. The table was laid ready for tea, and I felt instantly at home and so proud of what Kim had achieved. The place was wonderful.

I'd met Graham before I went away, and I wasn't mad about him at the start. He was into real ale, cricket and Jimi Hendrix, none of which were my thing, but I could see how good he was for Kim and how much they cared about one another. I was glad it had worked out for them and grateful to Graham for offering me a place to stay.

After tea he went off to the pub for a couple of hours, discreetly leaving us to catch up. As we sat and chatted I scooped Carrine into my arms and cuddled her. Kim sat nearby, watching me, her face glowing with pride. I was thrilled she had given her daughter my name and promised Kim that if ever I had a daughter I would do the same.

We stayed up talking for the next few hours. I told Kim all about my adventures and she told me about the pregnancy and wedding. There was a lot of laughter. Neither of us mentioned the court case or our parents. All that was behind us now and we had good things to look forward to. I longed to ask Kim about John, but I held back, afraid of what I might hear. I would leave it to Kim to tell me any news when she was ready.

I had virtually no money so I needed to find a job as soon as possible. A couple of days later I met up with Sherri, who told me she'd been for a job, but didn't want it and that if I called quickly the vacancy might still be available. It was as a recep-tionist/telephonist for a company at King's Cross, and the pay was a whopping 39 pounds a week – more than I'd ever earned before. I called, went for the interview and got the job. It was convenient, too. I could catch the number 73 bus, just outside Kim's flat, which would take me all the way there. It all seemed perfect. I started a couple of days later and soon settled in. I was still relying on Kim and Graham for somewhere to live, but at least I was earning and could give them some rent.

I had thought a lot about John since I got back, and wondered whether I should contact him, but I was unsure of how he would feel. Kim told me he was still around and she wanted to get us together again. But would he still want me? I hoped and prayed he would.

One night a couple of weeks after I got back, Kim asked me to baby-sit while she and Graham went on a rare night out. I'd just settled Carrine down after her feed when the doorbell went. I opened the window, and out of the shadows a familiar figure looked up at me. It was John. This was Kim's doing, I was sure of it.

My heart was in my mouth as, having thrown him the key, I waited for him to make his way to the door. As soon as I opened it I knew I was still in love with him. But I couldn't tell whether he felt the same way. His smile was warm, but the look in his eyes was sad.

I made us a cup of tea, and for a while we made small talk. I wanted to find the courage to tell him I'd made a mistake and to ask him to forgive me for going off and leaving him.

I took a deep breath. 'John I have something important to tell you,' I began, but before I could finish he turned towards me with bitterness and hatred on his face. 'Don't bother with your excuses. I suppose you slept with every man in sight.'

My mind was racing. He'd got it all wrong. I hadn't done anything to shame him or myself. I just wanted to tell him how stupid I'd been, but tears filled my eyes as I took in what he'd said. I began to shake and panic. I suddenly felt resigned. John didn't want me back and it seemed as if nothing I could say would change what he now felt for me. I slowly died inside, I couldn't fight for what was no longer possible. I took another deep breath and asked him to leave, and he looked glad to be going. As he left, I sank on to the armchair and sobbed. Then, with the sickness inside of me slowly welling up into my throat, I knew I had to swallow my pride and chase after him. I couldn't let it end like this, I had to try to get him back. I raced down the stairs into the street. It was raining hard and a strong November wind was pushing the rain into swirls across the street. Squinting in the wind and rain I could see him in the distance. I called his name, but he kept walking. He wasn't going to turn around. I stayed rooted to the ground, with the rain soaking me to the skin. I had lost him, John had gone.

Kim

It was a shock for Jenny seeing Monteagle Court again after such a long gap, but I was used to it. I knew nothing would ever change. The dirt would always be there, the cupboards would always be empty, and Dad would always bully and brutalise Mum and the kids.

I worried so much for Carole and Chris. Every day they came home from school grubby, badly dressed and cold, to face a tea of jam sandwiches and crisps and an evening trying to keep out of Dad's way.

Once I moved into the flat with Graham I made Mum bring them round once a week for a decent meal. Chrissie would often stay and Graham treated him like a son, taking him to football matches and to cricket, which he loved. Graham's friends included him in their sporting games and treated him with affection and respect, neither of which he had ever received from his own father. He became a regular at our flat, often staying the whole weekend, and he would spend hours playing with his baby niece. Carole, on the other hand, was withdrawn, shy and insecure and even when I invited her to stay, she would usually choose to go home.

Jenny's return from her travels was a joy for me. I was used to spending a lot of time alone with Carrine; Graham was at work all week and often played football at weekends, so it was great to have Jenny's company. We spent hours trying on each other's clothes and talking over cups of tea; no matter how long we talked, we never got bored with one another. Jenny had changed in the time she'd been away. She seemed stronger and more adult. She still laughed and knew how to have fun, but there was a more serious side to her.

She thought more intently about things and was more reflective.

She also looked different. She had toned up and grown her hair longer and she looked better than ever. Jenny had always managed to look good. When we were scruffy kids I remember someone once saying Jenny could wear a bin bag and still look good, and they were right. She was tall and blonde with a wonderful curvy figure and good skin, and she turned heads wherever she went.

As for me, I was dark-haired, as tall as Jenny – five foot nine – and very slim; after I had Carrine I weighed eight stone. Graham's friends used to say there was more meat on a sparrow's kneecap than on me, although the pregnancy had increased my bust by a couple of sizes, which I was pleased about.

I was surprised that Jenny hadn't asked about John since she'd been back. I had hoped she would but she didn't, and I wondered if she was afraid of what I might say. While she'd been away I had kept up my friendship with John – he'd even been a guest at our wedding. I had always kept him informed about Jenny and what she was up to, but as the months went on his interest started to fade. I could only imagine that he had accepted that they were never going to be together again and moved on with his life. But I still didn't want to give up on them. Deep inside I truly believed that they were meant for one another and that love would conquer all. So I set up the blind date, inviting him round to my house when I knew she would be on her own, without telling either of them. But my hopes came to nothing when their relationship ended that night for good.

I was gutted that they hadn't been able to patch things up, but John had been hurt when Jenny left and no one could blame him for refusing to pick things up where they had left off. He'd moved on and Jenny had to accept his rejection.

It wasn't easy, though. For weeks after that night she used to sob her heart out when she was feeling low, and nothing I could say eased the pain. John had been Jenny's first love, and losing him was heartbreaking.

3
Keith

Jenny

For the next few weeks I hardly knew what to do with myself. I realised how much I had counted on John being there for me when I got back, and when he walked away that night it hit me hard. I had been so smug to believe I could win him back. I went through the motions of going to work, coming home, eating and sleeping, but inside I felt empty and lost.

Kim did her best to comfort me. She and Graham couldn't have been kinder, but nothing seemed to lift the heavy depression I felt. Christmas was coming and one evening Kim suggested we go out with the baby for a walk and a bit of late-night shopping. I needed to buy some presents, so I agreed and we headed off to Dalston. By eight that evening we were tired and thirsty and had spent too much money. So we made our way up the Kingsland Road to Centreprise, a trendy coffee shop, that also sold books and cards and showed local artists' work. We made ourselves comfortable in a quiet corner and chatted about our plans for Christmas over a cup of tea.

For a while we were oblivious to other people in the shop, but I suddenly had a feeling that someone was watching me. I turned around, and standing at the counter was a tall slim man who was staring at me. He was smiling, and when I turned and saw him he winked at me and then came over. 'Don't I know you?' he said. I was puzzled, he did look familiar, but I had no idea where from. Then it dawned on me. We had met before, when my friend Stacey and I had gone on a double date with him and his friend. I had only been fourteen then and he'd been seventeen. Although I'd liked him he'd wanted more than I was prepared to give on a first date. I'd said no, he'd walked me home and we hadn't seen one another in the four years since then.

He now re-introduced himself as Thomas George Keith Hemmings, but said he liked to be called Keith. He was good-looking and charming and soon I was engrossed in conversation with him. Kim decided to leave and make her way home with Carrine, while Keith offered to take me for a drink and see me home later that night. We set off for a pub nearby and at closing time he walked me home. I invited him in to Kim's, and we stayed up chatting all night. By morning I was mesmerised by him.

It was the beginning of a passionate romance.

From the start we saw one another almost every day. Keith would phone me all the time, and when we parted he'd say, 'I'm missing you and I've not even left you' or 'I don't want to sleep tonight, I'd rather be talking to you.' He brought me presents, told me I was gorgeous and acted like a man head over heels in love. Every time I saw Keith or spoke to him on the phone, he would tell me how he had heard a record on the radio that was one of our special songs. My grief over losing John was put to one side as I threw myself into this new, exciting relationship.

Everywhere we went people seemed to know Keith. He would take me to a club and word would go round, 'Keith's here.' I couldn't believe how popular he was or how many people he seemed to know. He'd walk in with his arm round me and tell everyone, 'This is my lady, isn't she special?' I was proud to be with him and I glowed with all the compliments he showered on me.

Keith had charisma. His background was Irish-Italian and he had dark hair and eyes and a smile that sent girls weak at the knees. Girls were often hovering around him, but he only had eyes for me. I knew he could have had his pick of women wherever we went, and I felt great, knowing that this charming, clever, charismatic man had picked me.

My only disappointment was that Kim and Graham didn't appear to take to him. I put it down to the fact that Keith smoked the odd joint and they disapproved. But whatever it was, they were never keen to be in his company, and although they were polite to him they didn't encourage me to bring him round. To be honest, if Kim had doubts about Keith then I didn't want to see or hear them, as I was totally swept away with my handsome Prince Charming. He made me feel good and I was in love, head over heels and besotted. In a very short time I was hooked and felt I needed him, body and soul.

I had slept with Keith on our second night together. We were hungry for each other, and as we explored each other's body he was totally considerate of my needs as a woman. I was not as experienced as him, but he guided and helped me; I knew it could only get better, and it did. Each time we made love, I felt a sense of satisfaction and warmth that I had never experienced before. At times it was so intense that I was breathless with the feelings I had for this man. I was completely and utterly in love.

Looking back now, it's easy to see that perhaps part of the reason for Keith and me being so passionately attracted to one another was that we shared something far less obvious than physical attraction or a sense of humour. We both came from deeply troubled backgrounds, and I'm sure that, in some ways, this was a powerful draw. We found it easy to talk to one another – whatever we had to say was accepted by the other, with a smile that acknowledged a deep understanding of how each of us felt. Keith had been born out of wedlock to an Irish girl, Bridie, who left him with her mother and came to England to find work. When he was nine his mother sent for him and he left his grandmother's home in Ireland and came to live with his mother and her new husband, Stanley Hemmings. The couple went on to have three daughters, Keith's sisters Margaret, Sandra and Pauline. Stan and Keith always had problems getting on. Their home became a pressure cooker and Keith and Stan fought constantly. By the time he was a teenager Keith was roving the streets and getting in with local gangs.

Of course in the early days of our romance I heard about his tempestuous relationship with Stan, but I didn't know any of the rest. I did wonder why Keith didn't have a regular job, but he'd laugh and say he did a bit of this and that. In fact, when we were out, the only time he left my side was when he'd say, 'I'm off to sort out a bit of business – back in a while.' And to be honest I didn't think much of it. I could see that Keith was a big fish in a small pond, that people respected him and that he always had lots of cash, and I was proud to be his girl. I was very naïve, and for a long time I didn't put two and two together but now I suspect that his 'bit of business' involved buying and selling cannabis.

By the time I worked things out, weeks later, it was too late. I was hooked on Keith, and he was a drug that I needed to take on a regular basis. Nothing I could have learned about him would have put me off. I told myself that even if he was involved in something a bit shady he wasn't doing any harm and that it could only be a bit of dope to consenting adults. In a way I saw the possibility that he was involved in something illicit as glamorous — it made him even more attractive — and I decided to close my eyes to any other aspect of the seedy world he moved in.

Instead I threw myself into looking good for him, spending my spare cash on new outfits and getting my hair done. He was the most attentive man I'd ever met, always complimenting me on what I wore and the way I looked. He phoned me several times a day and he wanted to know all about everything I did. After a childhood spent being ignored, it was like water in a desert to me. I drank it in, thanking my lucky stars that I'd met the perfect man. Despite what others said or thought, Keith loved me and nothing would persuade me to leave him or the safety of his strong, loving arms. Keith and I would love each other and be together always, and we would prove them all wrong.

Kim

I was suspicious of Keith from the start. Admittedly he looked cute, but his charming patter and his cockiness made me uneasy. Couldn't she see that it was all front? I had never seen Jenny so instantly hooked and it worried me. The last thing I wanted was for her to get hurt again.

Keith had no job, yet he appeared to have plenty of money, which made Graham doubt his character immediately. And he openly admitted to smoking dope, which bothered both of us.

When he came round he'd lie on the sofa while Jenny ran around trying to make him comfortable, bowing to his every demand. She started buying brands of beer he liked and cooking his favourite meals, and she'd spend hours getting ready for him every time she saw him.

I felt helpless. I hated the fact that this man was taking my sister away from me when I had only just got her back. And I was convinced he was no good for her.

I tried telling myself that this was what Jenny wanted and I should just stay out of it. I knew she wanted a husband, a child and a home that she could call her own, but I didn't feel Keith was the one to give her these things.

I couldn't help feeling that something wasn't right. Although Keith was attentive towards Jenny, he didn't seem to treat her as if she was the most important thing in his life.

Though I never said it to Jenny, Keith's attitude reminded me of Dad. It was hard to explain why, there were just little similarities, like his creepy way of smiling, the rubbish he talked to make himself sound big and the way he lounged on the sofa and expected Jenny to be at his beck and call.

I tried to put my worries aside, but it was impossible. I'd also begun to resent Keith coming round and making himself at home in our flat all the time, and I decided to tell Jenny what I thought of him.

It was on a rare afternoon that Jenny and I were spending together on our own. We hardly ever got time together any more, because she was usually rushing to get ready for Keith. I didn't hold anything back – I told her how worried I was, why Graham and I didn't like him, and of my fears that she was getting into something that wasn't right for her.

I told her what others thought of him too, and how I suspected he was involved in dealing drugs and drink.

I might as well have saved my breath. Jenny was hurt and angry. She told me she loved him, he was 'the one' for her, and she couldn't believe that I didn't want her to find happiness.

It was our first major row. Nothing I said or did would change her mind. She was totally besotted and determined to make her own decisions. What did I know about what she wanted or what was good for her? I just knew that I resented him, even more so now that he'd been the cause of our first real argument.

I couldn't help contrasting Keith with John, who was so caring, not only about Jenny but about everyone around her. I believed that Jenny was still in love with John and that she was desperately trying to recapture, in Keith, the hopes and dreams she'd had with John. What she had with John was extraordinary: she knew that, I knew that and John also knew it. But she threw that away, looking for an answer when all the time she had it, right in the palm of her hand.

After that row there was nothing more I could say. I felt sure she was making a big mistake, but I didn't want us to fall out, so I kept quiet. But I didn't ask Jenny to baby-sit so often, preferring to stay in rather than ask her, because she would often end up inviting Keith round and I didn't really want him around. Graham felt the same way: we didn't want him smoking dope in our home and we didn't trust him. Whenever we came in to find Keith in the flat we said very little. Graham would sit and read his paper or go off to bed, while I would try to politely smooth things over, but Jenny sensed the atmosphere and knew that Keith was beginning to wear out his welcome with us.

I knew I couldn't tell Jenny how I felt, but I also knew that, deep down, she knew. We often had an uncanny way of communicating without the need for words, and this was one of those times.

Jenny

One night Keith and I went to a club where I bumped into some old friends I hadn't seen since before I went to Barry Island. They came over yelling 'Jenny's back!' and hugged and kissed me, full of questions and wanting to catch up. As I talked to them Keith's hold on my arm tightened and he muttered in my ear, 'You're supposed to be out with me.' It took me a minute to realise that he was jealous. Suddenly he wasn't the centre of attention – I was. 'When I take you out I expect you to be with me, not half the fucking club,' he went on. 'Who was that bloke kissing you on the cheek?'

I tried to soothe things, taking him off for a dance and telling my friends I'd see them later. On the dance floor Keith held me a bit too tightly and kept whispering in my ear, 'You know you're mine, don't you?' I was flattered. He loved me so much; he just couldn't bear to share me.

Perhaps I should have taken more notice of the early warning signs, but I was so trusting, and as odd as it may sound, these outbursts made me feel even more wanted. I was sure that they were just his way of showing love and that perhaps, because of the insecurities of his past, he just needed to hold on to me more tightly.

However, Keith's jealousy started to surface more often. We'd be in a pub or club and he'd say, 'Who's that bloke you're looking at? Do you know him?' He'd be pointing at a complete stranger, someone I'd glanced at in passing. I'd reassure him that I hadn't even noticed the bloke, but as time went on and this happened more and more often, I began to keep my eyes on the floor when we were around other people, hoping that Keith wouldn't find any cause to be jealous.

Despite my efforts it only got worse and soon I couldn't talk to another man – even an old friend – without Keith getting upset. His compliments turned to criticism, and the flattery that had once made me so proud to be on his arm, became controlling. He'd turn up to take me out and say, 'Why did you put that fucking skirt on, you know it makes men look at your legs when you wear it.' Another time he'd say, 'You look fab,' but as soon as we went out and he saw another man looking at me he'd say, 'What are you doing wearing that low top, showing off your tits?'

I used to tell myself it was just that Keith loved me and he couldn't help getting jealous. In a way it made me feel wanted and needed, and I'd try even harder to please him and to get it right. I didn't realise that, by looking at the floor in the pub, by avoiding talking to other men and by changing what I wore, I was suppressing part of myself, shrinking myself to try to fit in with him.

We started having arguments. I tried so hard to get it right for him, but if another man even glanced at me Keith would say I provoked him and it was my fault. He'd shout at me or sulk and refuse to speak to me until I apologised, even though I hadn't done anything wrong.

After one argument we had, Keith flounced off and didn't call me the next day. That evening Kim and Graham invited me to go with them and some friends to see a band. We got home early, around ten thirty, and were having a cup of tea when the doorbell went. I went down and it was Keith. He was furious that I'd gone out without him. He demanded to know where I'd been and who I'd seen. I realised he must have come round earlier to see me and the baby-sitter told him I was out. Startled by his anger, I told him that as he hadn't come round I'd gone out with Kim and Graham and a few of their mates. I told him it was just a quick drink and that, after all, I was with Graham and Kim.

He seemed to be deep in thought, calmer now and almost relaxed. 'Did you have a good time?' he asked. When I said yes, his face changed and became ugly and twisted. He suddenly grabbed me by the throat and pushed me back against the shutters of the door, so that I hit my head on the metal grooves. Frightened, because he could see he'd hurt me, he said, 'I shouldn't have done that, but you made me do it.' Then he pulled me to him and hugged me. I was shaken, but he talked quietly to me, telling me not to do things to make him angry, and that he loved me and was scared I would meet someone else and leave him. I assured him I would never leave him, and that he was my life and the only man I would ever want. Eventually, he seemed convinced enough to leave, and I promised to meet him the next night, saying I was tired and needed to have a good night's sleep.

He left and I made my way back upstairs, stunned and in pain. Keith had been so changeable that I couldn't follow his moods; one minute he was menacing, the next calm or even apologetic. All I knew was that he'd been violent towards me and hurt me.

This was the moment when I should have ended it. I knew it, deep inside, but as I've said, Keith was like a drug that I was addicted to. So I went upstairs, drank my tea and didn't tell anyone what had happened. As I sat there looking at Kim and Graham laughing and chatting, I felt an urge to tell Kim, but she would have told me to give Keith up immediately. She would have reminded me of Dad and his violence towards my mother, but I was convinced that this was not a trap I was going to fall into, and that Keith was different from Dad.

I was wrong. After this incident Keith began hitting me regularly. It never took much to spark him off: he'd often hit or shove me in the street on the way home, always accusing me of making him do it. It was never a full-fisted punch, just a push or a slap. He said he did it just to keep me in check, and I told myself that there was nothing going on that I couldn't handle. Besides, I actually believed that Keith's violence was my fault, because I wasn't being what he wanted me to be.

I hid what was going on from Kim. She knew we argued and perhaps she suspected Keith was violent, but I was too ashamed to tell her the truth. When Keith gave me a black eye or a cut lip I hid it from her, or pretended I'd hurt myself. But I knew that soon she was bound to work out what was happening. I decided I had to find another place to live, away from her questions.

Poets Road was a quiet, tree-lined road near Newington Green, not far from Kim's flat. There were rows of terraced Victorian houses that had been divided into flats, let mainly to students. I heard there was a room up for rent there and managed to see it before anyone else. The two other girls in the flat were students, and they were happy to let me have the room. It was tiny but adequate, and I soon settled in.

I didn't really get on with the other girls in the house. They were older than me and always made me feel uncomfortable when I used the communal rooms. This wasn't helped by Keith's late-night visits, when he'd bang on the door, shouting for me to let him in.

By this time Keith and I were arguing constantly and he was often violent, but still I couldn't let go of the relationship. When things were good they were really good: we'd laugh together, make passionate love, and I'd feel certain he was my soulmate. I was convinced that if I could just make him really happy he'd stop being violent and everything would be all right.

At the time I saw no similarity between Keith and Dad. Dad never showed any remorse at all, but Keith would cry and say how sorry he was. Dad was a monster all the time, while Keith could be charming, helpful and loving. So I just didn't make the obvious link.

Of course it's easy to look back now and see that with Keith I was doing what I'd done as a child with Dad – trying so hard to make everything right and taking all the responsibility on myself for what he did. But I was too involved with Keith to be able to step back and see what was happening. I refused to admit there was a problem, and the nice things he did always seemed to make up for the beatings. Late at night he would play the *Average White Band* album for me, telling me it was our special record. He would hold me close and tell me how much he loved me, and for the next few days we would be blissful.

Kim

I was relieved, in a way, when Jenny decided to move out and found herself a flat to share in Poets Road, which was, coincidentally, the same road Graham and his friends had been living in when we met. Before she left she had often arrived home in tears after an argument with Keith, and I hoped that when she moved out she might decide to stop seeing him, but she carried on and their relationship was so stormy that she often sought sanctuary at our home.

Jenny would come to us crying, then she'd dry her eyes and settle down for the night, only to be woken at three or four a.m. by the constant ringing of the doorbell and screaming up at the window. She'd go down and see him and they'd make up yet again. She worshipped him, I could see that. Yet I felt he owned her and didn't give a damn about anyone but himself.

Life for me was completely different. The closest Graham and I came to arguing was debating who would make the tea. We were settled and very happy and we both doted on our daughter. Graham had self-respect, principles and a determination to provide for his family, and I wished Jenny could find someone as good as he was.

We were united in our views on Keith and both felt Jenny was heading for a roller-coaster ride of grief and trouble. But there was nothing we could say or do to change things and I wasn't going to abandon her.

I suspected that Keith had hit her, but whenever I took the plunge and asked, Jenny was always adamant that he hadn't, just as Mum had been time and time again when Dad had hit her.

I encouraged her to socialise with us, hoping it would show her that there was another way. She only came out with us when Keith allowed her to, and I suspected that his giving her permission was just another way of controlling her while he went off and did what he wanted.

Two of Graham's friends worked for the Ministry of Defence, and he played Sunday league football for the Home Office with them. We took Jenny along to football social events, hoping she might meet a decent, hard-working man who would give her all she wanted. But it was useless: her heart lay back in the East End with Keith. When she wasn't with him she moped about and seemed to be in a world of her own.

When we were children one of our escapes was daydreaming. Trapped in the hovel of our childhood home, surrounded by filth and haunted by the nightmare of Dad's demands, we often sat on the window-sill, Jenny at one end and me at the other, gazing up at the stars and dreaming of where our lives would take us. I felt so sad to think that Jenny had escaped from our father straight into Keith's arms. All I could see was Jenny turning into our mother and the whole thing happening all over again. I worried about her chances of survival if she insisted on staying with him.

Jenny

Our brother Laurence liked Keith. Of course he had no idea what was going on – with him we behaved as though everything was fine. By this time Laurence was working for the same company as me, in King's Cross. He was in the accounts department, and I enjoyed having him around and travelling home together.

Laurence had met a great girl called Margaret, and he'd left the house he and Alf lived in and moved to a flat in Muswell Hill with her. He would often invite us over for dinner and try to think of some way for Keith to earn a living, since Keith had decided that he'd like a regular job. I think Keith saw Laurence doing well and liked the idea of living a more stable life. I was pleased, and hoped it would be the start of something new and challenging for Keith.

After a few months Laurence and Margaret decided to get married and buy a house together, so Keith and I took over the flat in Muswell Hill and decided to really make a go of things. Laurence had got a new job with a marketing company and I was back working for the Alfred Marks employment agency, but this time in Mare Street, Hackney. I was good at my job, I was on a decent salary, and the added commission I was earning was enabling me to save some money.

I also had a good circle of friends. I liked the girls I worked with, Michelle and Roxanne, and I still kept in touch with Debbie from Cornwall and of course my old school-mates and Sylvia, with whom I'd shared the flat before I set off on my travels.

The flat in Muswell Hill was always immaculate. I would do the housework before and after work. I was determined that wherever I was living would always be clean and tidy and that there would always be food in the cupboards.

It was Auntie who had taught me how to be clean and look after things. Her cupboards had always been full of food and there was always love and warmth in her home. Unlike my mother, who had only taught me how it felt to be hungry, tired and unloved.

For a while everything seemed to be going well. Keith had apparently given up his shady dealings and had temporary work as an electrician for the London Underground, and I really thought we'd turned a corner. But it wasn't to last. He was jealous of my friends, my money and my popularity. He hated me earning more than he did and he resented me having good friendships, perhaps because so many of his were based on his underground connections rather than being genuine ones. It seemed as though he felt he had to compete with me all the time, and before long he was soon back to his old ways, because it was the only way he could earn more money than me, and trying to control everything I did.

He often screamed at me, saying the world had done him wrong and that he wasn't being given a chance. This, of course, was not true. He was ruining his own chances by smoking cannabis every night and drinking heavily. I'm certain that a lot of his violent, unpredictable behaviour was caused by drink and drugs.

He would call me incessantly at work, dogging my movements and checking on what I was doing. When we went out as a couple I was made to sit in a corner and look at the floor. If I lifted my eyes or looked around he would become enraged, dragging me outside and screaming at me, and pushing or shoving me.

I did my best to cover up his behaviour, embarrassed that the girls at work and my other friends might suspect that my wonderful relationship had massive holes in it, and that Keith was not a Prince Charming after all.

One night we went to the local pub to meet up with Laurence and Kim. The pub was busy and everyone was having a good time. A friend of Kim and Graham's was in the pub, a bloke called Phil who had always had a soft spot for me. Phil wasn't my type at all, but he was friendly and funny. He paid me a lot of attention that night and, as the evening progressed, Keith became more and more enraged, though he hid it from everyone, including me.

At the end of the evening we made our way out of the pub. Keith said good night to Laurence and Kim and even shook Phil's hand. We started to walk back home, and Keith's arm was around my shoulder as he hugged me close. Suddenly he wrapped his arm around my neck and squeezed so hard I could hardly breathe.

'You fucking bitch,' he said as he punched me full in the face with his other hand. I tried to struggle but the blows continued to rain down on me until he finally released his grip and I fell to the ground. He continued to scream abuse at me and kicked me several times in the stomach and buttocks. As I lay there, bleeding, he told me to fuck off and walked away, leaving me to pick myself up and stagger home alone. He was waiting when I arrived at the flat, but he ignored me, and nothing was said about what he'd done.

I had to return to the flat. There was no way I could go to Kim's. This was the first time Keith had beaten me severely and I was in shock. What he had done this time was so much worse than the previous slaps and pushes. It had been a full-on assault, and totally unexpected.

When I got in I made my way silently to the small bathroom. As I bathed my face Keith came in and slid his arms around my waist. 'I love you, baby. Why do you make me hurt you?' he said.

I looked into the mirror above the basin and saw his reflection looking back at me, with tears in his eyes. He looked like the Keith I had fallen in love with, and he promised that it would never happen again. Despite the warning bells ringing so loudly in my ears, I chose to believe him.

This beating was followed by others, and they became more and more frequent, but I continued to forgive him. I couldn't give him up.

When the morning after the night before came round, he would play love songs for me and beg for forgiveness. As Bob Marley sang 'Waiting in Vain' I would give in and end up making love with him, convincing myself that this time everything really would be all right.

And it would, until the next eruption, a few days later. It reached the point where the slightest little thing could trigger his temper, and a terrible beating would follow. Things might have been better if I hadn't fought back, but I refused to be a punch-bag when I had done nothing wrong, and I fought him with everything I had. But my attempts at retaliation just seemed to fuel him. As time went on I realised that he got a kick out of getting the better of me, and that fighting back only led to worse injuries. I became tired and scared. I was trying to work out the best way to survive, and it occurred to me that perhaps acting limp and lifeless might give me better protection.

On one occasion I had been out swimming with friends and Keith was angry when he got back and I wasn't there. As he rained punches down on me I felt exhausted, as though I just didn't care any more. It was the same feeling I'd had when I was a child and Dad beat me black and blue: I felt like a floppy rag doll that was slowly becoming immune to the violence. But if I thought this time that my lack of response might help, I was wrong. It only aggravated Keith. As I lay on the bed, swollen, bleeding, weak and tired, I just wanted to be left alone to sleep, but out of the corner of my eye I saw him take a matchbox from his pocket.

'Hey baby, look what I picked up for you.' He threw the box towards me. 'Pick it up and open it

. . . now,' he shouted. Something told me this was not going to be pleasant. He screamed again: 'Open it, bitch.'

I did as I was told. As I slid the box open I saw two enormous hairy legs. I screamed and threw the box across the room. I hated spiders and Keith had squeezed a large spider into the box, knowing it would terrify me. 'I'm gonna keep this for you,' he said. 'If the good hiding I give ya don't keep you in line, then perhaps this will.' He laughed loudly and I froze with fear. Eventually he went out, but left the box on the table, slightly open. He had now resorted to terrorising me mentally as well as physically.

4

Joy and Pain

Jenny

One hot sunny morning in late July, we made love. This time it was more intense, more loving and beautiful than it had ever been before. We lay in each other's arms, and when he said things would be different, I truly felt they would.

Over the next few weeks I felt nauseous and I was tired all the time. I put it down to the contraceptive pill. It was still in its infancy in those days, and I'd tried many brands but always ended up spotty or suffering bad headaches. I had persevered, but this latest one was making me feel really rough.

Keith and I were back in the usual round of arguing and making up; it had become a way of life. Work was busier than ever, which was hard when I was feeling tired so much of the time. I'd even missed a few of my regular visits to Kim, which was unusual for me as I loved to see Carrine and take her out in her pram to give Kim a break.

One day in late September, while we were at work, Roxanne said something to me that changed my world. 'Jenny, are you pregnant?' she asked. For the first time everything clicked. I had missed my period and I had put on weight, but I had just assumed I was tired and a little run down.

I wasted no time in going to see the doctor. A few days later I rang up to get the results. The test was positive; I was pregnant. Roxanne was waiting for me to put the phone down. 'Life will change for you now,' she said as she went back to her desk.

I sat at my desk staring at the phone, my mind racing with torrents of thoughts and emotions. Suddenly I realised I was happy to be pregnant, and I grinned. The joy of knowing that I was having a child outweighed by far any fears I may have had for the future. I was immediately swept away with thoughts of marriage and a happy family and began to daydream about telling everyone.

The person I was least sure about telling was Keith. Things had been rocky, as usual, and I wasn't sure how he would react. Nothing prepared me for his joy and the whoops of delight when I told him. He thought it was wonderful. Although I was delighted by his reaction, I felt disturbed too. I couldn't put my finger on why, exactly, but when he held me to him, I felt trapped. As his arms held me tighter than ever, I wondered what he really felt. I was now carrying his child. Something that would tie me to him for ever.

our eyebrows. I knew that after they left we would discuss our true feelings about this piece of news.

Jenny would have been very hurt if she had known how we really felt. I was devastated, knowing that Keith would have a lifelong hold over her now. Even if Jenny managed to leave Keith, the baby would always bring him back. But she was my sister and she would get my support whatever happened. We had both shared too much in the past for me ever to judge her or let her down.

Jenny was now earning a good living and she assured us that everything would be fine. She had already worked it all out. If she carried on working, with Keith helping to put money away when he could, they would eventually get a better flat and make a decent home for both of them and the baby.

I nodded and smiled as Jenny told me of her plans, but privately I wondered how long this fairy tale would last.

Jenny

Once I'd got used to the idea that I was going to have a baby, nothing was going to be enough for my child, when he or she was born. I continued to work and saved as much as I could for all the things the baby would need.

The next few months were hard. Roxanne and I had moved to an agency in the City, and it was up to us to generate business. After a really busy morning, I would put my head on my desk and fall asleep during my lunch hour. The travelling to and from work was hard, and by the time I got home and had cooked an evening meal, I was too tired to do much else. But Keith didn't seem to care. Once the novelty of my pregnancy had worn off he was back out at his all-night parties, and he showed little interest in my swelling tummy and aching feet.

I often called round to see Kim. She would always run a warm bath for me and supply me with plenty of tea. She knew things were not right, but I just didn't want to burden her with my problems. I knew Kim would have listened, but I also knew, when I looked into her eyes, that she knew everything anyway.

I would often think about Auntie and wonder what she would have made of all this. Had I let her down? She would have been so happy about the baby, but she'd have been horrified at the way Keith treated me.

Autumn passed quickly and winter set in. By this time it was clear that things were not working out at Muswell Hill. With Keith not working, I just couldn't afford to keep it going, and I was exhausted trying to manage the long journey to the City and back, and work a full day, as well as cook and clean, with no support from Keith.

If it had just been a matter of money we might

have looked for a cheaper place together, though they were hard to find. But I was paying the bills and doing all the work while Keith made no effort at all, and it was too much for me. So eventually we agreed to give up the flat. It seemed easy for Keith to let go of our life together, perhaps because he knew that with a baby on the way he would always have a hold over me. But for me it was hard, as I didn't want to have a child on my own.

Keith returned to his mum's house and I went to stay with Kim. She was brilliant at making me feel good. We spent lots of time sorting baby clothes and talking of good times, and I marvelled at the way she ran her home and had lots of energy and enthusiasm for everything. It wasn't easy for her putting me up, as money was tight and she and Graham needed their space and time together. I often worried about getting in the way, but neither of them ever said a word. I always paid something towards my keep, not that they asked, but if they refused my offer of money I'd often buy something that they needed for Carrine.

Carrine was now a year old and walking. She was remarkably bright for her age and Kim was so proud of her. Kim was still a little too thin, but she had a lovely figure and she looked good. I would often baby-sit while she helped out downstairs in the small grocery shop in the evenings and at weekends. It was nothing permanent, but the small amount they paid her helped, and I loved being with Carrine. I spent hours playing with Carrine while daydreaming about my baby and wondering whether I would have a boy or a girl.

I felt safe at Kim and Graham's, and it was a relief to be away from Keith's attacks, but he continued to arrive unannounced and try to cause trouble. One night after everyone was in bed, the doorbell rang. As I made my way to the window, Graham beat me to it. 'Clear off, or I'll come down and you'll be sorry. I can put up a better fight than Jenny,' he shouted. I was mortified. Graham knew what had been happening, and I felt so ashamed. He had always been so quiet and never said a word to me. But as my shame lifted, my gratitude grew. Graham had stayed out of things as long as he could, but now he'd had enough. Keith went away that night and the next morning I stumbled out an apology. Graham smiled. 'Just look after you and the baby,' he said.

Kim and Graham's support meant a lot to me, but I still felt very alone. Perhaps that's why a few weeks later I made up with Keith again. He said he had made changes, and I wanted to believe him, but deep down the truth was that I was afraid of having my baby alone and, despite everything, I still felt I needed and loved him, and I clung to the dream of a happy family. It just didn't occur to me that Keith might ever hurt our child, otherwise I would never have gone near him again. I believed that once the baby came, Keith would love it so much he would be totally different.

This time he had been to see Laurence. The two of them still got on well and together they had come up with a plan to make lots of extra cash for Christmas. Laurence had bought a very large consignment of Ravenhead glassware. It was beautiful stuff and he had everything from boxes of glasses to elaborate bowls and ornaments. Keith put up half the money and before long they were up and running, selling in the markets. It was an amazing success; the glassware was selling quicker than they could re-stock, and money was plentiful.

I had been invited to spend some of the Christmas holiday with Keith's family, and I agreed. Again I began to believe that he and I could make things work. Despite everything, I loved this man and I truly felt he loved me. I wanted my child to know its father and I desperately wanted to have a family life that was good and solid and different from my own childhood. I wanted to believe I could make everything work.

Keith bought lots of gifts for the baby and we made sure that everyone had something special for Christmas. Even better, there were no arguments in the run-up to Christmas, and Keith had started to treat me well. At last I felt happy and I looked forward to a really special Christmas Day.

Keith's mum Bridie was a real darling, but I was not keen on her husband Stan. Keith and Stan hated one another. Stan would ply Bridie with drink to get her drunk and cause arguments, and Christmas was no different. What started off as a nice day ended up in a huge row. Keith stormed out and I followed him, and on Christmas night we found ourselves walking the streets. I tried to calm him down but he became more and more agitated. He'd been drinking too, but I was sober because of the baby. As we walked along, his temper erupted and I became the butt of his punches. Before I knew it, I was knocked down, bruised and bleeding. Panic set in and I began to scream, 'My baby, my baby!' I looked towards Keith. He laughed, then he walked off without glancing back, leaving me lying in pain on the ground.

For a few minutes I couldn't get up. My back hurt, my lip was bleeding and I was in shock at Keith's callous response to my fears for the baby. I wrapped my arms around my tummy, praying that my baby wasn't hurt. With tears streaming down my face, I made my way to the only place I knew I would be safe. Kim's.

Kim

I was so excited about Christmas. Carrine was fifteen months old and able to recognise all the

Christmas lights and presents. By this time she was stringing words together, and I was really looking forward to being with her and Graham on Christmas morning.

Jenny and Keith had made plans to spend Christmas at Keith's family home, so I packed up all her gifts, including some small little things I had bought for the baby, and kissed her goodbye on Christmas Eve, wishing her a happy Christmas.

We had a great day. Carrine loved opening her presents and lots of friends popped round to see us, full of festive spirit. I always made an extra effort at this time of year, as the memories of our childhood Christmases were very vivid in my head. I was determined that there was no way anyone would spoil Christmas ever again for me and my family. For a start Carrine would get to keep all her presents. She would never have to sell them to strangers, as we had, down in Petticoat Lane market on the first Sunday after Christmas.

Every year it had been the same. Dad would show us toy catalogues before Christmas and ask us what we wanted. He'd order the gifts – of course he never paid for any of them – and then almost as soon as we'd opened them we'd have to put them back in the packages and cart them down to the market, then stand there till we'd sold them all. Dad took all the money, and the most we could hope for was that he'd spend some of it on some dinner for us.

Christmas had always ended in tears for us, but hopefully Carrine's smile would remain. She would never need to ask if she could take off the wrapping and actually play with a toy, or to give up a new game to prevent a festive beating from her father. I would make sure that her day would be free of arguments, fights and fear.

On Christmas afternoon Mum brought Carole and Chrissie over to exchange gifts. Chris jumped at the chance to stay on with us, but Carole wanted to return home. Chris played for hours with Carrine; he was a great uncle to her and Graham loved having him around. In the evening Carrine and Chris went to bed exhausted but happy, and full of dinner and chocolate. Graham and I cuddled up on the sofa; the day had been full-on and I was all too ready for a bit of peace.

A few minutes later the doorbell rang. Going to the window I knew it could only be one of two people: Jenny or Mum. I peered down to see Jenny, her arms round her tummy, tears streaming down her face and blood at the corner of her mouth. I didn't wait for her to get to me; I ran down and met her coming through the gate. Putting an arm around her I led her upstairs, where Graham had already put the kettle on and made himself scarce.

I insisted Jenny see a doctor, so we went together to the local casualty department. It was quiet in there. Christmas night usually was, as I knew only too well. I remembered how often we'd ended up taking Mum to casualty at Christmas, us kids scared out of our wits by what Dad had done to her.

Jenny told them she'd had a fall down some stairs, and she was given a check-up and reassured that the baby was fine. As we left, the doctor called me over and, resting a hand on my arm, he said kindly, 'If your sister continues to sustain injuries in her house I suggest she moves . . . soon.' I knew he had seen too many injuries and heard too many excuses to be fooled by a woman trying to cover up domestic violence.

It felt like my childhood all over again. There in front of me was my sister Jenny, but all I could see was my mum from all the Christmases before. Weary, broken and disillusioned, Jenny sobbed as she told me the story. I was angry with her as well as with Keith. By going back to him she had put herself before the baby, believing, just like Mum, that everything would get better, even though it never did.

I told her that she was to stay at our flat, and that Keith shouldn't matter any more; all she needed to worry about was herself and the baby. He was just like Dad; he couldn't bear to see anyone having fun or getting attention, and when things didn't go his way he used his fists to make his point. She had to stay away from him and build a life for herself. He hadn't hurt her too badly, but I knew it would only get worse. I begged her to remember what she had witnessed all her life and think about whether that's how she wanted to end up.

I hoped my words had got through, and I believed they had. Jenny agreed to stay with us, and went back to work after Christmas feeling stronger and saying she was determined to get her life in order without Keith.

Then, just after New Year, she rang to say she was working late to earn some extra cash for the baby. I should have known. Keith had begun turning up outside her work, waiting for her with flowers, chocolates and baby gifts and pleading with her to take him back. He promised he'd changed his ways and swore undying love for her and, as always, Jenny fell for it, hook, line and sinker.

She attempted to convince us he was different, and although we didn't believe it, for her sake we accepted him back into our lives and our home yet again. Jenny desperately wanted stability and a complete family. She was never one to rely on handouts, and she felt a stable family unit was the best hope for her and her unborn child. The trouble was, she was hoping to find that stability with Keith, and I was so afraid that he would never give it to her.

I had begun working part-time in the evenings for a bit of extra cash and to get out more. I was still only seventeen and my whole life was Carrine and Graham. I had been helping out in the grocer's downstairs for some time, but I wanted something more, so I took on a part-time job at Sainsbury's in Dalston. It was a new store that stayed open till seven each evening, after which staff worked till nine filling the shelves for the next day. One evening I had just finished work and was walking to the bus stop to catch the bus home. As I walked along Kingsland High Street I saw a figure ahead of me that I recognised instantly as Keith, and he had his arms wrapped around another woman.

As I approached I felt I could hear my heart beating, it was thumping so hard. Keith and the woman disappeared into the doorway of a closed shop. As I passed I pulled up the collar on my coat, but I couldn't take my eyes off them. They were all over each other, kissing at full throttle. I kept my head down and walked on.

My mind raced. Not only was this man hitting my sister, but he was cheating on her too. What was I to do? Should I tell Jenny, who believed that he had changed his ways, or keep quiet and attempt to convince myself that things would work out? I decided I had no choice but to tell her, although I had no idea how to do it. I didn't want to appear to be saying 'I told you so', and I didn't want to be the bearer of bad news so late in her pregnancy.

I paced up and down and tried to avoid her in the

flat, but she knew something was wrong. As I stuttered through the story I could barely look her in the eyes. I dreaded seeing what little life she had left in her eyes disappear for good. But Jenny surprised me. Although she had tears in her eyes, as I blurted out what had happened I could see the anger rise in her. From that moment on she became totally different. Very matter-of-fact and business-like. That same evening she decided not only what she was going to do, but how. From then on, she told me, her every decision would be for her baby first and then herself.

The next day, after slipping out of work early to avoid Keith, she went and signed on a housing trust waiting list; it was her first step in finding a home for herself and the baby.

The next few weeks were horrendous. Keith appeared outside the flat in the early hours every night, drunk and shouting threats. When he had sobered up during the day he left flowers and baby gifts on the doorstep. But Jenny didn't relent, and I began to believe she might really be getting over Keith. Her whole heart and soul was devoted to the child she hadn't even seen yet.

building, bleak and grey. I went up some steps to a forbidding front door. Inside, the smell of disinfectant was so strong it made me feel queasy. A thin woman in Salvation Army uniform greeted me and led me across cold linoleum floors, past large wooden doors and up a wide stone staircase. The staff were pleasant enough, although their starched uniforms were imposing and they ran the home according to a strict set of rules. The whole place was cold and unfriendly.

Most of the girls were put into four-bed dormitories, but I was told that because I was still working and needed my sleep, I could have a room to myself. The 'room' turned out to be a small section of a long rectangular room, divided into ten of these cubicles by plasterboard partitions. In each 'room' there was a bed, a three-drawer chest and a small wardrobe. The only light, apart from the fluorescent tubes on the high ceiling of the main room, was a table lamp perched on the chest of drawers in my cubicle. The bed was pushed close to the large old-fashioned radiator, and a cot was provided, as these cubicles were often given to women who stayed after the birth of their babies.

The home was full of mothers-to-be, mostly very young, all with their own personal stories of unhappiness and despair. Most were unmarried, but a few were married women who had got pregnant by another man and been sent here to get rid of the baby. Almost all the girls there were going to have to give up their babies – most of them had no choice. There was one girl I made friends with who wanted to keep hers, but her mother kept phoning to insist that she must give the baby up.

I will always remember the young West Indian girl with the lovely smile, who was quiet and rarely spoke. She was in one of the dormitory rooms near to mine, as she was still at school and she needed to continue her studies. One of the other girls told me that she was fourteen and pregnant for the third time, by her own father. I was shocked. How could something like this happen? Why wasn't this girl helped or protected? Each time she gave birth her baby was sent away to be adopted. She knew that it would happen again this time, and late at night I would listen to her crying in the dormitory.

There was a big day room where the girls would sit, most of them knitting clothes for the babies they would soon be losing. Social workers would come in and out of the home, which was run by Salvation Army women. Meals were served at long refectory tables.

I hated being there, I felt I didn't belong. I wasn't going to give my baby up, I was planning our life together and this was just a stopgap for me.

I was back in contact with Keith again, though I was much more wary around him by now. To be honest, I still hoped it would work out between us, but I knew I had to be realistic. Taking care of my baby came first, and that meant holding out for a place for us to live that was in my name. Sometimes Keith would call and take me out for the day. The year had started off cold, but by spring the weather was blistering hot, with air so close and humid I could hardly breathe. One very hot day Keith took me to the boating lake at Whipps Cross and rowed the boat out to the middle of the lake. There was a cooling breeze and I felt so much better.

At other times he would take me back to his mother's house for the night. It was a huge house and Keith had a big room. He would take me up there and play me 'our songs' while he kissed my bump and wondered whether the baby would like the music. He could be so kind – making me tea, rubbing my feet, and even getting up in the night and going to an all-night hot food stall in Ridley Road market to get me an egg and bacon sarnie, then running home so that I could eat it while it was still hot.

We sometimes had several days like this before he erupted again, set off by something trivial or someone who'd upset him. I never knew how he would be from one day to the next. I was a nervous wreck a lot of the time, too scared to speak and terrified of what he would do next. Still I couldn't let him go. I hoped and believed that he would change once the baby came along.

Getting to work was an effort once I was heavily pregnant, although it was a relief to get away from the home during the day. But as my due date grew closer the travelling became too much for me and I had to give up work.

I needed to get out of the hostel. Being there all day was too depressing, and I couldn't stand listening to the tears of the other girls at night. We all had our nightmares, and I dreaded being in that place when my baby was born.

There was no place to go except back to Mum and Dad's. Kim had told me I could go back to live with her, but if I wanted any chance of a home for myself and my baby, I knew I would have to be in the worst possible place, and that was Monteagle Court. The thought of returning was making me feel ill, but the need to provide for my baby was stronger than my dread of going back. Chris offered me his room and despite everything I knew I had to go through with it. I had no choice.

Chris had the small room that had once been Laurence's and I cleaned it from top to bottom and made it as nice as I could. The rest of the flat was as disgusting and filthy as always, but I did my best to ignore it – apart from the bathroom, which I cleaned too – and shut myself away to prepare for my baby.

While I had time on my hands I went to visit Mrs Wagner, who'd taught me English at Haggerston

Secondary School. She'd always had a soft spot for me, and she gave me a gorgeous Silver Cross pram. I spent hours cleaning and polishing it, ready for my baby.

Sherri, my old schoolfriend, was working as a barmaid at the Spread Eagle pub in Shoreditch, and sometimes I would go and visit her for something to do. If things were really bad at home, I would go round to Sherri's home, and her lovely mum always let me stay. I never received any lectures at Sherri's, the whole family were supportive and kind. They had been like a second family to me when I was still at school and used Sherri's home as a bolt-hole to escape from Dad. Now they were happy for me to go back as often as I wanted, and in the last days of my pregnancy I spent most of the time with them or with Kim.

My due date, 22 April, came and went with no sign of my baby. Soon afterwards I was admitted to hospital with a severe chest infection, no doubt the result of the filthy conditions at Monteagle Court and the poor diet I lived on there. The infection cleared up, but at my next pre-natal check-up, on Tuesday 10 May, the consultant decided to induce the birth two days later.

On Thursday 12 May I left Monteagle Court on my own and made my way back to The Salvation Army Mother and Baby Hospital in Clapton Pond, where I was admitted. I had no idea what was going to happen to me, and although I wasn't frightened I longed for it all to be over.

These were still primitive times, and before the induction I was shaved. I hated it, but the enema they gave me next was far worse. As it took effect I was busting for the toilet, but so were three other expectant mothers. It was a real fight to get in there!

Next I was given a bath, but the water only just covered my ankles and was lukewarm. Sitting in it I felt the need to break wind, but when I did it was not what I expected. The bath-water turned a nasty green colour and the smell was awful. I was so embarrassed and didn't know what to do, but when the nurse walked in she dismissed it as nothing, and when I was clean and dry she took me to a bed on the labour ward.

It was packed. Women were screaming with pain, and at that point in the morning I became scared. Thankfully Kim arrived just then to stay with me for a while, which helped. The hours slowly went by. Keith eventually turned up late that evening to announce he was now working nights and would return when he could. Kim stayed as long as she could, but in the end she had to go, and I lay there listening to the screams of the other women and wondering what was going to happen.

By early Friday morning my pains were terrible but nothing had happened. A doctor arrived to break my waters in the hope that it would speed things up. But hours later there was still no sign of my baby. The pains grew worse and I was heavily sedated but still conscious of the contractions. This carried on throughout the day, and by evening I was in a great deal of pain and talking nonsense. Another doctor arrived to examine me and discovered that the baby was facing my back and had the cord around its neck. It needed to be facing forward for the birth, and the cord had to be released or the baby might have breathing difficulties. They decided to turn the baby by hand and it was pure torture, one of the worst things I have ever experienced.

By the early hours of Saturday morning the contractions were very frequent and, after 36 hours in labour, I was told my baby was about to be born.

I was wheeled to the delivery room, alone and frightened. Keith and Kim were both due to visit me, but where were they? It was only later that I discovered they had been sent away, having been told that I wouldn't be ready to deliver for another few hours. Keith had gone home to bed after his night shift, and Kim had been told to phone the hospital later in the day.

The pain was unbearable but I was told not to push. I heard the midwife shout at another nurse to cut me, and I was given an episiotomy, to make it easier to get the baby out. There was no time to anaesthetise me, and the whole hospital must have heard my screams. Finally I was turned on my side and told I could push, and minutes later I looked down and saw a thick mop of black hair and eventually a lovely little face, with eyes and mouth wide open.

My daughter was delivered at 7.43 a.m. on Saturday 14 May 1976, weighing seven pounds three ounces. She was put into my arms, and as I held her for the first time the most amazing sensation swept over me. She was mine and no one would ever hurt her. The morning sun filtered through the window and a sun-ray lit up her face. I looked towards the light and thanked God.

My ordeal wasn't over. After I had cuddled my baby my legs were placed in stirrups ready for the doctor to stitch me up. At that point the midwife entered the room to tell me my husband was out-side. I was so excited, Keith had come back and would meet his daughter. The next moment I got the shock of my life when in walked a huge black Rastafarian with a multicoloured hat on his head and dreadlocks down his back. 'Dat not my woman,' he said, and I replied, 'And he's not my husband.' The midwife had been convinced that my daughter was mixed-race, as her hair was so dark and her skin was a deep olive. It was a genuine mistake, but one I could have done without.

After the stitching had been finished I was

pushed to the ward and helped into bed. I lay holding my daughter for a while, just looking into her sweet face. I didn't want to put her down, but eventually exhaustion got the better of me and I dropped off.

I didn't sleep long or deeply. I kept waking up to make sure my baby was still in her cot at the bottom of the bed. At every opportunity I picked her up for a cuddle and attempted to nurse her. Breastfeeding wasn't easy. I had too much milk, and in order to release some of it, the nurses decided to put me on an expressing machine. I felt just like a cow being milked. I sat upright in a chair while my nipples were placed in suction teats. Then the machine was switched on and my nipples were pumped in turn. As I jerked backwards and forwards, a horrible spurting sound could be heard and the whole thing was horribly uncomfortable. A nurse walked in, giggled, and said, 'My goodness, we have enough for the whole of special care.' I walked back to the ward feeling lighter, but very sore.

Later that morning Keith arrived. He looked at our baby and his first words were 'Is it a he, she or what?'

'It's not a what,' I replied. 'You have a beautiful daughter and she's going to be called Martine Kimberley Sherri.' During my pregnancy I had read a book about star signs. Martine was a Taurus and ruled by Mars. Martin was the boy's name for those born under Mars and I simply added an e. Kimberley was for my sister, and Sherri for my closest old schoolfriend.

Keith cradled his baby daughter, and as I watched them I knew that while I still felt deeply for him, I could never love him as I had before. He had betrayed me and our baby, and although I wanted him in her life so that she would know her father, I really did not want him in mine. As he looked at me and smiled, I heard a voice shout out, 'Hey baby, how did you do?' It was my Rastafarian 'husband'! He gave me a thumbs-up and laughed before he went on his way. It took me ages to explain to Keith who he was and what had happened.

Before long Laurence and Margaret, Kim and Carrine and Mum all arrived and everyone began fighting for a cuddle with my gorgeous baby. Keith looked uncomfortable, as he always did when he wasn't the centre of attention, and it wasn't long before he left.

By the next morning accommodation was uppermost in my mind. I had endured Monteagle Court while I was pregnant, but there was no way I was taking Martine there. The next few days were spent calling the council from the hospital, trying to secure a home for me and my baby. After a week in hospital, I was discharged and I made my way to a bed and breakfast hotel in Finsbury Park, where I had been told I should stay while waiting to be allocated permanent housing.

Kim

Jenny had made the decision to break from Keith, and I was proud of her for this. It wasn't easy, because he was the father of her unborn child and she didn't want to sever the ties completely. I wondered if she could really manage to keep him at arm's length while still allowing him to see the child.

When she first moved into the Salvation Army hostel Keith didn't know where she was. He would call round to our flat and beg us to tell him, but we didn't, because we felt it was up to her whether she wanted to contact him. He soon found out somehow, though, and would often visit her. I felt he was simply keeping his fingers in the pie. Keith would never pass up the chance of another place to crash in the future, especially somewhere he could demand sex, food, money and alcohol.

It was a brave decision for Jenny to move back into Monteagle Court before the birth. It showed me that she was more determined than ever to get her life in order. I could never have done it, and the thought of her having to share the same roof as Dad made my skin go cold.

Jenny looked on it as a small price to pay for eventually getting a proper home for her and the baby. Chris had given up his room for her and she spent hours cleaning it. She scrubbed the bathroom too – Mum and Dad rarely used it, so she was able to keep it clean. Staying under their roof was so hard for her that, unbeknown to anyone apart from Chris, she would sometimes slip out at night to stay with us, returning really early in the morning so they would never know that she wasn't there every night.

We both knew that if Dad had thought he had any hold over Jenny that he could use to jeopardise her chances, he would certainly have threatened to use it and probably demanded money to keep quiet. Staying out of his way and ignoring his disgusting habits was the only way to succeed.

Jenny would stay with me during the day. Worried, I would ask her how she was managing to inhale the same air as him, let alone be under the same roof. She would always reply very matter-of-factly that she was only doing it until the birth, and then she would be out as quickly as possible. I knew that ignoring the horror of the place was the only way she could get through the whole experience.

Jenny had finally given up work, having saved some money for her new flat. We spent a lot of time gathering things in preparation: saucepans, crockery, cutlery, bedding and all the bits and pieces she would need. At the same time I was busy sorting out baby things for her which she preferred to keep at my house. We both knew that if baby clothes were taken to Monteagle Court they would soon take on the sour, dirty, pungent smell we had always associated with 'home'.

When Jenny was taken into hospital to be induced, I went straight to meet her there. Outside the ward I bumped into Keith, who was so full of the joys of spring that I assumed he must have had a joint before he arrived. I couldn't stay long because I had Carrine with me, so I left Jenny, promising to return the next day with rolls and crisps to save her having to endure hospital food.

The following day I returned armed with a bag of goodies, but as children weren't allowed into the labour wards and I had Carrine with me, I couldn't see her. I managed to talk to one of the sisters on the ward, who told me that Jenny wasn't in labour yet and probably wouldn't be until Saturday or Sunday. I promised to come back the next afternoon and went home.

On Saturday afternoon I popped down to Mr Ali in the grocer's shop below our flat and asked to use his phone to ring the hospital. When I was told that Jenny's baby had been born, I let out a huge cheer. They wouldn't tell me over the phone what sex it was – I had to wait until I got there. I sat on the bus with butterflies of excitement, wondering how the birth had gone and whether I had a niece or a nephew.

As soon as I got to the hospital I could see Keith, sitting by the bed holding a little bundle. I ran round and gazed at this dark-skinned loo brush! She had so much black hair and such olive skin that I had to agree with the nurses that she did look mixed-race. She was sucking on her bottom lip, with her eyes wide open, when I said my first 'hello' to her. When I introduced Carrine to her cousin Martine, Carrine peered into the bundle and said 'Herro Bartine.' We all laughed, and even now I still call Martine 'Bart'.

Jenny was tired but still aware of everything going on around her, and her gaze never left Martine, especially when Keith held her. Even though her child was only hours old, I could see that Jenny had all the protective instincts of a mother. Little did she know then how fully those instincts would be tested in the years to come.

Keith played the doting father extremely well. With a broad smile across his face he promised everything Martine could wish for. Jenny and I just looked at one another.

Once Keith had left, I took the baby and Jenny went through the saga of the birth for me. I felt so sorry for her and so grateful that Carrine's had been such an uncomplicated birth.

As I was about to leave I placed Martine back

into her mother's arms. Carrine jumped up, wanting to kiss 'Bartine' goodbye, and Jenny reached out and grabbed hold of my hand. 'Kim,' she said, with tears in her eyes, 'promise me if anything should ever happen to me you will fight for Martine and bring her up as your own.'

I told her not to be so stupid, nothing was going to happen to her. But she tightened her grip and said, 'Promise me,' and I told her she didn't need to ask.

Jenny hadn't finished. 'I don't want anyone else to have her, please don't give her up without fighting for her,' she begged. I told her to stop being silly, she wouldn't need me to fulfil the promise, as she would always be there for Martine.

As I left the hospital I couldn't help thinking about what she had said. Was Jenny telling me she didn't think she would survive much longer? Was Keith still hitting her? I was frightened and worried.

Sharing my worry with Graham at home later, I was relieved when he said without hesitation, 'Of course we would take her, you couldn't let her father bring her up.'

Jenny

The bed and breakfast hotel in Finsbury Park was no more and no less than I had expected. My fellow guests were unmarried mothers, homeless families and recently discharged hospital patients. All of us were on benefits and waiting to be housed. I was given a very small room on the top floor, next door to a young mother with three children under five. We were allowed no cooking facilities except for a kettle, and all meals, apart from breakfast, had to be taken elsewhere. We were expected to vacate the rooms during the day.

When I first arrived I sat on the bed cradling my baby and wondered how long this grim place would be our home. I prayed it wouldn't be for long, but I knew it might be weeks or even months.

Keith wasn't allowed into the hotel, but he'd often creep in to see me and Martine after his night shift as an electrician at the Royal Opera House, before heading off to his mother's to sleep.

I spent most of my time with Kim and Carrine. After feeding Martine and getting her ready in the morning I'd catch the bus over to Kim's flat. The single-decker 231 bus was notorious for its bad timekeeping, and I knew the wait would be horrendous on the first day when I saw that someone had scrawled on the timetable, 'Died waiting'.

I soon knew how they felt. It was almost always a long wait. But eventually I'd get to Kim's, where she and Carrine would be waiting for us. It was late May and the weather was wonderful, so we often went out for the day with the girls. One of our favourite places was the playground at Highbury Fields that we knew so well from our childhood visits to Auntie. She lived nearby and would often take us over there on a sunny afternoon.

There was a paddling pool where Carrine would splash, under Kim's eagle eye, while I would lie in the shade nearby just gazing at my adorable bundle.

Dozing on the grass, I'd remember the wonderful times I'd had here with Kim and Laurence. When we were old enough to come on our own, Auntie would make us a packed lunch of spam sandwiches, crisps, boiled eggs, an apple and an orange each and a large bottle of orange squash for us to share. What a wonderful feast that was. We would spend hours in the pool or playing in the adjoining playground.

Mostly the memories were happy. But there was one incident, when Kim and I were on our own there, which was far from pleasant. I was eight and Kim was six at the time. We'd been to the swing park one very hot day, and as our curfew drew near we headed back through the paddling pool and out on to the road.

A man came towards us, with two small dogs. Kim went to pet the dogs and the man started talking to us. He had thick, slicked-back hair that looked stuck to his head and a small thin moustache. His eyes appeared like two slits in his face, there were bits of dirt in each corner of his mouth and he wore an almost overpowering aftershave.

He was asking what two pretty little girls were doing out alone in Highbury Fields. I had never felt unsafe in the area before, but this man made me nervous, and as soon as he invited us home to his house for tea, alarm bells went off. Kim was still wrapped up in fussing the dogs. The man looked at me, and all I could see was Dad. Panic set in. I grabbed Kim and said we had to go. When I looked back from down the street he was staring after us and rubbing his penis through his trousers. I felt sick and ran back with Kim to the safety of Auntie's.

I wanted to tell Auntie what had happened, but I knew that if I told her, Highbury Fields would be out of bounds and I couldn't bear that. I told Kim to keep our secret, and neither of us ever told anyone. Once again we were the silent sisters.

As the weeks passed Martine blossomed and was eating well. So it came as a surprise one night, back at the hotel room, when she began to vomit violently. By morning she was still vomiting and had diarrhoea too. I took her to the local surgery, where we saw a doctor who didn't seem too worried and told me it was just a stomach upset which would soon pass. But by late that day she had developed a high fever and was still vomiting. Frantic with worry, I managed to contact Keith at his mother's before he went to work, and he immediately came over to the hotel. We decided not to hesitate any longer and called a cab to take us to the nearest accident and emergency department, at the Whittington Hospital in Archway.

As we entered the emergency department, a nurse came over and immediately ushered us into a cubicle. The paediatrician arrived, took one look at Martine and admitted her immediately. She was put into isolation, and Keith and I could only sit nearby and wait for the diagnosis. I was trembling with fear, and tears filled my eyes as another doctor arrived to see her, and then another.

I was even more terrified when the Matron approached me and placed her arm around my shoulder. 'Mrs Ponting,' she said quietly, 'your baby is very sick and we suggest you stay.' I couldn't take it in. What was she saying? I looked at Keith, who began to sob.

6

Everyday Violence

Jenny

We were told that Martine had gastroenteritis and had become extremely dehydrated. The matron explained that the next few hours were critical – our baby might not make it. She was in a little cubical in a children's ward right at the top of the hospital, and I was allowed to sit beside her cot all the time. Keith stayed too, bringing endless cups of tea to get us through that long night. When slowly the sun began to rise on a new day I gave thanks – Martine was still alive and fighting. I called the little grocer's shop underneath Kim's flat and asked Mr Ali to run and fetch her urgently. Mr Ali and his wife were wonderful, and seemed happy to act as a telephone exchange for me and Kim. As soon as Kim heard what had happened she came to the hospital to offer support.

The gastroenteritis and dehydration had caused Martine all sorts of internal problems. It was going to take some time, but as I gazed at my beautiful baby, I knew she wouldn't give up. She was a real fighter.

She was in hospital for more than a month and I seldom left her side. I expressed milk for her when she was too sick to feed, and watched over her, leaving only to go home for a change of clothes.

Keith came to visit regularly and Kim was marvellous, coming to the hospital whenever she could. We would talk as we sat beside Martine, who continued to grow stronger each day. She had lost a lot of weight, but as she put it back on, her cheeks plumped out again and at six weeks old she looked as gorgeous as ever.

One day a man approached me in the special care unit. 'You have a beautiful baby there. I'd love to take some photographs of her for a billboard advertisement I'm doing. Would you mind? It's for the new Labour Party campaign.'

I was flattered and proud and happily agreed. Once he'd finished the session the photographer gave me a business card. 'Call these people and start that baby in modelling. She's perfect.' I took the card and said goodbye to him, but I hadn't taken what he said very seriously and soon forgot all about it.

A few days later I was on the bus when I looked out of the window and saw my baby on a giant poster. I was amazed at how quickly it had appeared. There she was, lying on her little mattress, wearing a nappy bigger than she was, while a slogan underneath declared, 'The Future is with Labour'.

I never got paid for the poster, but a few weeks later a big envelope arrived at Kim's, addressed to me. Inside were some lovely shots of Martine and a card from the photographer, reminding me to start Martine in child modelling. Kim told me she had spoken to him after he had taken the photographs and asked him to send me some of them. It was so typical of Kim to realise how much it would mean to me. Keith, of course, wasted no time in telling everyone about his daughter's poster debut. His pride in his daughter and his constant support at the hospital made me feel that, despite everything, there might still be a chance for us. Could the fear of losing his baby have made him turn over a new leaf?

After nearly four and a half weeks in hospital Martine was given the all-clear and discharged. I took her back to the bed and breakfast hotel, vowing that I'd get us a permanent home as soon as I could.

I sometimes took her round to see Keith's mum, Bridie. I got on well with her and she was always delighted to see her granddaughter. One day, not long after Martine came out of hospital, I went round to Bridie's for a visit. I was surprised when she looked a bit uncomfortable and told me Keith was in his room and needed to talk to me. She said she would take Martine out for a walk, while I went up to see him. I was puzzled, as I had expected Keith to be sleeping, after his night shift. This was all very odd. I went up to his room and found the door locked. I asked him to let me in, but he refused. I could hear a girl giggling in the room with him. I couldn't believe the way he was treating me, especially after our baby had narrowly missed death. Then I heard a rustle and looked down to see a green appointment card popping out from under the door. I picked it up and read it. When I saw what it said I banged on the door and begged Keith to open it, but he and the girl just laughed.

I rushed downstairs and into the street and looked for Bridie and the baby. She was just turning the corner and I called after her. I ran up and grabbed the buggy from her, angry and in tears.

'Did you know?' I shouted.

Bridie looked embarrassed and crestfallen. She spoke softly in her rich Irish accent. 'Yes, Jenny, I did, but I wasn't going to bail him out this time. He's my son and I'm so ashamed of him. He needed to tell you himself.'

She looked at me with tears in her eyes as I marched up the road, sobbing. The card Keith had shoved under the door said that he had VD – a sexually transmitted disease. I knew it was likely that I had it and possible that the baby could be infected. At that moment I wanted to die.

I couldn't take it in. When Martine was in hospital Keith had been so loving. He had stayed with me and comforted me and, vulnerable and afraid for my child, I had gone to bed with him. I still couldn't understand why he made me feel all the things I knew I shouldn't. I still loved him, and when we made love I never wanted him to leave me.

I had hoped that living through the near-death of our daughter had created a new bond between us and we could be each other's strength. But, as always, Keith had shattered my hopes in the cruellest way. It was clear that he had another girlfriend who had given him the VD, and despite this he preferred to be with her, leaving me stranded and alone and letting me know in the most cowardly way possible. He couldn't even face me, and as I thought of the two of them giggling in his room, my hatred for him and his new girlfriend filled every bone in my body.

I wasted no time in phoning for an appointment at a sexual health clinic. We called them VD clinics in those days, and having to visit one was about the most embarrassing thing I could imagine. And it was even worse, having to take my baby with me.

The clinic was based at the back of Homerton Hospital in a small, run-down building. I felt humiliated, and as I gave my name to the nurse I wanted to blurt out that I had done nothing wrong, that I was clean and that it was the father of my baby who had betrayed me with another woman. But I said nothing and just waited where I was told.

The other women in the waiting area read old magazines and rarely raised their heads. Eventually my name was called and I pushed the buggy into the consulting room. Various tests were carried out on me and the doctor swabbed my baby's private parts. After I'd shown them the card I'd received from Keith, they told me that Keith was quite badly infected and that he could have passed something on to the baby simply by changing her nappy if he hadn't washed his hands. This made my blood run cold, because Keith often changed Martine's nappy after her feed. I was told to return the following week and I left feeling devastated by the whole experience.

I made the return journey to the clinic a week later, praying I wouldn't meet anyone I knew. The results of the tests had come through. Martine, thank goodness, was given the all-clear. I wasn't so lucky, I had been infected and was prescribed a course of antibiotics. I went home in a daze, too scared and humiliated to tell anyone. My heart was truly broken and I wanted nothing more to do with Keith.

I'd had no word about being re-housed, so I started the rounds of appointments with the local councils and housing associations. No one seemed interested, but eventually they moved me from the bed and breakfast hotel to a half-way house, another interim step on the road to getting a permanent place. The house was situated close to London Fields and I was given a small room at the top. There was a shared kitchen on the landing, a shared bathroom, and the whole place was bleak, dismal and very dirty. I spent a week cleaning, but despite all my efforts the room had a stale stench and nothing could disguise the peeling wallpaper.

Living in this run-down, neglected place with no prospect of a home for us, there were times when I felt true despair. I would sit and cry and wonder how I was going to cope. I was lonely and afraid and there seemed to be little hope of anything changing.

Mice were a continuous problem. As I lay in my bed at night I could hear them scurrying around the room. I spent most of the night staring into the dark, terrified that they would get into Martine's cot. By morning they would have managed to eat some of her cot blanket, and the cereal in the cupboard in the kitchen would be strewn everywhere after they'd chewed the corners of the boxes.

I followed the same routine almost every day. I would wake early, feed Martine and then get both of us ready to face whatever lay ahead. Usually I would spend hours in the local housing offices, trying to get them to move me to a more permanent home. Each time I was offered nothing and I would feel more dejected than ever. Sometimes I felt like giving up, but every time I would dig a little deeper and try to find the determination and courage to help me carry on and believe things would get better.

Kim was my salvation. She would often spend days with me, trying to help, and she would come with me to help plead my case with the council. I was getting nowhere. Hackney Borough Council had refused to house me, but a kindly housing official had told me to try the Greater London Council, which often took cases that local councils could not help. I phoned the GLC and made an appointment to see a housing officer.

In the days before my appointment I kept everything crossed. The GLC's houses and flats were not pretty, often pre-war and unmodernised, but I was ready to live anywhere rather than stay where I was.

With Martine in her pram, I made the long journey by bus and tube to the GLC housing offices at King's Cross. There, at the end of a dingy corridor, I found the door I was looking for. I knocked and was invited in. Sitting behind a desk was an elderly man wearing small, round spectacles.

It didn't take long to explain my situation to him. I pleaded with him to help me and my baby find somewhere decent to live. He smiled at me and said he would write to me with his decision in a few days.

He had listened and seemed kind, and I left feeling hopeful. A few days later a letter arrived offering me a flat on the Pembury Estate in Hackney. The Pembury Estate was notorious. It had a reputation for violence, drugs and crime of every kind. Many unmarried mothers were placed there and then forgotten. I knew it wasn't going to be easy, but at least it was a chance to have a home of my own, somewhere to start us off. With Kim's help I moved into No. 44 Sandgate House on 14 December 1976. It was a two-bedroom flat on the second floor and it was cold, damp and filthy. It needed to be cleaned from top to bottom and I didn't have a lot of time, Christmas was coming and I wanted to make it special for my baby.

I scrubbed and cleaned for three days. I got a fire lit, and with my bits and pieces in place and a Christmas tree up in the lounge it almost seemed like home.

Kim and I both needed extra money for Christmas, and for a few weeks we had been 'home working' from Kim's flat – putting cards and envelopes together in packs of twelve. For every pack we got twenty pence. As Christmas approached we worked night and day, determined to make enough to buy presents and treat our children.

Keith had been round to see my new flat and said he wanted to spend Christmas with me and Martine. Since the VD episode things between us had been very strained. He had made endless promises and excuses, but I knew deep down that I would never forgive him and that something inside me had finally died.

I knew I had to handle him carefully. He would never give up his right to see Martine. She was his excuse for turning up whenever he felt like it, and there was nothing I could do to stop him, so I kept my feelings to myself and tried to keep things as pleasant as possible between us.

I agreed to make Christmas dinner, hoping that we could make our daughter's first Christmas really good. Surprisingly, he kept his word and we gave Martine her presents and then sat together as a family, eating our festive meal. For a little while I dared to believe that we had started on the road to being a complete family. But as usual, the good times didn't last. On Boxing Day Keith announced that he was going out and that I should be waiting for him on his return. The old fear gripped me and, too terrified to argue, I did as I was told. For the rest of the holiday, I sat and waited while Keith arrived and disappeared at will. I never knew when he would be back, or what kind of mood he would be in. I didn't dare go anywhere, knowing that if he came back and I wasn't there he would erupt into a violent fury.

One night he asked me to save him dinner. I did, and placed it carefully on a saucepan full of hot water to keep it as fresh for him as I could. As the hours went by with no sign of him, I switched the gas burner off, placed a plate over the dinner and went to bed.

I never really slept well in those days. I would sit bolt upright in bed at the smallest noise, waiting and listening for Keith. I was living in constant fear, never knowing what to expect, and always worrying about what would happen next.

When he finally arrived home in the early hours of that morning, he said the dinner on the saucepan was nasty and overcooked and insisted I get up and cook his dinner all over again. I knew he was waiting for me to argue but, as I peeled the potatoes all over again, I knew that I would do whatever he asked, just to keep my baby safe.

By the time New Year arrived I was a nervous wreck. Keith disappeared over the New Year and I spent it alone with Martine. She was such a delightful baby, always smiling and playing quietly, and I loved the peaceful time I had with her on my own. I didn't want to be with her father any more, but I didn't know how to escape from him. He could come and go as he pleased, walking out on me one day and returning the next, knowing I had no money and no means to get anywhere, other than walking. He would take whatever money I had and leave me alone to wonder where the next meal or Martine's nappies and milk would come from. I was trapped, and very unhappy.

Kim, as loving and dependable as ever, often came round with food parcels, milk and money. But I felt bad relying on her. This was not the life I had hoped for, and I knew that things would never get better unless Keith left us alone.

I was determined to get Keith out of my life, and I had a plan. The first step was to find a job. Kim had agreed to baby-sit while I went out to look for work. I didn't want to leave my baby, but I knew it was the only way to earn the money I would need to escape from Keith. It would take a while, but with enough money, I could leave London and find a new life. I had never had any trouble finding work and I soon got a job as a barmaid. Although he didn't like me going out, Keith would often agree to me working as he saw it as a way to get more money to line his pockets. Although I wasn't earning a lot, it was cash in hand and I managed to save a little by lying to Keith about how much I was actually earning.

The winter months passed, spring arrived and it would soon be Martine's first birthday. She was already walking and beginning to talk and was a happy, healthy little girl. I loved to dress her in pretty clothes, but although I worked very hard, I never seemed to have enough money to do all the things I wanted to do for her.

A couple of months after Martine's birthday Kim came round with wonderful news – she was pregnant again, and Carrine would have a brother or sister next spring. I couldn't wait to be an auntie again.

Kim had enough on her hands with Carrine to look after and now the pregnancy, and she couldn't manage Martine every day as well. Luckily for me, Chris, our younger brother, was now almost fifteen and he offered to baby-sit for Martine in the evenings so that I could keep working.

Chris adored Martine. She was such a good baby and I would return home from a late shift to find her fast asleep next to Chris – they looked like two angels.

Chris had worried me lately. He seemed a little withdrawn, but when I questioned him he shrugged and said it was nothing. I knew life wasn't easy for him. Chris was a deeply sensitive boy, and living at home was a nightmare for him. As well as the filth, the poor food and the sight of Mum being regularly beaten by Dad, Chris had to put up with Dad hitting him, picking on him and putting him down. Chris had real depths, but Dad had no interest in him – unless it was to humiliate him.

I tried to encourage Chris to stay with me as often as possible, but Chris was afraid of Keith and was reluctant to stay. It seemed sometimes as if there was nowhere he could run.

Carole would visit me too, and at sixteen she had developed into a very pretty young woman. As she grew up she appeared to escape from home at every opportunity. Sometimes she came over and baby-sat for Martine too, but Carole was a deeply tortured soul, and I never found it easy to communicate with her.

One Friday night, when Chris was baby-sitting, I returned home after a busy night in the pub to see Chris peering over the balcony, looking very anxious. When I reached the second-floor landing he rushed towards me.

'I couldn't stop him, Jen, I couldn't stop him,' he gasped.

I grabbed him by the shoulders. His face was ashen white and the tears were rolling down his face.

'He's taken the baby. He just pushed past me and took her out of the cot. Jen, I couldn't stop him.' Chris was rambling now, obviously in shock and feeling total desperation.

Horrified by what he was saying, I told him to stay where he was and ran as fast as I could to the local phone box. As I dialled 999 my whole body was shaking and all I could think of was my baby. My beautiful baby, my life, the only reason I went on, was gone. The emptiness was like a huge, awful void. I could hardly speak as the operator answered the call.

The police were very prompt and very kind. I explained the whole story of my relationship with my baby's father. In fact they knew me already because they'd been called out on many occasions by neighbours when Keith had beaten me. They'd done what they could, but in those days these incidents were classed as domestic disputes and there was not much they could do. They'd advised me to take out a civil action against Keith, as it was my only option, but I'd been too afraid. But now Keith had abducted our daughter things were different and the police could act.

A policewoman made me tea and sat me down in the kitchen to think about where he might have gone. After we'd drawn up a list of places we made our way to the patrol car. Chris waited at the flat with another officer, in case Keith returned.

For the next few hours we visited places I thought he might have gone. We went to his family and friends and to all-night cafés. He had a small child and he had to be somewhere, but everywhere and with everyone we turned up a blank. When we called on his mother she was worried sick and looked deeply ashamed of him yet again. We also called on Kim, who was sitting nervously at her flat waiting for news and secretly hoping Keith would turn up there with Martine.

I was becoming more and more frantic. Keith had no bottle and no clean nappies with him, and it was a chilly night. I kept thinking of Martine – was she cold, frightened, missing me? Taking her was the cruellest thing he could have done to me.

Our last call was at Keith's sister's flat in Downham Road. Margaret wouldn't open the door and I pleaded with her through the letter-box to tell me if she knew where my baby was. The reply was no, but as we turned to leave, I heard the bolt on the door slide. Margaret's partner Ginger popped his head out.

'He was here, but I told him to leave. He headed off to your mother's house.'

Thanking him, I raced back to the police car. All the way I prayed that Ginger was right and that my daughter was safe.

We reached my parents' home around five in the morning. Mum came to the door, holding Martine, who had apparently slept through the whole thing. I grabbed her from my mother and held her tightly to me. Her little face was peaceful and her dark lashes lay on her pale skin as she slept. My princess was safe, in the last place I'd expected to find her.

The police eventually caught up with Keith, who told them a grotesque pack of lies. He accused me of not letting him see his child, and of mistreating her by leaving her with my brother whilst I worked as a prostitute.

I had hoped that they'd be able to charge Keith, but he was Martine's father and they told me there was nothing I could do. They advised me, yet again, to seek legal help in keeping him away from us, but I was still far too frightened. I knew that if I took action Keith would find me and punish me, and I wasn't going to risk it. I may have been quietly confident with the police behind me, but once they had left I felt alone again and the determination to take action against Keith drained away as the fear kicked in.

By this time I was desperate to leave Sandgate House. It was depressing and ugly and I wanted something better for Martine, with a place to play or a garden to sit in. But it seemed an impossible hope; the council would never move me.

One day a letter arrived. The whole of the estate was to be modernised. We were to have new kitchens and bathrooms, and the old coal fires were to be replaced with central heating. I couldn't wait! I had also found a company that sold cheap televisions, and with some of my savings I bought an old colour set. It had no aerial, which meant using a coat hanger, and the picture was a permanent green colour, but at least we had something.

A couple of weeks later work began on the renovations to the flats. The workmen were all very sweet, but one in particular had a soft spot for me. He often helped me upstairs with Martine and the buggy and my bags of shopping. His name was Callum and he was in charge of re-covering the floors in the kitchens and bathrooms of all the renovated flats. He was dark and quite handsome and we would spend the last hour of the working day chatting. I found him easy to talk to, he was a good listener, and I had told him about the problems I had with Keith. He always showed me kindness and offered words of comfort when I needed them.

One sunny day, Callum was visiting me in the flat for a cup of tea. He was just finishing and getting ready to go home when I heard the strip blind rustle. I thought it was the summer breeze, but as I glanced towards the living-room door I saw Keith standing there, with a face like thunder. I was startled, as I hadn't seen him for a few weeks.

'Who the fuck are you?' he shouted at Callum, who remained calm and stood up. He looked at Keith and without turning his head towards me said, 'Do you want me to go, Jenny?'

'I think it's best,' I muttered.

As he went to leave he turned and looked at me. 'Are you sure, honey?'

I nodded and Callum sighed and walked out. He and I had become great friends, and the tone he used was almost a challenge to Keith not to touch or hurt me. He was the sort of man who would want to protect any woman in trouble. But he also knew that, in the end, this situation with Keith was something I had to work out for myself.

Keith looked furious, but then his manner changed. 'Where's my princess?' he asked. I told him Martine was sleeping, and he swaggered towards me as I sat frozen on my chair. He straddled my legs and pushed his groin into my face. I was terrified, dreading what might happen next. My mind was racing and I tried desperately to think of some way to escape, but I was powerless against this man, just as I had been against my father. Memories flooded back of the abuse I had suffered as a child, and I knew no one could help me. I was praying that someone would arrive at the door to interrupt him, but no one came. It was only then that I realised that I was to be punished for what Callum had said. This was Keith's way of telling me I was his and that it didn't matter who tried to fight for me, they would always lose.

'Undo my trousers, baby, and get my dick out and then suck it hard,' Keith ordered. I refused, but he grabbed my head by my hair and repeated his demands. Unable to fight him, I did as he said. The oral sex was violent and unpleasant and as soon as he had climaxed, I sank back on the chair, gagging. He threw his head back and laughed. 'Very good,' he said and then went down on his knees to look me in the eyes. His breath stank of alcohol and he had tobacco stuck to his lips. His eyes were wild, and I knew then that he was high on drugs and hadn't finished with me. All I could think of was that Martine was sleeping and that any noise could wake her.

Keith looked long and hard at me as he spouted vulgar and disgusting verbal abuse. He seemed to get excited by humiliating me, and knowing I couldn't fight back. 'Open your legs, bitch; it's time for your examination,' he spat.

He placed his fingers roughly into the gusset of my knickers and ripped them apart, shoving his fingers into me. After what seemed like hours, he stopped and knocked me sideways on to the floor. As I lay on my side he pulled me up on to my knees and straddled me again, smacking my backside and asking me to wail. I was no more than a dog to him. When he finally stopped slapping me he turned me over to have full intercourse. With one hand covering my mouth and the other pinching and squeezing my breast, he climaxed again and fell to the floor. As he got his breath back, he stood up and gazed down at me. Then he placed his boot over my stomach and stamped hard. The pain was unbearable, but again I stifled my sobs.

'I'm going to sleep now, wake me with a decent meal and a cuppa, slag.' He walked out of the room and into the spare bedroom, slamming the door. I rolled over, holding my stomach, and coughed. Blood spurted out into my hand. I needed to get to the hospital and I knew I couldn't make it alone, or leave Martine. I had to have help.

At that moment, with perfect timing, Kim arrived. By the time I'd managed to let her in, Keith was snoring loudly in the spare room. I was in agony and Kim was horrified when she saw me, but there was no time to go into what had happened – all I needed to say was 'Keith.' Martine stirred and Kim went in to get her up from her afternoon nap. I needed medical attention urgently – so with the two girls in the buggy, and Kim's shoulder to lean on, I managed to walk to the local hospital, Homerton. The walk was horrendous and I had to stop often to take a rest, but eventually we made it to the casualty department.

Kim stayed patiently in the waiting room while a kindly doctor examined me. Two of my ribs were broken and I had severe bruising. The doctor was lovely: he sat next to me and told me he was concerned; it wasn't the first time I had turned up in casualty in a bad way. He knew he wasn't allowed to report such incidents, so he tried to encourage me to seek help.

I wanted to take his advice, but I was so scared. I knew that if I attempted anything things might get even worse. Keith would always return, no matter what I did, and maybe the next time he was out of control, he might hurt the baby. I couldn't cope with that. It seemed better to leave things as they were.

When I was patched up and discharged, Kim took me home with her as she felt it was just too dangerous for us to return to the flat. Graham was waiting and he said little as Kim helped me to the sofa. I could see he was angry, but he made no comment. Kim cooked supper, bathed the two girls and put them to bed, and then we sat quietly, not saying a word. What was there to say?

I knew I would have to return to the flat sometime, and though I was still very sore and finding it painful to move, the following evening I decided to go back. I needed a change of clothes and to get Martine back into her routine. And I wasn't going to be frightened out of my own home, not even by Keith.

The flat was empty when I arrived back and, for the next few days, peace was restored. I tried to settle back into my routine, but I was never really able to. I was constantly on my guard and forever looking over my shoulder. On the Friday evening, a few days after the attack, Chris arrived to baby-sit. I had decided to go in to work. I needed the money and couldn't afford to miss it. I applied my make-up carefully, trying to cover the all-too-obvious bruises. It was painful and hard to breathe, and I had to hold myself when bending down, but I had no choice. I had no money and little food and so, with the help of a tight bandage and strong pain-killers, I went and suffered in silence.

Work was good therapy for me, and the atmosphere in the pub on a Friday night was always great. The other barmaids carried me through the evening; they were so sweet and kind to me and they never asked questions. I was popular and good at my job, and despite my bruises I still received a steady stream of attention from the men in the pub that evening. One guy in particular always tried to chat me up. He was tall and good-looking and his name was Marc. He had a sympathetic ear and towards the end of the evening he offered to give me a lift home. I was tired and it had been one hell of a week, so I agreed.

As we pulled up at the flats, something told me not to invite Marc in for a coffee. I climbed the stairs and reached the door, which was slightly ajar. As soon as I realised Keith was there again my heart started to pound. Chris didn't want to leave; he was afraid of what Keith might do, but I assured him I would be fine and sent him home.

Once Chris had left I waited for Keith to erupt, but surprisingly he didn't. He'd heard about the extent of my injuries and he was full of remorse for what had happened. He actually begged for forgiveness. As usual his unpredictable moods stunned me and I felt I had no choice but to forgive him.

Kim

Jenny had worked hard to get her flat and to look after Martine. She was now supporting herself and her baby and had her independence. But I knew that Keith continued to turn up unannounced whenever he wanted, demanding money and sex, and I had my suspicions that each time he went one step further in his violence towards her.

I tried to make Jenny see sense and take legal action to stop him, as he was making her go backwards instead of forwards. But she always thought she knew best and that she could cope with his demands. I worried, though, that his behaviour towards Jenny was beginning to affect Martine. She would cower when Keith was around, hiding behind Jenny's legs and whimpering. Jenny had protected her as best she could from witnessing the beatings and drunken calling cards, but she couldn't hide everything from Martine, who must have heard Keith's rantings and who often saw her mother bruised and injured.

It was for this reason above all others that I nagged Jenny to do something, but she continued to deny to me there was much of a problem. She attempted to play down Keith's behaviour and even accused me of exaggerating. I was left wondering whether she was ashamed of what he was doing, so ashamed that she couldn't even tell me, the one person she truly trusted. As children our way of dealing with the abuse was to keep quiet and never talk about it, and it seemed Jenny was still doing the same thing.

She tried to make everything all right and to blank out Keith by giving Martine special treats and a 'normal' childhood, hoping that Martine would forget about the bad times. But hard as Jenny tried, she couldn't stop what was going on affecting Martine.

On a visit to London Zoo with the girls I talked to Jenny about violence. Since our father's court case we had never discussed any details of our childhood with anyone, not even one another. Our attitude was: it happened, move on, there's nothing that can be done now. But on that warm and sunny afternoon in Regent's Park I broke the silence and asked Jenny what she used to think when we were awoken by Mum's screams, the sounds of her head and body being punched and her muffled cries for help. Jenny recalled being scared and frightened, and with tears in her eyes she said she used to pray that he wouldn't come into our room. I asked her to think how Martine must feel, hearing what went on when Keith called round to demand sex and beat her mother.

Jenny stared ahead and didn't answer for a long time. The girls were playing happily and she watched them for a while before replying, 'Do you think she really understands what happens when he calls round?'

'Jen, look at what it did to us,' I answered. 'We heard everything, didn't we? If we could have chosen then to be anywhere else do you think we'd have stayed around to witness that?'

She looked at Carrine and Martine playing, and with tears in her eyes she admitted she didn't want Martine to have to witness anything like the horrors we remembered.

I didn't need to say anything more to Jenny. I trusted she would sort out the problem with Keith once and for all, for her daughter's sake. Suddenly Carrine and Martine began screaming with glee as the elephants and camels came trotting past on their way to give children's rides, and we rushed to the queue to take our turns.

Graham and I had settled down very happily. We got on well together and had a warm and loving relationship. We were rarely tactile in public, apart from linking arms, but when we were alone we would often cuddle up on the sofa together. And when I was washing up or bathing Carrine, Graham would come up behind me and kiss me on the cheek or the back of the neck. I treasured those moments, I felt loved and very secure.

Graham was very much settled in his work as a shipping manager, and I had found an evening job at a greeting card factory. I worked Monday to

Friday, from six until ten, while Graham stayed with Carrine. She was a dream and we both loved being with her.

We had talked about having a second child, and with Carrine getting older and me beginning to feel broody, we decided the time was right to start trying.

Soon afterwards I had confirmation that I was pregnant, and Graham and I were both elated. I was just nineteen and this baby would complete the family I had always longed for. Graham wanted a son, to continue the family name and share in his passion for sport. I wanted a boy as well, just because we already had a girl. Money would be tight, but we were both working, so we knew we could manage. We had all the equipment a baby would need, so it would just be a case of an extra mouth to feed. We couldn't wait.

7

Riding the Rollercoaster

Jenny

During those painful weeks while my broken ribs healed I thought long and hard about taking legal action against Keith. When Kim had told me of her concerns for Martine it shook me. Of course I'd worried desperately for Martine myself, but it was even worse hearing it from my sister. I knew Kim wanted me to make sure Keith couldn't come near us again, but I had no faith in the law at all. The police had several times dismissed Keith's behaviour as a 'domestic', so the only option I had was to take civil action. And that wouldn't put Keith behind bars; it would only result, at best, in an injunction, leaving him free to take revenge on me. The thought terrified me, and I convinced myself I was better off trying to handle Keith in my own way.

To cheer me up while I was recovering, Kim announced that she and Graham wanted us to join them on a week-long holiday to Devon. I was a little worried about money, but Kim put my mind at rest by insisting that she and Graham would treat us. It was the answer to my prayers.

For the time being I decided not to mention the holiday to Keith. I didn't know how he'd take the idea of us going away, so I kept it to myself. It would be the break I so badly needed and a real treat for Martine.

As the holiday drew near I still hadn't drummed up the courage to tell Keith we were going. In the end I decided to go without telling him. I was too afraid that he'd do something to stop me going. I knew he'd almost certainly call round while we were away, and if he did I'd have hell to pay when I got back. But at least I'd have my holiday and it would be worth it. I packed our suitcase late on the night before we were due to leave and prayed Keith wouldn't come round. But my luck was out. He turned up at two a.m., drunk and abusive – but not too drunk to notice the suitcase.

After making his usual sexual demands and giving me a few thumps for trying to deceive him, he forced me into the kitchen, naked, and ordered me to make him tea. As I fumbled with the teapot, he grabbed me and held me against the kitchen wall. I prayed silently that he would soon leave me alone and go. I thought I might get a few hours' sleep before meeting Kim and Graham at the station.

I was wrong. Holding me by the neck with one hand, he reached behind with the other to open the kitchen drawer. He took out a large knife and began to wave it in front of my face.

'Looking to get another bloke on the firm are ya? What if I cut that pretty face of yours, then what, eh?'

I was too terrified to move. The blade was scraping against the skin on my face and I knew that if I made the slightest movement I'd be cut. Sweat was pouring down my face and I was rigid with fear. Slowly he put the knife down. But before I had time for relief he clenched his fist and struck me full on the mouth. Stunned, I felt the blood trickle down from my lip, then my legs gave way and I sank to the floor.

When I came round I managed to pick myself up, but I was in a lot of pain. Apart from the beating, my vagina was sore and throbbing. Keith must have raped me while I was unconscious and had left me in agony. When I crept through to the front room there was no sign of him. I checked the bedrooms. I thanked God he had gone. I looked at the clock. It was five a.m. and I was due to meet Kim and Graham at Paddington Station in a couple of hours. Keith had done his best to stop me going on holiday, but I was determined he wouldn't win.

I managed to have a bath and dress myself and then get Martine up and ready with time to spare. I set off, pushing Martine in the buggy with one hand and carrying our suitcase in the other. I had a long walk and then had to haul the buggy and the luggage on and off the bus. I was exhausted and in pain; looking back, it was willpower alone that got me to that station. As I approached Kim, Graham and the baby, my legs started to give way. I fell into Graham's arms and Kim took Martine. Once on the train and with a cup of hot tea from the buffet car, I fell into a deep sleep.

Kim

My earnings from my evening job enabled us to save a little money and go on the holiday – the first we'd had as a family. We booked a week in a holiday centre in Dawlish, Devon, and Graham suggested asking if Jenny and Martine would like to join us. 'She'd love to,' I told him. 'Don't you think you ought to ask her first?' he said, but we both knew that it would be a treat for Jenny, and besides, Martine would be company for Carrine.

When I told Jenny, she was worried that she wouldn't be able to afford it, but after I explained that we'd pay the fares and the accommodation and it would be just as cheap to feed three adults as two, she happily agreed. Her only worry was Keith: she didn't want him finding out or he would be sure to try to put a stop to it. She hoped she could keep it from him, but when she met us at the station it was evident that Keith had left his calling card. She had a bruised lip and was obviously in pain. She was struggling along with the baby in the buggy and the case, and we could see she was in a bad way. We were just glad that she'd made it.

Once we got to Devon the whole family had great fun. Jenny and I rented bikes and went off sightseeing, and for once she could relax in the knowledge that Martine was safe. We returned four hours later, saddle sore and vowing never to ride bikes again!

There was plenty of free entertainment in the clubhouse at the centre, and in the week's diary of events we saw there was a children's fancy dress competition. As we didn't have much money, Jenny and I scoured the area for ways to make costumes for the girls. Eventually we cut four leaves off a tree, stuck them on Carrine and Martine and entered them as Adam and Eve. They came second and we were really proud, although Carrine cried because she was old enough to understand and she didn't want to be the boy.

Later in the day there was a show for the adults, with a magician, and we all went to watch. As soon as the show began, the magician headed straight for our table and chose Jenny as his assistant. She was cut in half and then made to disappear, only to return ten minutes later with a phone number and the promise of a date she didn't particularly want – with the magician.

It was all good fun and a far cry from the misery she had to endure back in London. I was glad, as I wanted to show her how different things could be for her and Martine in a decent family environment.

The holiday did seem to have a positive effect. Jenny came home looking good and feeling so much better. And on the way home she told me she wasn't going to let Keith hurt and abuse her any more.

Now that I was pregnant again, Graham and I realised our flat above the greengrocer's was far too small. I had already signed us up on the waiting list for the Samuel Lewis Housing Trust a while back, and not long after the holiday we heard that we were being given a flat.

It was a two-bedroom flat on the fourth floor of a block in Dalston. It wasn't a lot bigger than the flat we already had, but it was better designed and more modern. The toilet was in the bathroom instead of down a flight of stairs, it had central heating and was easy to heat and clean, and it was newly decorated. All we needed to add were carpets.

It did mean we had more stairs to climb, but at least we'd have our own front door. No more throwing keys down to visitors, who then had to find their way through the back alleys to get to us. I loved it, and I was pleased because it was much nearer to Jenny. Unfortunately it was also closer to where Keith lived, at his mother's home, which we weren't happy about. In fact Graham wasn't too pleased with the flat at all; I think he had hoped for better things for our children. There was nowhere for them to play, and he didn't relish having neighbours on both sides or being on the fourth floor.

Excited as I was about our new start, when the time came to move I was sorry to say goodbye to the old flat. It had been my first home and the place where it all began for us as a family.

Jenny

I returned home from Devon relaxed and happy. For a whole week I'd been able to laugh and enjoy myself without constantly looking over my shoulder, and it had done me so much good. As I got closer to home I became more and more nervous, but when I opened the door of the flat, I was relieved to find it as I had left it. For the moment I had peace, but I knew it wouldn't be long before Keith reappeared.

I soon got back into the old routine. Callum was still around, being his usual cheerful self. We'd become good friends and he often dropped in. And

I made friends with a girl called Lisa who lived in the flat directly below mine. She had married young and had a baby and then met someone else. She confided in me that like me, she was still getting grief from her ex, though not on Keith's scale. She called upstairs to my flat to introduce herself and her beautiful baby girl, Kerry, who was just a few months old. Martine loved their visits; she would sit in a chair and hold Kerry on her lap, beaming with pleasure, and I was glad to have company. Lisa became a good friend, we often went to the shops together, and sometimes Kim would join us.

Around this time Kim and Graham moved into their new flat. Kim had managed to get it with the help of our old friend Stacey, who lived on the Amhurst Road Estate. Kim was offered a flat only a short walk from both Stacey and me.

I envied Kim and her new flat; it was so much nicer than mine. My next-door neighbour, Astra, who I hadn't known well, had moved out and sold the keys on to someone who only wanted the flat for all-night parties. This was a common occurrence on the Pembury Estate. Night after night, I would try to sleep, but it was almost impossible with the noise going on next door. I would wake exhausted and try to grab a few hours during the day, but again this was virtually impossible with all the workmen milling around. As the night closed in again, I prayed that it wouldn't be a party night.

would kill me one day. It comforted me to know that if the worst happened at least Kim would make sure my baby was safe.

One particular day, a few weeks after our holiday, death came closer than ever. It was the day Elvis died – 16 August 1977 – and Martine was fifteen months old. I'd been to the shops with her, and everyone, young and old, seemed to be in shock at the news about the King of Rock. I went home, and settled Martine down for her nap, made myself a cup of tea and started to doze off in the chair. As I sat with my eyes closed, I became aware of someone's presence. I opened my eyes to see Keith standing there. When the weather was good I often left the front door open, with a strip curtain across it, to let the breeze circulate, so Keith had been able to walk straight in. And in any case there was never anything I could do to keep him out. If I didn't let him in he'd batter the door down.

It was late afternoon and he'd obviously been in the pub. His clothes and breath stank of stale beer. He had a joint hanging from his mouth and he just stared at me. I sat up slowly, but as I did, he punched me full on the face. I started to scream, but he put his hand over my mouth and hissed, 'Shut it.' My screams became whimpers.

He ordered me to undress. He seemed to love this power he had over me, and I could only follow his instructions. Naked, I felt vulnerable and humiliated. He threw me on to the floor, and as I fell I caught my face on the corner of the coffee table. Suddenly I could not see out of my left eye. I began to panic, but he laughed and ignored me. As I tried to touch my face with my hands, he pulled them down, pinning my arms with his body. One of his hands came over my mouth and the other started to open his flies. Once he had entered me, with one hand still over my mouth, he brought his other arm up across my throat. I was being slowly suffocated and I could feel the breath leaving me. Within minutes, I passed out.

As I came round, Keith was still on top of me. He must have realised what was happening and I can only assume he panicked enough to release his grip. He lifted himself off me and ordered me to sit on the chair. I must have looked a terrible sight. I could feel blood pouring from the wound on my eye.

'You're pathetic, d'ya know that,' he spat. 'If it wasn't for that kid, I'd finish you.' I looked at the floor. If I made eye contact with him I knew he would see how I really felt. Inside I was raging, I wanted to kill him. I felt at breaking point and suddenly I knew I could take no more. In a mad dash I made it to the kitchen and grabbed a knife. I wanted to plunge the knife into him and as I did it I would laugh! But Keith was too quick for me. As we fought for control of the knife, he twisted my arm to make me drop it, but I held on. The knife cut into the flesh on his arm, causing a deep gash. He prised the knife out of my hand and threw it into the sink, then he looked at his wound, laughed and grabbed me by the hair to drag me back into the front room.

At that moment I heard the bedroom door open. Rubbing her eyes and carrying her bottle, Martine tottered into the room. She looked at me and started to scream. Keith grabbed her before I had the chance to. She wriggled and pushed his face with her little hands.

'Now we'll see who's boss in this house,' he yelled. He moved to the front door, which was still open, and stood on the balcony holding Martine. My heart was in my mouth. I grabbed a housecoat to cover my nakedness and followed him out on to the balcony. He held Martine by her feet and swung her over the balcony wall so that she dangled, upside down, in midair. We were two floors up – if he let go he would kill her. My sobs turned to panic and hysteria. Until now Keith had never hurt Martine and I'd told myself he never would. But this man was capable of anything. Martine just hung in midair, not moving or making a sound. I begged and pleaded. 'You can have anything – money, me, whatever you want – just please don't hurt my baby.'

Lisa appeared around the corner and screamed.

Callum came running up the stairs in the opposite direction and slowed his pace as he approached Keith. Quietly he spoke. 'Don't be a fool, mate. Give the baby back.'

Keith glared at Callum, but suddenly his demeanour changed. He pulled Martine back to the safe side of the balcony and hugged her. Through sobs I heard him whisper to her, 'Forgive me.'

Keith pushed Martine into my arms and ran towards the stairs. All of us were in shock. I held my precious baby close and sobbed. Callum led me inside and Lisa put the kettle on. Before long the news had spread around the estate and everyone was gunning for Keith. I begged them not to do anything. I knew it would make him even worse.

This incident, more than any other, galvanised me into action. Now that Keith had threatened Martine I could not risk him being around her. I had to get away – I would never let him touch her again.

The very next day I made the trip to see the estate manager at Stacey's flats. I knew how bad I looked and I hoped he would feel sorry for me. By this time I had no pride left, I just needed help. Stacey came with me to his office and she was simply marvellous. The manager asked where I was living and I lied. I said I was back at my parents', and he said he would arrange for a duty officer to come and visit me.

I wasted no time in returning to Monteagle Court and setting up the room to make it look as if I was staying there. I didn't want to lie or fool anyone, but I knew that if I told the truth I wouldn't get help. I couldn't take any more chances. Martine and her safety had to come first and I would do whatever it took.

A few weeks later the letter arrived at Monteagle Court to say that the officer would be visiting. I made sure that everything was in place and Martine and I were ready. The officer was a lovely lady, and when she saw the filthy state of Monteagle Court, she said she would recommend me for re-housing immediately.

Sure enough, a few days later a letter arrived offering me No. 68 Samuel Lewis Flats. It was a top-floor flat, with four huge flights of stairs to conquer before reaching it, but I didn't care. This was my chance to escape from the Pembury Estate and all the memories.

The only people I told that I was going were Lisa and Callum, who offered me the use of his van to move my things. Within a week Martine and I had left Sandgate House and were installed in Samuel Lewis Flats.

Kim

Yet again Keith had come into Jenny's life and turned it upside down. When she got the chance of a new flat I pleaded with her not to let Keith or his family know where she lived. If she continued to have contact with them she would never be free of him. She listened quietly and promised me that she wouldn't let anyone who knew Keith know where she was. I was relieved, both for her sake and for Martine's.

On 15 March 1978, which happened to be Jenny's 22nd birthday, our son was born. He had been due on 1 March, and once he was two weeks overdue I was told he would have to be induced.

I went into St Bartholomew's Hospital the day before, where they took me through the procedure and showed me the epidural needle they planned to insert in my back. I was amazed at the size of it and lay awake all night worrying.

The worry obviously worked wonders, because by five in the morning my labour pains had started and my baby was born by seven. Unfortunately Graham missed the birth as the nurses guessed that I would be ready to deliver at nine and told him to return then. By the time he came in I was up and about and I walked down to the nursery to introduce him to his son.

Graham looked at him and said, 'Bloody hell, is he ours?' He had weighed nine pounds ten ounces at birth and looked a lot older and bigger than the other babies. His little face was all screwed up and he had deep olive skin and enormous brown eyes. When Jenny met him later that day she nicknamed him Chief Sitting Bull, and although I was a little upset, I had to admit that the name suited him.

We called him Daniel Michael after two of Graham's closest friends. Graham might have liked to name our son after another good friend, who was also the best man at our wedding, but his name was Ron – the same as my father's – so he never stood a chance.

I didn't want Carrine to feel left out, so I had arranged for Graham to get a present for her, and when she visited we slipped it under the baby's cot and told her Daniel had brought it for her. The present turned out to be a pair of football boots – I'm not sure what three-year-old Carrine made of them, but Graham thought they were great, and there was the added bonus that when Carrine outgrew them she could pass them on to her little brother.

Not long after Daniel was born we heard that Laurence, who'd been doing really well in his career, had got a great new job in Colchester, Essex. He and Margaret were buying a house in Wivenhoe, a small village just outside the town. Once they'd moved in they invited us down for a weekend. We loved the place, which seemed so clean and peaceful after London. While we were there we noticed that new houses were being built nearby and the developers were offering first-time buyers the chance to secure one for only two hundred and fifty pounds. It sounded too good to miss, but that amount of money was still an awful lot for us. We pondered all weekend over whether we could find a way to raise the money. In the end we managed to borrow some from Graham's parents and some from Laurence, and with what we had saved we scraped it together.

A few months later, in the autumn of 1978, we were packing up all our belongings again and heading off to Wivenhoe to start our new life in a three-bedroom house that cost twelve thousand pounds. Our house was in the same close as Laurence and Margaret's, a new home that had only been finished three months before we bought it.

I was excited about our new start and looking forward to better things for all of us. Graham and I were both happy that the children would be in a healthier, safer environment. My only regret was that we were leaving Jenny behind with Martine. But as long as Keith didn't find them, I knew they'd be all right. Jenny was a fighter and a survivor and she'd make it.

Jenny

Stacey introduced me to lots of other women on the estate. One of them was Pam, who was to become a very good friend. Pam had three very boisterous boys and a drug-taking partner, Tom. Everyone in Lewis Flats had a story, but it was a good little community and soon I had a bunch of girlfriends who all looked out for me. When times were hard we would help each other, and for the first time in ages I had begun to feel safe.

I knew there was always the risk that Keith would track me down. He would be furious to find me gone and would question everyone. But most people didn't know where I was, and those that did were loyal and would never tell him.

The weeks turned into months with no sign of him and I began to get back to my old self. Carole had started to visit me and would baby-sit for Martine on the rare occasions when I went out with the girls. We were all single parents, apart from Stacey.

Kim was nearing the end of her second pregnancy and I was delighted when Daniel was born on my birthday. I rushed up to St Bart's to see them both and immediately stuck my nose into the cot by the side of the bed. I stifled a giggle, for lying there was a huge bundle, with no hair and a bright red nose. 'Cripes, Kim, he looks like Chief Sitting Bull,' I said, and I burst out laughing. Kim was really upset, but I told her I was only joking, and that he would improve with age – and he did.

When Daniel was a few months old Kim came round to tell me she and Graham were going to buy their own home in Essex. It sounded like an incredible deal, and I didn't blame Kim for wanting something better, but I was going to miss her so much. However, life was so much better now that I was away from Keith and I had Pam and Stacey and my other new friends. I knew I would be OK and I promised her that Martine and I would visit soon.

Martine was a bright child and I loved being with her and watching her learn. When she wanted to do something she would go on trying until she managed it. The first time she walked, at ten months, she had pulled herself to her feet over and over again until she succeeded, and it had been the same with everything else. She loved books and would sit looking at them for hours – she had never damaged a book, even when she was tiny. And she was very good at keeping herself busy. She liked her own company and would play by herself quite happily.

Once Martine turned three I got her a place in playschool, starting the following September. In another year she would join the nursery class at school.

Our life together seemed settled, but it wasn't to last. One night, at a Tupperware party in the house of a friend called Frances, the doorbell went. As Frances opened the door, I heard Keith's voice. He showed her a fake ID and said he was searching for his long-lost family. He described me and Martine.

As I sat there I froze, my fear obvious to everyone in the room. I covered my mouth and closed my eyes. I heard Frances apologise and say she knew nothing about us. The door closed and she came back into the room. We all remained quiet, in case he was still outside.

A plan was hatched to get me to my flat unseen by Keith, who was obviously patrolling the estate looking for me. Pam offered to go back to her flat and ask Tom to come and get me and walk me home. A little while later she arrived with Tom, who seemed very calm. He explained that Keith was downstairs and that he knew him and he was an alright bloke. He couldn't understand why I was frightened. I tried to explain to him, but he would have none of it, insisting that Keith wouldn't harm me. It only made sense later, when I found out that apparently Keith knew Tom through the drugs business! After he left Frances's flat, Keith had happened to knock on Tom's door and he, not knowing any better, had told Keith where I lived. Pam felt terrible about what had happened. I didn't blame her, but my cover had been blown and panic and despair returned to my life. Keith knew where I lived, and the nightmares began again. Soon things were no better than they had been before. I didn't know what to do – it seemed there was no escape.

I knew I had to get away, so I contacted Laurence in Wivenhoe. He said he would make some enquiries and try to find me a flat with a job. I didn't want to go – we were settled with good friends, and I had some nice little cash-in-hand jobs that earned me a bit extra – but I felt I had no choice. A few days later, Laurence was in London and after he'd finished work he came round to see me. He told me that a local political party social club in Colchester was looking for a live-in barmaid. It was the perfect opportunity for me to get away. And at least he and I would see more of each other, and I'd be near Kim and Graham too.

I got the job, and with a heavy heart I told my friends. I would miss them, especially Pam. She was brilliant and promised to visit as soon as she could. Tom had gone and she had met a new man, a policeman. They were in love and I was so happy for her.

Stacey had fallen out of love with her husband and was seeing someone called Brian, and soon afterwards she left to set up home with him. Everyone seemed to be moving on.

Callum had been a regular visitor to the little flat and we had grown fond of one another. But we both knew it could go no further, because he was married with a family of his own. It was hard to say goodbye, but once again he helped me move, turning up in the van to take me to Liverpool Street Station. We said a tearful farewell, and as I boarded the train with Martine I wondered what lay ahead.

Kim

Everything should have been perfect in our new home, but almost as soon as we moved there I began to feel very isolated. Graham had a rail season ticket so that he could travel to London for his job. But it wasn't just on weekdays that he used it – he took full advantage of it by going to London at weekends to carry on with his football in the winter and cricket in the summer. He wasn't interested in joining local clubs.

He was leaving the house at six in the morning and returning at seven every evening on weekdays, and then at weekends we hardly saw him because of his sports. After three months I hardly remembered what he looked liked, and I became more and more lonely. I didn't have any friends in the area apart from Margaret, who was at work during the day. The only solace I found was in getting the telephone connected, which enabled me to keep in touch with Jenny and my friends.

At least Chris came to stay regularly. Graham would often pick him up after work on Friday and bring him home. He loved the children and was always easy to have around. But gradually I began to notice a difference in him. He developed lots of spots around his mouth and nose and he often appeared glassy-eyed. I didn't know what was going on until I discovered from Jenny that he'd got in with the wrong crowd and started sniffing glue. It was a dangerous thing to do, and we were all worried.

I knew how hard Chris's life had been. He was the only one left at home now so he was taking all the flak from Dad. I talked things over with Laurence and we both agreed to give him the chance of a new life in Colchester with us. After all, we'd had Auntie to lead us in the right direction, but Carole and Chris had no one.

We moved Chris into our house, assuring Mum that she could keep the family allowance money, which was all Dad cared about. Laurence got him a bit of work helping with a milk round for the holidays, we found him a new school, and at first he appeared to settle well. Then one day, a few weeks after he arrived, two police officers knocked on the door asking if I was Chris's guardian. I said yes and they went on to explain that they had found empty glue canisters and plastic bags over at the nearby waste ground and suspected Chris. It seemed he had been bunking off school and sniffing glue. I was very upset that he had done this when we'd tried so hard to help him.

I wasn't happy having Chris around Carrine and Daniel when he was high on glue, so we agreed that he would spend most of his time with Laurence, in the hope that Laurence could be more of a father figure to him and help him sort out his problems.

We told him it was his last chance, and for a while it seemed to be working.

In the meantime I was also very upset to hear that Keith had found Jenny and was giving her as much trouble as ever. When Laurence managed to find her the live-in bar job it seemed the ideal solution, and I was over the moon that she was going to come and live near us. The only condition was that she wasn't to tell Keith where she was going, but Jenny didn't want him to know any more than we did. It would be another new start for her, and we all hoped that this time it would work.

8

Big Decisions

Jenny

I spent my first weekend in Colchester cleaning. The club was huge and very dusty. I'd taken the job without going for an interview, just on Laurence's recommendation, and almost as soon as I saw the place I wondered what I'd let myself in for. I was expected to keep the hall, corridors, stairs, snooker hall and toilets clean, as well as working behind the bar.

My quarters, above the bar, were two large rooms, a bathroom and a very small kitchen, and like the rest of the place they needed a good clean. I did my best to settle us in and make it look nice, but the whole place seemed grim.

I made my first appearance behind the bar on the Monday lunchtime. It was very busy and no one seemed to care that it was my first day, they just carried on talking loudly and demanding more drinks. I was even asked when I was going to start doing lunches, and I wondered how on earth they thought I'd fit that in as well.

The cleaning and bar work took the entire day, and by the time I finished and crawled back upstairs, I was exhausted. I hated the whole place, but I didn't dare say anything to Kim or Laurence after they'd gone to so much trouble to move me up there.

Kim had offered to baby-sit until I got Martine into a nursery. I hoped that would be soon, as she already had Daniel and Carrine to look after and I could see she was beginning to feel the strain. And the journey to Kim's house was a nightmare. I had no transport, so I bought a second-hand bike through a newspaper advertisement, and attached a baby seat to the back for Martine. Just getting to Wivenhoe took me 45 minutes, and I had to do the round trip twice a day. So it was a great relief when Martine was offered a nursery place and my biking days came to an end.

Martine settled in well and made lots of friends. I, on the other hand, was miserable and very lonely. I hardly got a chance to see Kim or Laurence because I was working such long hours, and no one in the club seemed interested in making friends. My problems got worse when some money went missing from the club whilst a member of my family from London was staying. The first I knew about it was when I got back one morning from dropping Martine at nursery to discover that the place had been ransacked. I was devastated and despite the fact that I had had nothing to do with the theft, I was asked to leave. I had to sort out somewhere to live. With Laurence's help, I went to the local council offices.

It was a wonderful surprise when they immediately offered me a small cottage in the old Dutch quarter of the town. The cottage was ancient and dilapidated, but it would do. Within days I'd also got myself a full-time job at Ratner's, the jewellers.

Although I worked every Saturday I got every Thursday off, which gave me a chance to visit Kim. She had begun to look tired and fed-up and had started to lose weight. I was worried about her, so I was glad when she told me she had found an evening job. She needed something more in her life. Graham had his work and all his hobbies, while Kim had very little.

I was also concerned for Laurence and Margaret. They didn't seem happy either. Margaret confided to me that things were not going well. It was hard to know what to say. All I could hope was that it would blow over.

Kim

It seemed to me that Jenny had done really well. I had no idea that she wasn't happy at the club. All I could see was that she'd got herself a nice little job and a lovely flat and she was based in the centre of Colchester, so she could make friends. I, on the other hand, was still feeling really low and missing Graham. Carrine had started school, which restricted my movements during the day, and because we lived out of town, all I had was my nine-month-old baby to keep me company.

I decided to get myself a job and was really pleased when I was taken on as an evening barmaid at the Wivenhoe Conference Centre. The centre was in the university grounds and I was employed from six until closing time, Monday to Friday, and occasionally at the weekend for special functions such as weddings. A local fifteen-year-old girl came in and baby-sat for the first hour in the evenings, until Graham got home and took over.

The job at the conference centre turned out to be more responsible than I had first thought. I wasn't just a barmaid; I was in charge of the bar, the ordering and stock-checking, and the serving of wines at dinner. I also took on responsibility for the running of the bar and the wine orders for wedding receptions and special occasions.

I loved the job and got on really well with everyone. The person who had the job before me had been there for years and was well respected, and I was hoping it would be the same for me. Because it was a conference centre we had different customers every week and I started to meet really interesting people. I realised there could be more to life than washing, cleaning and looking after children, and I began to wish I could find a career of my own.

I didn't realise it at the time, but over the next few months I slipped further and further away from Graham. We barely saw one another, we were both working so hard, and while he assumed our family life would carry on in the same way, I was becoming independent, earning my own money and gaining self-respect. I had even started to build up a circle of friends. One week we had a group of social workers at the centre. They came from all over the country for a conference on alcoholism, and I found their company fascinating. I loved hearing about their work and all the cases they dealt with. I began to wonder whether I could ever do a job like that.

One of the social workers, a Scottish guy named Eddie, sat talking to me one evening and explained that you could get into social work by doing a course in psychiatric nursing. I was immediately interested. I could see myself nursing, even though I hated the sight of blood.

After the social workers left I began to daydream about becoming a nurse. I was still only twenty and I knew I wanted something more than being a wife and mother. I was brought back down to earth by the problems we were having with Chris. No matter how hard we tried to help him, Chris continued to sniff glue, and was found on numerous occasions lying semi-conscious on the local waste ground where he now spent most of his days.

Neither Laurence nor I knew what to do. If Chris wouldn't even try to change, how could we do anything for him? In the end we told him that if he didn't stop he would have to return home to London. We hoped it might shock him into stopping, but sadly it didn't and a few weeks later, with heavy hearts, we had to admit there was nothing else we could do, and he returned to live with Mum and Dad.

Jenny was also having terrible trouble in Colchester. She was devastated when a family member totally let her down by stealing from the club. It was so tough for Jenny to stay in Colchester but she decided to stick it out because what mattered far more was that she was away from Keith. In the five months she had lived in Colchester she hadn't once needed to call for assistance from the police or seek sanctuary at our house. She was still adjusting to the fact that she didn't need to sleep with the light on and a poker under the bed. I was so pleased for her. The physical scars Keith had left were fading fast, and I hoped that in time the mental scars would also be gone.

Eventually she was offered a quaint cottage opposite the main park, and as it turned out she was much better off. The cottage was nicer than the rooms she'd had in the club and she preferred the job she found at the jeweller's.

Meanwhile my marriage was getting deeper into trouble. One night while I was working behind the bar at the centre as usual, the phone rang. It was Graham, asking where the ham was for his sandwiches. I should have done the shopping that day, but I'd used the money to go over and see Jenny. I felt guilty, but at the same time Graham had no idea how lonely I was and how badly I needed to see another adult face sometimes when I was stuck at home.

I explained that I couldn't talk, as I was busy, and I would see him when I got home. A few minutes later Graham rang again and said, 'I asked where the shopping was.'

At that moment something in me snapped. I lost my temper totally, said all sorts of angry things to Graham and then yelled, 'I won't be coming home, you sort the kids out for once.' I slammed down the phone and realised I was shaking uncontrollably. The last time I had snapped like that was the night I had confronted Dad about Carole.

Looking back I can see that on both occasions I had bottled up all my feelings instead of talking about them. With Dad, talking wouldn't have been an option, but I could have talked to Graham and in many ways I wish I had. The trouble was that I was so young, and so used to keeping things to myself. So I had never told Graham how unhappy I was, or how lonely I had been and that I always felt I came second to his friends and the sport he loved.

In those few seconds on the phone my whole life changed. Suddenly I knew I was not going back to Graham and the children; I was going to return to London, train to be a nurse and make something of my life.

That night I went to stay with a friend, and the next morning I caught the bus to Colchester and went to Jenny's. I knew Graham would have to miss work to look after the kids, and by this time I was scared and I felt there was no turning back.

I was afraid that if I stayed I'd never make anything of my life. Now I can see that I could perhaps have stayed with Graham and still achieved what I dreamed of. But for that to happen we would both have needed to change, and Graham, I felt, was quite happy with what he had and life the way it was.

Jenny soon let me know that she disapproved of my decision to sort my life out at the expense of losing my husband and children. She was afraid I would regret it. I told her I was feeling lonely and undervalued, but she didn't seem to understand. And with hindsight I can see that for her to hear I was leaving my children must have been shocking. I think I was numb at the time and just couldn't take in what I was doing.

I phoned Laurence, who gave me the same reaction, telling me Graham was a good man and I should go home. But I refused, and Laurence reluctantly agreed to take me back to the house to get some clothes and a toothbrush.

When we arrived, Laurence went in first. He then came out and told me Graham was there with both the children, but didn't want to see me. They stayed shut in the front room while I went upstairs and packed a few things. I was shaking all over, knowing that I was leaving our home, that my husband was downstairs with our children, and that when I walked out this time it would be for good. But I was angry and frightened and I was determined not to give in. Five minutes later I fled, bag in hand, and Laurence drove me back to Jenny's. It hurt that I couldn't say goodbye to the children, but they were too young to understand and I was afraid they'd only be more confused.

I knew Laurence was right: Graham was a good man. But in my head there was more to life than what I had, and no amount of talking and advising was going to make me change my mind. And there was something else. Deep down I didn't believe that it was me Graham really loved and wanted. I knew he loved Carrine and Daniel, but I felt I was just someone to look after the children and cook the meals. I honestly thought he wouldn't care that much if I went.

Of course I was desperately torn about leaving the children. But I couldn't possibly take them with me, with no money and nowhere to go. I promised myself that I would see them again as soon as I could, and that I would find a way to make them proud of me.

Jenny lent me some money and I went to collect what I was owed from work. Then I went to the station and caught the next train to London. I had started by walking away and ended up running so fast that even if I'd wanted to stop – and part of me did – I just couldn't. I went so fast that I literally didn't look back.

Jenny

When Kim arrived at my cottage and told me she'd left Graham, I have to admit I was stunned. I knew she had been unhappy lately, but nothing prepared me for her announcement that she was leaving her husband and children to go off and 'find herself'. Looking back on it now, I feel far more sympathy and understanding for her than I showed then. At the time, all I could think of was the children and, if I'm honest, myself.

I'd already had one hell of a week with a visit from Pam and her boyfriend. I'd made up a bed for them in the front room and we managed, although we were all a little squashed. It had been tiring, but great seeing them, and after they left I realised how much I missed them.

Now Kim was leaving too. Nothing I could say would change her mind. She asked to borrow money, and even though I didn't agree with what she was doing I couldn't say no. She had helped me so many times. When she left I felt really sad. I hoped that what she was doing would turn out to be the right thing.

Only days later I received a visit from Margaret. Laurence had finally told her that he did not want to be married any longer. Margaret was distraught and asked to stay with me until she could sort herself out. I liked Margaret and wanted to help out. I told her she was welcome to stay as long as she needed.

It seemed desperately sad that all three of us – Laurence, Kim and I – already had broken relationships behind us. I wondered how big a part our painful childhood had played in making it so difficult for us to be truly close to another person.

Kim

I cried all the way to London, and when the train pulled into Liverpool Street my face was red and blotched.

I knew a lot of people wouldn't understand how a mother could walk out on her kids. I wasn't sure myself. I just knew that I felt I'd never had a life of my own and I had to find what was missing. Graham was a wonderful father and would look after them. And whatever happened I would always be their mother – no one could take that away from me. I would see them whenever I could, and one day, perhaps, they would be able to live with me again.

Jenny and Laurence were the only real family I had known, until I met Graham. They'd been there for me no matter what, so it was hard knowing that they disapproved of me leaving Graham and the children.

I had nowhere to go and not much money, so I headed over to Hendon to see Danny and Irene. Danny was an old friend of Graham's – our son had been named after him – but they'd become friends of mine too and I hoped they'd help.

Irene was lovely and took me straight to the pub. Even though she was Graham's friend first, she listened without judging me and never once said I had done wrong. I was afraid to phone Graham, so she called him to say where I was, and for the rest of the evening we got slowly drunk together as I spilled my heart out.

I wasn't sure where to start, now that I'd actually left. I felt totally lost without Graham and the children. I thought of them and wondered how they were every moment of every day. I had got so used to being part of a family and feeling safe. Now I was alone, with no job, very little money and no family around me. And it was my own fault.

A few days later we went to the pub again, and as we chatted the barman handed me a drink and said it was with compliments from the gentleman at the end of the bar. I looked round to see Eddie, the Scottish social worker I had met at the conference centre. I went to talk to him and it turned out that he lived nearby. He asked me to meet him for a drink again and I agreed. He was a friendly face, and I badly needed friends.

Graham had asked me not to contact him. Instead he asked Laurence to act as intermediary. Graham had decided that he had to continue with his job, so as an interim arrangement until the house had sold and he could move back to London, the children had gone to stay with his parents in Coventry.

A few weeks after I left, Graham wrote me a letter. This was the first direct communication between us. He told me how hard it was to write, and that he couldn't see me because seeing me would break his heart. He said he loved me and understood that I had to go for myself. He promised he would always care for our children and that I could be part of their lives whenever I wanted. Reading his letter I was touched by his generosity of spirit. I realised he really had loved me and I felt so sorry to have hurt him, but for me it was too late to turn back. I had started my new life and I was determined to prove to everyone that I'd done the right thing and could become a success.

The pain of wanting to see the children never ceased, and once they were settled in Coventry, Graham was generous about arranging for me to see them. Laurence would collect them and bring them down to London and then take them back again.

Their grandparents made sure they wrote to me too. I would receive scribbled notes from Carrine, who was now five, or cards she had made at school. Daniel's auntie would help him to contribute to the cards and letters by crayoning right across the page.

Eddie and I met often and gradually became close. He was from Aberdeen, and I liked his soft accent and dashing good looks. He was intelligent (he read *The Times*, which impressed me), charming, witty and confident. He was good for me too, because he built up my confidence. Where Graham had been quiet and steady but not prone to giving compliments, Eddie gave them all the time. He told me I was gorgeous and beautiful and bright and could do anything I set my mind to. He gave me flowers and chocolates and helped me to believe in myself. Graham had always done the crossword in the *Mirror* and I could never do it. But Eddie did it with me, teaching me how it worked and giving me a huge boost. He made me feel important and wanted, he was interested in my opinions, and he had a way of making me feel I was on a pedestal and no one could tip me off.

Within a few months I was staying at Eddie's flat so often that he suggested I move in with him. He was divorced – he told me his wife had found him in bed with someone else, but at the time I didn't see this as a worrying sign.

Eddie was about to embark on a course at Kent University, in Canterbury, and when he moved down there I went with him. Once we had settled in Canterbury Eddie advised me to seek some voluntary work as a first step towards getting into nursing. I became a volunteer for Kent Council on Alcoholism, answering the phone and talking to people who dropped in.

At the same time I put in my application to train in psychiatric nursing at St Augustine's Psychiatric Hospital in Chartham, just outside Canterbury. When I was accepted I was thrilled. The school of nursing suggested that prior to my training start date it would be good to get some experience, and I was offered an auxiliary post in the hospital, which I gladly accepted. I was placed on the psycho-geriatric medical ward, which meant dealing with elderly patients who had psychiatric problems as well as medical ailments.

During my first week I was asked to feed an

elderly man his lunch. The sister had explained that the gentleman had suffered a severe stroke and eating was quite a problem. She explained that it was a very time-consuming task, as his food had to be liquidised and he regularly dribbled it back out of his mouth. I set about the task and chatted whilst feeding him. I always believed that I should treat people the way I would like to be treated. After an hour the sister came and asked how I was getting on. I explained that I kept putting the food in his mouth but he really didn't appear to be swallowing any of it, the whole lot just dribbled out and ran down his chin. She peered at the old man, picked up his hand and, after a few moments, said very calmly, 'That's probably because he's dead, Nurse Deacon.'

By the time I began my nursing training I'd had nine months as an auxiliary and plenty of experience which stood me in good stead.

My contact with Jenny was now infrequent, but I heard that she was back in London. Laurence was already there, after breaking up with Margaret, and both Carole and Chris were back in Monteagle Court. Meanwhile Graham had sold the house in Essex and also moved back to London with the children. He had a child-minder for Daniel and had managed to stay in the same job.

One of the first things I'd done on coming to Kent was to save up for driving lessons, and when I passed my test I bought a little Renault. I went to see the children as often as possible, and after every visit I felt torn and asked myself if I was doing the right thing. The children always seemed happy to see me and never questioned why I wasn't living with them any more or where I was going when I left. As I said goodbye they didn't cry – but I did, once the door was closed behind me. But I had made my choices and had to stick by them, no matter how painful that sometimes was.

Jenny

It wasn't long before Margaret and I were the only two left in Colchester. Kim had gone back to London, and then Laurence and Graham sold their houses and went back too.

Some weeks after everyone had moved back, Margaret came home one night and introduced me to George. He was in the army, stationed at Colchester Barracks. It was instant love, and Margaret was happier than I had seen her in a long time. Soon the two of them were an item, and one night Margaret announced that she was moving on and going to live with George. A few days later she was gone, and once again I found myself alone with Martine.

My days were now spent working, and my nights were spent alone in front of the television. I was miserable and very lonely. Nothing had worked out the way I had hoped and, rather than stay in Colchester on my own any longer, I made the decision to return to London.

So Martine and I were uprooted again and we boarded the train again, with just two suitcases. Friends had offered to put me up, but beyond that I had no idea what I would do. I left my furniture in Colchester until I could find somewhere permanent to live.

By this time Martine had become a real little performer. I knew she loved an audience, but I was to find out just how much on our journey back to London. It was an early train, full of commuters going to work. Half-way through the journey the train suddenly ground to a halt and the guard announced that we would be delayed because of signal failure. As far as Martine was concerned, that was her cue to perform. She stood on her seat and announced to everyone in the carriage that she would be singing for them!

Aged four, she sang three songs to her stunned audience of smartly dressed men and women. When she finished the silence was broken by rapturous applause, and she was given over two pounds. I was a little embarrassed and was re-lieved when she sat down, but it was something Martine continued to do throughout the next few years. It was very clear that Martine had decided she wanted to be a performer and nothing was going to stop her.

Back in London I used my old trick of pretending to be homeless and living at Mum and Dad's. I approached the new Islington and Hackney Housing Association for help. Anyone could see that Monteagle Court was no place to raise a child, and within days of the housing official's visit I was offered a flat.

I expected another grubby flat several storeys up in a tower block. So when I was offered a clean and pleasantly spacious two-bedroom maisonette I thought I'd landed in heaven. The top half housed a lovely single parent called Polly, with her nine-year-old son, and I had the bottom half. It was in Greenwood Road in Dalston and was perfect. It even had a garden for Martine. I really felt I had made it at last. We settled into our new home and loved it. Martine went back to the same school she had left a year earlier, and I soon had three jobs on the go. I also had my old friends back and was feeling much happier. Despite my desperation to avoid Keith, I had always stayed friends with his mother Bridie and his sister Sandra, both of whom lived a few streets away from my new home.

I saw no reason to stop them from having contact with Martine; they gave me a lot of support and would always forewarn me if Keith was back in the area so that I could lie low. I knew I could trust them, and I wanted Martine to know her grandmother and her aunt as well as her cousin, Sandra's little girl.

For months everything went smoothly. Bridie would collect Martine in the morning and take her to school and also pick her up afterwards, which was a great help to me. I had an early start with my cleaning job, followed by my full-time job in Stoke Newington as a clerk. Then, two evenings a week, either Sandra or Chris would come over to baby-sit while I went back to my barmaid job. Chris knew he couldn't look after Martine if he sniffed glue, and he showed no sign of having taken anything on the occasions when he came over. I worked hard to try to give us a better life, but I always made sure I had time for Martine.

I had enrolled Martine in dance classes and she went three nights a week. I loved to go with her and watch, and it was a real thrill to see her receive her Highly Commended and Blue Ribbon Achievements in ballroom, old time and Latin American dance. And I glowed with pride when she was crowned Princess of the Ballroom.

I missed Kim, but we stayed in touch by phone and letter. She had now met Eddie and was settled with him in Canterbury, where she was training as a nurse. Sad as I'd been at her marriage break-up, I could see she was making a life for herself and I was glad for her. Laurence had also met someone new and was thinking of getting married again. Life seemed to be moving on.

Then, one Saturday afternoon when I was doing an extra shift at the local pub, a familiar figure appeared. It was Carole, now eighteen and looking stunning. The pub was packed, so I told her to wait until my shift was over so that we could go for a proper chat. She came back to Greenwood Road with me and we sat and talked for hours. She told me she was very afraid for Chris because his glue-sniffing had become worse. He had moved out of Monteagle Court and had found a flat to squat in with some friends. I had seen Chris quite recently, when he had come to baby-sit, and to me he seemed fine. He had found a girlfriend and he was enthusiastic about getting a job as a presser in the rag trade. I assured Carole that he would be fine. Laurence was still keeping an eye on him, and whenever Chris was baby-sitting for me Kim phoned to catch up with him, so I felt sure she was worrying unnecessarily.

9

Pure Terror

Jenny

After more than a year free of Keith, and just as I'd got used to a normal life, he reappeared. Once again he had asked around the area for me, using his fake ID, and saying he had just returned from the oil rigs and was looking for his wife and child. Someone tipped him off that his mother had been seen with a dark-haired child, and one morning Keith followed her. He discovered where we were living, and that night he turned up at the door. He begged me to open it, saying his mum had had an accident. Foolishly believing him and afraid for Bridie, I opened the door, only to be greeted by a fist in my face.

Martine was now five, old enough to understand what was happening and, no doubt, to remember some of the horrors of the past. I had never wanted her to know about Keith's violence, but perhaps in the end it was inevitable that she would see and hear some of the things he did. I know that his behaviour towards me, and his failure to be any kind of proper father to her, wounded her little heart. But she was brave and bright and on this occasion, as Keith pushed his way into the flat, she knew what she had to do.

I had decided early on to teach Martine how to use the phone in case of an emergency. It was Keith that I had in mind, obviously, but I didn't want to say this to her, so I prepared her for any kind of emergency. She was so quick to learn, and picked up everything I taught her very quickly. As I tried to fight Keith off, she flew up the stairs to call the police and told them her daddy had arrived and was hitting her mummy. I could hear her giving her name, age and address and I blessed her.

The police arrived while he was still there and he was given a warning and told to leave. Again the police advised me to seek an injunction, and this time I knew I had to.

The next day I was too bruised to go to work. Sandra came to see me and explained that she knew a solicitor who would help, and that I could get an emergency injunction within a few days. I made up my mind. This time I would do it.

I got my injunction within a couple of days and for some reason I felt safe with my piece of paper, stamped by the judge, telling the police that Keith Hemmings was to stay at least three miles away from me. When he knocked on the door a few days later, I stood my ground and told Martine to call the police again. By the time they arrived, however, he had gone, and this was the pattern that followed for the next few weeks.

Despite my new stand against Keith, life was far from normal. Wherever I went, whether it was to work, to the shops or to pick up Martine, I knew that Keith was watching me. The phone would go late at night and he would tell me where I had been and who I had seen that day. He would then tell me all the terrible things he was going to do to me. He even started to threaten Martine.

I got so scared at night that I would turn all the lights off and huddle in bed with Martine beside me. When I heard his familiar steps coming to the door, we would hide under the duvet, having piled furniture up against the door, as I felt sure he would kick it in when he got tired of banging on it.

One night, just as I was putting Martine to bed, the phone rang. It was my sister Carole. 'Jen, Keith's got me and I'm terrified. You must come. Please go to Mum's.'

I called Pam. She now lived minutes up the road, in another housing association house. She had been through everything with me; she knew about all the beatings and the calls to the police, and she had come with me to the meetings at the solicitor's offices. I think without her I would have gone mad.

Pam offered to have Martine. Next I telephoned Kim, who by now had passed her test and had a car. She said she would drive up from Kent and meet me as soon as she could. After dropping Martine off I made my way to Monteagle Court.

Kim arrived not long after me and we tackled Mum. She seemed uninterested and said Carole had gone off with Keith in his car and had seemed OK when she left. Kim and I decided to go to the police. It was obvious to us that Carole had been kidnapped and we needed to get her back.

We went to the police station in Mare Street, Hackney, where I met Sergeant Chris Coomber of the CID. I told him my story, half expecting to be given a few words of advice and then sent on my way. After all, the police had always said that what Keith did to me was a civil matter. But this time I was wrong. Kidnapping was a serious offence and this officer meant business.

I told him Keith had an old Ford Zephyr with a bench seat, which was unusual for the time. Sergeant Coomber said he would put out a warrant for his arrest immediately. He also gave me his direct line number and told me to call him if anything happened.

Kim and I left the police station feeling a lot better. However, Carole was still missing and we were worried. But it was late in the evening and there was nothing we could do, and so Kim came back with me to stay and we agreed we would make a fresh start in the morning.

Bright and early the next morning we left for Monteagle Court, where we waited for news. A few neighbours were aware that something was wrong, but Kim and I said nothing. The morning passed and we decided to try Keith's mother's place. Just as we were leaving, Carole appeared around the corner, shaking and frightened. We ran to comfort her, but she seemed strange and distant. She told us Keith had kept her prisoner all night and assaulted her. What exactly these assaults were she never said, but of course I had my suspicions. Apparently he had thought she was me and kept calling her Jenny. She said he was creepy and had mad eyes and had said he was going to come and get me and Martine and also Pam and her three boys. He told her he was convinced I was a lesbian, and that my time had come. He would be back for me very soon and would pour acid in my face and cut Pam up with a hatchet.

We gave Carole a cup of tea, while Kim went to phone the police. A squad car arrived an hour later to take us to the police station, where Carole was asked to make a statement and press charges. Another warrant was released, this time for threats to kill and kidnap. For my protection, until Keith was caught, a panic button was installed at Greenwood Road and a strong chain was put on the front door. I was told to take Carole home with me and tell Pam to stay at home.

There was nothing more Kim could do, so after making me promise to keep her updated at all times she went home.

The next few nights were pure hell. None of us wanted to venture anywhere. After a couple of days Pam suggested we come over to her and, thinking we'd be safe all together, I put Carole and Martine in a cab for the five-minute journey. Once we got to Pam's we decided to order some pizzas and watch a video. We all sat together in Pam's large front room, terrified, with the boys at our feet and Martine on my lap. Carole sat nervously biting her nails. Suddenly there was a knock on the door. Panic broke out, Carole ran to hide in Pam's large chest freezer and the boys grabbed Martine to protect her. Pam and I stood up and looked at each other.

'I've had enough of this,' she said, reaching for a large hammer from the cupboard. 'He's not terrorising anyone any more.' She instructed her eldest son Gary to call the police and we both made our way down the stairs to the front door.

The plan was simple. She would stand on a box with the hammer. I would open the door and then run, and as Keith chased me, she would hit him over the head and knock him out. Fear was making both of us shake, but we knew what we had to do. I opened the door and darted down the corridor and up four stairs before I realised no one was chasing me. I turned to look at Pam and she turned to me, and at that moment we heard a voice say, 'Pizza.'

Our laughter was close to hysteria. We paid the poor delivery man, made our way back to the front room and sat down to eat. We were still laughing when there was another knock at the door. Thinking we'd make idiots of ourselves if we panicked a second time, we went on eating while Marc, Pam's second eldest son, went to the window and opened it.

'Who's there?' he asked. We all recognised the angry voice that shouted back.

Marc reeled. 'It's him this time, and he's got a big axe!'

We scurried to our feet. Gary picked up the phone again to dial 999, but thank God we had forgotten to cancel the last call and they had taken it seriously. We could hear the siren outside as the police car approached. We were desperate to get Keith caught, but he heard the police car and Marc saw him jump a wall and make his way round to the back garden. We ran to the kitchen window to look out of the back. It was dark, but we could still make out his figure. More knocking, and the police rushed in. We shouted to them that he was in the garden and they charged outside.

A few minutes later, Chris Coomber arrived. As

he got there the officers came back from the garden; Keith had managed to escape. We felt so deflated. Our one chance to get him had gone, but Chris assured me that they would get him, and soon. As we saw the officers out, we noticed that there were two objects on the porch floor. One was an axe, the other a glass jar full of what turned out to be acid. Keith had meant what he said.

I couldn't stay with Pam for ever, so I had no alternative but to return home. Carole decided to stay with me for a few days, too terrified to go back to Mum and Dad's, but in the end life had to go on. Carole went home, Martine went back to school and I went to work. It was hard, but with the chains on the door and my panic button I did feel a little safer. I decided to not go anywhere at night, and every evening I put on the panic button, locked the front door and secured all the windows.

Kim

I couldn't believe my ears when Jenny telephoned to say Keith had reappeared and had kidnapped Carole. After all Jenny had been through I found it incredible that she had let him know where she lived. I didn't realise until later that she hadn't let him know – he'd tracked her down.

I briefly told Eddie what was happening and then set off for London. It was late at night and I was heading back to the place I vowed I'd never set foot in again, Monteagle Court. I felt angry and began to think that Jenny was just like Mum. She'd taken Keith back time and time again, and this time was one too many.

I was getting on with my life, I'd escaped my past, and the last thing I wanted was to re-live it. I'd spent years watching my mother being beaten senseless; now it was my sister. I decided that unless Jenny got serious about getting away from Keith I wasn't prepared to help any more. If it wasn't for her I wouldn't have to return to Monteagle Court, but here I was heading down the motorway, back to the place that had been my hell as a child, bringing back memories that I would rather forget.

When I got there I was cool and detached. I felt almost like a professional, coming in from outside and viewing it all for the first time. The place looked filthier than ever – the carpet glistening with dirt, cigarette ash smeared over it around Dad's chair, cup stains all over the arms of the grubby furniture. The curtains had so many brown condensation rings on them, I had to look twice to check it wasn't part of the pattern. In the middle of all this sat Dad, who turned and glanced at me without any acknowledgement and then shouted, 'Miriam, where's the fucking tea?' Then he turned back to the TV and sat picking at the dirty, cracked skin on his feet, with a cigarette between the fingers of his free hand and saliva accumulating in the corners of his mouth.

Chris was there and he looked ill. He had grown very tall and he was painfully thin, with skin so yellow it looked almost jaundiced. He cuddled me and said he'd missed me and asked after Carrine, Daniel and Graham.

As we embraced I whispered, 'Are you OK, babe?' and he replied, 'Yeah, so so.'

After refusing an offer of tea from my mother I took control of the whole situation. I asked questions and demanded straight answers, and as soon as I understood from Jenny what had taken place I decided we would go to the police and then return in the morning, as we could do no more that night.

I kissed Chris goodbye and told him not to worry about Carole. After all this time I still felt guilty at leaving him there. He was now six feet tall and seventeen years old, but to me he was still my little brother.

It had been about six months since I last saw Jenny, and although we spoke regularly on the phone she hadn't once said that she was back in touch with Keith. Once we had got into the car, I lost it. I told her what I truly thought about the whole Keith situation. Jenny started to cry, saying I didn't understand, but I'd heard that too often. I said it was simple. She had returned from Colchester and got a new flat and Keith never needed to know where she was. End of story.

Jenny explained that she had never contacted Keith directly. She told me she'd been in touch with his mum and sister and he'd tracked her down by following his mum. She sobbed and sobbed. We went back to her flat, and over several cups of tea she told me everything. All the details she'd held back over the years, of the fights, the beatings, the rapes and the assaults she'd suffered – it all poured out. She explained that she really hadn't wanted Keith to find her, but she thought she was acting in Martine's best interest by contacting his family.

I felt frustrated that it had taken Jenny this long to tell me the whole truth about all the things Keith had done to her. I couldn't understand why she had forgiven him time and time again, what kind of hold he must have had over her. I told her it was time, once and for all, to get him out of her life. Jenny agreed. But we'd been here before, and nothing had really changed. So would it this time?

Jenny

One evening, a few days after Keith had given the police the slip in Pam's back garden, I got home from work exhausted. It had been a long day and I was ready for a hot bath and an early night. Martine played with her toy castle and her dolls, while I cooked supper. I could hear her making up all the dolls' voices and I smiled, her imagination never ceased to amaze me. The phone went. It was Pam, checking in. She often phoned in the evening to make sure I was safe. The days since the last incident had been hard, and neither of us had slept well since. A few minutes after Pam's call, Kim phoned. She had taken to phoning twice a night to make sure I was OK. It made me feel better knowing that my sister and friends were worried about me.

I was feeling apprehensive. Keith had been very quiet lately and I wondered what his next move would be. His close shave with the police might have scared him off, but I knew that sooner or later he'd reappear, and I wondered whether the chains and the panic button would be enough to keep him out. Keith loved to show that he was above the law, that injunctions and warrants for his arrest meant nothing to him, that he did exactly as he chose.

I knew he'd be back, and I had a strange feeling it would be that night. I thought about leaving the flat and going to a friend's place. I was trembling with fear. But while half of me wanted to run as fast as I could, away from Greenwood Road and the dangers, the other half wanted to stand my ground and make sure that Keith got what he deserved.

All that evening I experienced a strange mix of emotions. I was terrified, but brave; crying, but

Kim and I have always been best friends, as well as sisters. This photo was taken in 1974, on Hampstead Heath, about a year after I had finally escaped my parents' house.

Above left: Jenny and Keith. He was a charming bloke, at least at first but I always worried that Jenny was hiding the truth about him from me.

Above right: This is Jenny in 1976, so happy to be pregnant with Martine despite the fact that by now things with Keith were awful.

Left: Just look how overjoyed Jenny was with her daughter! This was taken in Highbury Fields, a place that always held happy memories for both of us, thanks to Auntie.

Above left: Kim was pregnant with Carrine and finally escaping the horrors of the past. I couldn't have been more pleased for her.

Above right: Graham was a good man, and for a while he and Kim were very happy.

Right: Kim and Carrine on the beach in 1975, complete with beaming grins and lollipop!

This was taken in my Newington Green flat. Jenny is holding Martine and I'm giving Carrine her bath. The girls were brought up side by side.

Our beloved younger brother Chris, giving Carrine, his new niece, a cuddle.

Left: Jenny, Chris and Carrine.

Right: Martine aged three, with Nanny Hemmings. Despite the fact that Keith was a poisonous presence in our lives, his mother was and is a wonderful woman and she and Martine were devoted to each other.

Far right: Kim with her fantastic kids, Carrine and Daniel. This was taken on a Bank Holiday outing in 1981.

Chris was 17 years old in this photo, with everything to live for. Less than two years later, to our absolute despair, he was dead.

This is me on the balcony at Pembury Estate. I can never think about that place without a shudder of horror when I remember Keith dangling Martine from it.

Martine and Carrine all dressed up as bridesmaids for Kim and Stuart's wedding. The girls had always stayed close.

This photo from the wedding is of our mum, Stuart and Kim and our older brother Laurence.

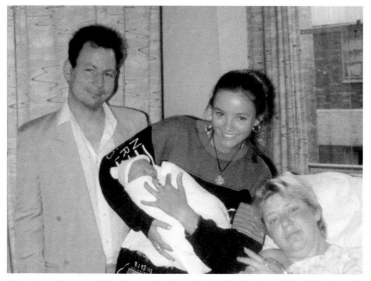

LJ was born in 1995. This photo, taken just after his birth, shows John, Martine with LJ and Jenny, looking a bit exhausted but over the moon.

A brilliant family holiday for Jenny and LJ, catching the waves in Barbados.

Left: When Jenny and Alan got married in January 2000, I knew my beloved sister had found real happiness.

Below: This photo, taken in France at Christmas 2005, really tells me how far Kim and I have come. But through it all, we've always been there for each other, and we always will be.

laughing also; and afraid of failure, but determined to succeed. Before going to bed, I double-checked every window and door. It was a hot summer evening, and a bit of air would have been nice, but I was taking no chances. I pushed a large chest of drawers against the front door. Martine was in a deep sleep. She'd been a little under the weather and I'd given her paracetamol syrup, which sent her to sleep very quickly.

I decided to go to bed and call Kim back just to check in and hear her familiar voice down the phone. She had seemed agitated when we spoke earlier, and I wanted her to know I was safe. I finished the call with my usual 'love you' and chuckled to myself. I knew it embarrassed Kim when I told her I loved her; she was so reserved, she could never bring herself to say it back. Not that it mattered, I knew how much she loved me. I snuggled down to sleep, thinking about what a good sister she was.

I was woken by a rough hand over my mouth, whilst the other hand reached under the duvet to grab my groin. I froze with fear. Despite all my efforts, Keith had managed to get in. How on earth had he done it? I looked into his face and was horrified by what I saw. If Keith had been frightening before, this apparition was terrifying. He laughed oddly and looked almost demonic – his eyes kept disappearing into his head. He was sweating so much that his normally clean hair was plastered to his head, but the corners of his mouth were dry. He looked possessed and I knew then that he must be heavily drugged. It was clear that he was completely out of control and my fear intensified. In this state he would be capable of anything.

'If you scream or try to get away, I'll kill you.' He removed his hand from my mouth and smiled a sickly grin.

I was frozen. 'What do you want? The baby's in the next room, please, Keith, please,' I begged in a whisper, conscious that Martine was only feet away.

As he bent over me, his breath stank of stale beer and cigarettes. In the past Keith had always been freshly washed and worn aftershave, but now he had a pungent, nasty body odour.

I felt this was a man I didn't know. The Keith I knew was violent and bad-tempered and often crazy with jealousy, but he could be easily read. But the man now in my bedroom was quiet, menacing and utterly cold.

In slurred words that were barely audible he said, 'You will do exactly what I tell you, and if you disobey you will be punished. I want to tie you to the bed and we are going to play a game . . . my game.'

I felt a wave of nausea sweep through me. Those words took me back to the nightmares of my childhood. I could feel my father's presence so clearly, it was as if it was him in the room. His acrid odour filled my nostrils and I could see his leering face, telling me we were going to play a little game.

Suddenly I was filled with rage. I had resisted my father in every way I could, and I would resist this man too. I made my voice as authoritative as possible and said, 'I won't play your game, get out of my house, the police will know you are here and will come and arrest you.'

He laughed, low this time. 'I have my secret weapon, girlie, she's in the next room and you will do as I say, or I'll make her watch to see what happens to naughty girls who misbehave.' He produced a knife and laughed again.

My eyes went to the panic button beside the bed, but again he laughed. 'You can press that button as often as you like, but no one will come. I cut the wires.' As his eyes rolled back all I could see in the dark were two white balls against his dark olive skin.

I searched in my mind for another way out, something I could do. But even as I did I realised I had no choice. I couldn't risk my little girl witnessing this ordeal or being hurt. All I could hope was that if I played along it would soon be over and he would leave.

Keith grabbed some scarves and tied me to the

bed. What happened next will remain with me always.

The first punch hit the side of my temple and I felt myself beginning to lose consciousness as he rained punches down all over my body. With my hands tied to the bed I couldn't move. I was trapped. He took a large bottle of vodka from a bag and began to gulp it down. After a few moments he took the bottle out of his mouth, wiped his hand across his face, paused, and then poured most of it over me. He laughed, then drank some more.

The first rape only lasted a few minutes, but Keith became more aroused and began oral sex. I couldn't control the thrusting of his penis into my mouth and began choking. As I thought I would pass out, he stopped. He lit a cigarette and took long drags, while he looked at me.

'You still don't get it, do you?' he said, and pushed the cigarette stub into the top of my thigh, twisting it deep into my skin. I felt my flesh melting, but terrified of waking Martine, I suppressed my screams and whimpered, as tears ran down my face. But Keith hadn't finished. He lit cigarette after cigarette, taking a few puffs from each before stubbing it as hard as he could into my body. Every time he did it the pain was excruciating.

Desperate not to scream, I bit down on the inside of my mouth each time, until my mouth was so full of blood I thought I would choke.

After he had run out of cigarettes he raped and assaulted me several more times. Then he turned me over and pushed my face into the pillow so that I could hardly breathe.

'I've had you one way, but I know you're still a virgin in another way,' he said, grinning. I was gasping for air and then I experienced a pain unlike anything I'd known before, as he penetrated my anus. I thought I would die and I blacked out for a few seconds. I felt blood trickling down my body, but I wasn't sure where from. Then, as Keith pulled out, he collapsed on top of me and soon began to snore.

Somehow I managed to squirm from underneath the weight of his naked, sweaty body. Using my teeth I managed to undo the scarves tying my hands. I was in terrible pain and bleeding in several places, but I could see the sun was rising and I knew that for the sake of my baby I had to get myself together and escape.

I staggered to the bathroom and slowly raised my eyes to the mirror. I stifled a sob as I saw my face. My eyes were so swollen that I could hardly see them, and my mouth was split in several places. I looked down at my body. There were welts on my wrists from where I had been tied and bruises all around my breasts, where he had bitten me. And all over my body there were livid burns. I suddenly had the urge to pee, and when I sat on the toilet blood came from both places. I found a sanitary towel and holding it tightly against me eased the pain.

I went back into the bedroom and dressed as quietly as I could. Keith still lay sprawled across the bed, comatose and snoring loudly. I looked at him, the man I had once adored and the father of my beautiful baby, and couldn't believe what he had done.

Even worse than my horror at the depths to which he had sunk, was my terror that he might do it again, and this seemed to push me beyond reason. Before I knew it I was upstairs in the kitchen with my hand tightly wrapped around a large carving knife. It was as though I was in some kind of a trance.

Suddenly everything became clear. I would kill him. It would be easy. I would tell everyone about the attack and say it was self-defence. I could hear myself becoming hysterical and starting to laugh loudly and I put my hand over my mouth to stop the noise. At that moment I could feel nothing. Even the thoughts of Martine that had kept me going through my ordeal disappeared. All I could think of was killing him. Keith was going to die, even if it meant I would become a murderer.

I walked to the top of the stairs and made my way slowly back down towards the bedroom. I held the knife so tightly that my knuckles went purple. I thought about plunging it deep into his back and then looking into his dying eyes to let him know it was me who killed him. It was me, the girlie, who couldn't say no to his games, it was me who would put an end to them for ever.

In my confused mind I wasn't just killing Keith, I was killing my father too – I would kill both the monsters who had abused me in such disgusting, torturous ways. They would die, and I would be free.

I reached the bottom step of the stairs and was about to cross the hall when I suddenly heard a voice calling my name softly, as if from a long way away. I froze. I didn't know where it was coming from. Slowly I moved to the door where I stopped and listened again.

Kim

Even though I had spoken to Jenny on the phone I sensed that something was wrong. I recognised in her voice, as she attempted to reassure me, the mix of confidence and deep fear that I remembered from our childhood when she used to say, 'It's OK, I'll be all right,' before being led away by Dad.

I had always thought Keith was a carbon copy of Dad. Now Jenny knew it too, and at last she was doing everything she could to get him out of her life and protect herself and Martine. But would she be able to keep him away?

As I settled down for the night next to Eddie, I felt so protected. We were getting on really well, and I longed for Jenny to meet a decent bloke and to enjoy the same feeling. I told Eddie that I wasn't comfortable that Jenny was in that flat alone with Martine, and that Keith could appear at any time. Eddie held me close and tried to reassure me that Keith wouldn't dare try anything with all the injunctions against him and the protection the police had given Jenny. He told me I was to stop worrying and get some sleep.

Still I tossed and turned all night. I thought of all the times she had saved me, and felt I needed to know she was all right.

After a very restless night I woke at dawn. Eddie had to leave early for lectures, but I was just beginning two weeks' study leave. I had time on my side and could have gone back to sleep. Instead I phoned Jenny. The line was dead. I contacted the operator who said there must be a fault on it. At that point I began to feel panic. What if Keith had got into the flat and cut the line? I threw some essentials into a bag and set off for Jenny's as fast as I could.

I told myself Jen was fine and I was just being silly, but as I turned into Greenwood Road and parked the car, despite the glorious sunny morning a terrible feeling of dread came over me. I tried to dismiss it and imagined Jenny opening the door in her nightie with her hair all messed up, saying, 'It's bloody early, what are you doing here? Mart's still asleep.'

As I neared the front door I could see the outline of someone on the other side through the frosted glass. My first thought was, she's up and about, thank goodness everything's fine. I tapped lightly on the glass front of the door, calling 'Jen' at the same time and expecting her to open the door. But the outline stayed there, motionless. I bent down to look through the letter-box and saw Jenny in the hall. But what caught my eye was her hand, which was level with the letter-box. She was gripping a knife with a long blade. I started to scream her name over and over, shouting at her to open the door, but Jenny didn't move.

My screams attracted the attention of several neighbours, who threw open windows and gawped at me with dishevelled hair and fags hanging out of their mouths. Jenny had become a local source of entertainment, just as the Pontings had all those years ago. I ignored them; all I cared about was getting the door open.

I looked through the letter-box again and saw Martine. I called to her, 'Mart, it's Auntie Kimmy, open the door.' But she was transfixed by the sight of her mum. She started to cry, tugging at Jenny's hand. I shouted, 'Martine! Martine!' She turned towards me and I told her to open the door, but she began to sob that she couldn't because there was a chest of drawers in the way.

I spoke to Martine through the letter-box, telling her that Mummy was OK but that I needed her to put the door on the latch, so that I could push it open from the outside. I told her to climb on the chest and do it for me. Still crying, Martine began to climb on the chest, but a moment later I heard the chest being pulled away and Jenny opened the door.

The sight that greeted me was pitiful. Jenny was so bruised and battered that she was barely recognisable as my pretty elder sister. Both her eyes were swollen, and her lip was bleeding in several places. She was ashen white and trembling, with congealed blood in her hair, and there was dried blood down her legs.

I said her name but she seemed to be in a trance. It wasn't until I put my arms around her and pulled her close that she snapped out of it and began crying uncontrollably.

Martine was standing in her pyjamas, still sobbing. I wanted to give her my attention but I knew I had to calm Jenny down first. I continued cuddling Jenny and tried to comfort Martine at the same time. Jenny was trying to say something, but the only word I understood was 'Keith'. I didn't want to think about the horrors that had gone on in that flat during the night. And I had no idea where Keith was or whether Jenny had done something awful to him. All I knew was that my fears had come horribly true, and as the reality of the scene hit me I too began to cry.

However, there was no time for tears. I had to think fast. The first thing was to get the knife out of Jenny's hand. Then I needed to make sure Jenny and Martine were safe and get Jenny some medical attention. In my panicked state I couldn't think of anything else, not even the danger we might have been in if Keith was still in the flat, or the opportunity to get him arrested by calling the police straight away. Jenny was still hanging on to the knife, so I pulled it from her hand and it fell to the floor. There was no blood on it and I realised that Jenny hadn't killed Keith, but must have been planning to. I understood why: part of me wanted to kill him too, for what he'd done, but Jenny had lost control, and she needed to know that he was just not worth it. I held her close and wiped her face with my sleeve. 'Think of your baby, Jenny. She needs you. Don't lose her because of him.'

I felt I needed to get them both away from the flat, so I pulled them out of the door and into my car and we headed for the safe haven of Pam's, a few streets away. It was only when we were there that Jenny said Keith was still in her flat, out cold on the bed. She told us the bare facts of what had happened, and as she finished she put her head on my lap and cried at the shame she felt for what he'd done to her.

Martine had cheered up as soon as we got to Pam's and was eating breakfast in the kitchen. Pam offered to take her to school and dressed her in jeans and a T-shirt belonging to one of her boys, while I phoned Eddie to say I would be staying with Jenny for a few days.

Once Pam had left with Martine and the boys, I took Jenny to the bathroom. As I bathed her wounds, I felt the anger well up inside me. She was covered in cigarette burns, and her body was cut and bruised all over. There were large welt marks at the top of her inside thighs, and the water in the bath turned a horrifying red. Seeing her in such a terrible state almost broke my heart.

At the time I didn't even think of phoning the police and telling them to go and arrest Keith while he was still at Jenny's flat. I was so shocked by Jenny's state that all my attention was focused on getting her the medical help she needed.

After the bath I helped her to dress in clothes I had packed and brought with me from home, and then we set off for the nearest casualty department.

statement he promised that he would get Keith and dispatched a police car to arrest him immediately. Kim and I stayed at the station until word came back that Keith was no longer at Greenwood Road – he had vanished once again.

I was still in a daze, but also worried and frightened for Carole. I knew that Keith would have woken and guessed that I had gone to the police. I was afraid of what he might try in revenge. I urged Kim to take us to Mum and Dad's to make sure that Carole and Chris were safe. Kim argued that I should be in bed resting, but I was insistent.

When we got to Monteagle Court, Carole was standing outside the door. She was relieved to see us but shocked at my appearance. She told us that Keith had called just half an hour before. He had acted strangely, calling her by my name, and had tried to coax her to go with him. Carole, cleverly, hadn't refused but had told him she needed to get some things together and to wait for her at the Royal Standard pub, which was just up the road. She was on the way to call the police when we arrived. Kim wasted no time in running to the callbox at the top of the road. She made a detour to get there, as the direct route would have taken her straight past the pub, and we didn't want to risk her being seen. We watched, from a safe distance, what happened next. Within ten minutes two large vans full of police arrived and they all jumped out and rushed into the pub. Keith was pulled out kicking and screaming. I decided to walk up the road with my sisters. We all wanted to let him know that it was the three of us who had instigated the arrest.

Kim, Carole and I linked arms and walked united up the road past him. Keith looked directly at me. 'You bitch, you haven't seen the last of me. I'll get you, I'll get all of you.' Just being that close to Keith made me feel afraid, but I still turned to Kim and smiled. He was in police custody, and for the first time in months I would be safe.

Kim

This was turning out to be a holiday I hadn't anticipated. The rest of my nursing class were going off to Spain and Greece, while I was spending it in sunny Hackney, heading for the casualty department. Still, if it meant that Jenny, Martine and Carole were safe and Keith would be put away, then I would gladly help. I knew I couldn't stay too long, though, as I had my first-year exams to study for.

After sitting silently in the casualty waiting area for some time, Jenny began worrying about stupid things. She was obviously deep in shock. With a swollen mouth and impeded speech she said, 'God, I left the door unlocked and I need to get milk and bread.' 'Don't worry,' I told her, 'Pam is popping round to sort it out.' She sounded like Marlon Brando from *The Godfather*, and I cuddled her, turning my head so that she wouldn't see the tears in my eyes.

Finally we were called through, and after examining Jenny the doctor told her that she had received a hairline fracture to her cheekbone just below the eye, swelling to the skull and possible internal injuries. She was still bleeding from the internal damage to her vagina and back passage and she had multiple cigarette burns, cuts and bruises as well as huge welt marks all over her body. It made me feel sick to think that one human being could do this to another. The doctor asked to take photos of her injuries and I agreed on her behalf, as Jenny lay motionless and appeared not to hear.

Suddenly she sat bolt upright, panic in her face, and said, 'Where's my baby? Martine, Martine!'

'It's OK, Jen,' I soothed. 'Pam's taken her to school, she's fine.' At that Jenny seemed to snap out of her daze and said she needed to get to the police station so they could get Keith. She got off the bed and, gasping with pain, attempted to dress. I was trying to convince her she needed to rest – the doctors had advised her to be admitted – but she was determined to make it to the police station sooner rather than later.

Once she was dressed we collected some strong painkillers and mild sedatives from the pharmacy department and then set off to Hackney Police Station in a cab. On the way there we bought sanitary towels from a chemist and then stopped off at Pam's. Jenny was bleeding so badly that she needed a change of clothes. Pam was horrified that Jenny wanted to go to the police station when she was in such a bad way, but Jenny insisted that she must.

Chris Coomber led us to an interview room, where Jenny sat opposite him at a desk and I sat at the back. I wanted to be there for her but, even knowing all I did about Keith and what he had done in the past, I wasn't ready for the story she told. I could feel her humiliation and shame and I wept for her as she re-lived the horrors of the night before. She kept her head bowed and spoke in a quiet whisper, without once turning to look at me.

Watching this painful scene, as Jenny answered the most intimate questions, brought back memories of the time when Carole and I had been interviewed by the police about the horrors that we had encountered at the hands of our father. Carole was just nine years old then, but she too had been frightened and ashamed, and I had never talked to those closest to me about the questioning all those years ago. I knew exactly how Jenny was feeling, the sense of shame and guilt, the feeling that it was somehow her fault. I had an urge to scream out in frustration, for someone to listen, understand and believe.

Jenny looked to me now just as vulnerable, young and crestfallen as Carole and I had all those years earlier, and I cried again, for Jenny now and for Carole and me.

When Jenny's story was finished they dispatched a car to find Keith, but he had fled. They assured us that his luck would run out, and a couple of hours later it did, when we went over to Mum's and Carole told us he was in the pub waiting for her.

As they took him away his arms and legs thrashed all over the place and he bellowed his threats of revenge, but we smiled as if we had won the pools. Relief, exhaustion and victory showed in our smiles and whoops of glee. At last Jenny could go home with her daughter and live in peace, and I could return to Canterbury to study for my exams.

Jenny

In the weeks following Keith's arrest, life improved in every way. Knowing that he was in prison on remand and that we were safe, at least until the court case, changed everything. I felt happier than I had in a long while, and as my injuries healed I made all kinds of plans.

I'd been having driving lessons for a few weeks, and not long before Keith's arrest I had taken my test and passed first time. In the days after the arrest Laurence helped me to get a cheap car and I became the proud owner of a pillarbox-red Mark 1 Cortina with column gear-change.

I'd been so afraid Keith would kill me that now he'd been put away for a while I felt as though I'd been given another chance at life. I decided to enjoy myself. I started to go out more, and Martine and I even went on a holiday in my new car, with Pam and her boys. We drove to St Osyth Caravan Park in Clacton on the Essex coast, the six of us singing along to songs on the cassette player as we drove. We were away for a week and we had a lovely time, on the beach, in the park's clubhouse and even fruit picking.

Back home again I met a lovely man. On a trip to the local grocer's, I virtually ran into him. He smiled at me and at Martine, and when I left the shop he was waiting for me outside. He started to chat me up, making me laugh, and when he asked me out on a date I said yes. He told me his name was Robert Walker, and he was a van driver.

Of course I was cautious, as I never, ever wanted to meet another Keith. But Robert turned out to be a really nice guy. He didn't live locally, but whenever he was in the area he would turn up and whisk me out for the evening. Martine wasn't keen on him, but that was because it had been just the two of us nearly all her life, and she saw Robert as a threat. I'm sure that she was also wary of men in general after witnessing what Keith had done to me. The only other men she knew were her uncles, Laurence and Chris, who were lovely, but being part of the family they were different from outsiders.

I didn't stop seeing Robert, in fact our relationship carried on for the next five years, but I made sure he wasn't often around Martine. I knew the relationship wouldn't go anywhere; I wasn't ready to settle down with any man yet, and Robert had another life and, I suspected, another name, elsewhere. But at a time when I badly needed love and affection, Robert gave them to me and it meant a lot to know he cared.

A few weeks after his arrest Keith was due to appear in the magistrates' court and I had been asked to attend, along with Chris, Carole and Kim.

Two days before the court case Chris came round to see me. He was due to turn eighteen in a couple of weeks, but he was as pale and skinny as ever. He brought me a record as a present, Phil Collins's song 'Missed Again', and I was touched. We talked all evening, but towards the end he said something that worried me.

He had asked me if I wanted him to baby-sit for Martine at the weekend and I'd told him, honestly, that I was concerned about his glue-sniffing habit. I said that he really needed to get help or I couldn't allow him to baby-sit again. As he cuddled Martine on his lap, he said quietly, 'I wouldn't hurt the baby, Jen,' and he sighed heavily as he said, 'Maybe I'm not meant for this.'

'Meant for what?' I asked.

He looked around. 'All of this,' he answered. I told him to stop being silly. But after he'd gone, I lay in bed and wondered what he had meant.

The day of the court case arrived. Laurence also came, to give us support. It was a preliminary hearing at the court in Old Street, to see if there was a case to be answered. I sat quietly and looked at Keith. He looked as arrogant and mean as usual, and though I tried to appear cool and calm I was still terrified of him.

The three magistrates spoke quietly to one another, and then one announced their decision. There was a case to be answered, and Keith was remanded in custody again to appear later at the Old Bailey Court to answer charges of threats to kill, assault, grievous bodily harm and withholding a person against their will. At last what Keith had done to me was being treated as more than a domestic dispute. The photos from the hospital showed how badly I had been beaten, and the evidence Keith had left outside Pam's front door, not to mention his abduction of Carole, had convinced the magistrates that there was a serious case for him to answer.

I felt satisfied as I left the courtroom. We were all pleased with the outcome so far. Now we just had to wait to see what would happen at the full trial.

After the magistrates' hearing, as we all sat together in the pub near the court, Chris looked as if he was somewhere else. Pam had been watching Martine for me and she brought her to meet us. As soon as Martine saw Chris, she ran to sit on his lap and he hugged her. Then he stood up, still holding Martine, and said he had to leave to get back to work. He kissed Martine and winked at me, and I said I would catch up with him later. The rest of us carried on chatting, and after an hour or so we all said our goodbyes and left to get back to our lives.

I headed for work. I'd lost my full-time job as I'd taken too much time off sick, but I'd found another part-time pub job which, along with the early morning cleaning job that I'd managed to hold on to, earned me just about enough to manage on. As always I was good at pub work and enjoyed meeting the customers. It was a busy Friday night and the place soon filled with workmen, celebrating the end of the working week. One of the regulars was a nice Irish guy called Liam and we'd become friends. He was sweet and attentive and would often ask me out, but I preferred to stay friends.

Carole hadn't wanted to go back to Mum and Dad's after the court case, so I invited her to stay for the weekend. The next day was hot and sunny. We opened the windows, put some music on and started to make a salad for supper. Pam called to say she would pop in and join us, so we decided to have a barbecue.

Carole and I were waiting for Pam, cooking and chatting, when the phone went. It was Dad. At first I couldn't make out what was he was saying, then it suddenly became clear. 'Your brother's dead.'

My mind raced. Was it Laurence? He'd had a weak chest, ever since he'd had pneumonia as a baby, after Dad had forced Mum to leave him out in the rain in his pram. Only Auntie's loving care had saved him, but the weak chest had later put paid to his dreams of a life in the Navy.

I asked Dad to repeat himself.

'Your brother Chris is dead,' he gabbled. I slammed the phone down.

By this time, Carole was sitting opposite me, leaning forward in the armchair. 'What is it, Jen?' she asked, her face anxious and her voice raised. I looked at her, tears streaming down my face. 'What is it?' she screamed at me, and then said, 'It's Chris. He's dead, isn't he?'

To this day I will always remember Carole's scream. It was the most terrible sound I've ever heard. She was absolutely distraught. I felt helpless, there was nothing I could do to comfort her.

I knew I had to get to my parents' house as soon

as possible, so after leaving Martine with Pam, Carole and I got in the car together.

As we arrived at Monteagle Court, I saw Laurence. Dad had called him at work, and he had arrived shortly before me. We both tried to make sense of what had happened. Apparently, Chris hadn't turned up for work and his flatmate, who worked with him, and who'd spent the night elsewhere with his girlfriend, had gone round to the squat where they lived to wake him. They worked together in a clothing factory and his mate had assumed Chris was sleeping in. When he'd found Chris he panicked and ran over to our mum and dad's. He told them Chris was dead and then ran off. We could only assume that he was in shock.

On this basis alone, without going to see what had happened or confirming that Chris really was dead, Dad had called all of us and told us our brother was dead. He had also rung the police.

Still hoping that there might be some terrible mistake, Laurence and I walked the short distance to Chris's flat, with Dad following us. When we arrived at the door of the flat a policeman was already there. The door was closed and the policeman told us he was going to break in. He threw his weight against the door, which gave way, and Laurence and I followed him in. The place stank of glue. At the living-room door, Laurence froze in his tracks. He blocked the doorway and shouted at me to leave. I stood my ground. 'Let me in,' I screamed, 'he's my brother.'

Laurence held firm. Despite the terrible pain he must have been in, he still thought of me. 'Get out of here, Jen, please get out, I don't want you to see.' He turned to me, tears streaming down his face. 'Please, Jen,' he said again. Past Laurence's arm I could see Chris's bare feet, on the sofa. I could tell that he was lying in a foetal position. My heart broke and I turned and left. Outside the flat my father was standing, looking at me.

'I hate you,' I said, and walked away.

I went back down the road to Monteagle Court in a daze. I couldn't believe Chris was gone. My beautiful baby brother was dead. By the time I got there Kim had arrived and was holding Carole in her arms, trying to console her. She looked at me. 'Is it true, Jen?' she asked. I looked at her and nodded and began to cry. We all stood together, silent with shock, unable to take it in.

I made my way into the flat, to where Mum sat at the table with a cigarette in her mouth. It was obvious from her appearance that she was in deep shock. I put my arm gently around her. As I held her close, I felt her let go and she started to wail. Her body started to shake uncontrollably and I shouted to Kim to come inside and help me. For the first time in many years I felt compassion for my mum.

Kim

I had caught up on my studies and prepared for my exams. And I had started an attachment at Canterbury General Hospital, which allowed me to attend an autopsy.

On the day of the autopsy I arrived early and smeared my nose with a strong-smelling vapour, as a colleague had warned me that the worst part was the smell. I sat at the back of the room, so that if I felt queasy I could leave without causing disruption.

The autopsy began with an explanation by the pathologist, before the procedure itself began. As he began cutting into the body before us I was mesmerised, totally fascinated by what we could learn from what seemed such a barbaric act. I was so engrossed that I failed to see the morgue attendant slip into the room. He whispered into the teacher's ear and after briefly looking around for me, he indicated that I should follow him out.

Eddie was waiting at the door. 'What are you doing here? Is someone hurt?' I asked. 'Kim, I have some bad news,' he said. I knew, straight away, what it was. 'It's Chris, isn't it? Is he dead?' Eddie nodded and put his arms around me.

We headed straight for London. It was strange how I knew instantly it was Chris. It's something I've never been able to explain, but I knew the moment I was called out of the autopsy.

Eddie had never been to Monteagle Court before, but I didn't have the energy to explain or apologise for what he was about to encounter. I remember thinking that he loved me, not my family, so it wouldn't matter. I sat in silence all the way, only speaking to give him directions.

I struggled to take it in. Chrissie, my little brother, was dead. I wept silent tears all the way, thinking of times when he was younger, seeing him in my mind's eye, smiling, playing football, playing with Carrine.

Was it really him? I felt a tiny flicker of hope that it might all be a mistake, not Chris at all. I thought of the time, not long ago, when I had cuddled him and asked if he was OK. I tried to remember how his voice had sounded, and the way his mouth moved, unable to believe that I'd never hear his voice again.

When we got to Mum and Dad's a few neighbours had gathered around a nearby door, and as I approached with Eddie following me, they fell silent and nodded to me. I was conscious that I still wore my nurse's uniform, even my hat was still neatly in place on my head. The door was ajar, but Carole was standing there. I put my arms around her, and at that moment Jenny and Laurence walked around the corner, followed by Dad. Jenny looked at me and I asked, 'Is it true?' She nodded and came towards me with her arms open. Through my sobs I asked how and what had happened and she explained as much as she knew.

Inside the flat Mum sat hunched and pathetic in a corner, already dressed in black, chain smoking and wiping her eyes every so often. I looked at this woman who had failed to protect her children from physical and mental abuse for so many years. Now she was crying over the death of her youngest child, when her others had virtually died inside years ago and she hadn't even noticed. She'd let us down so badly, yet I couldn't help feeling sorry for her. Chris had been her baby.

When I had left London I'd told myself that the past was behind me, I would never return to Monteagle Court again and I didn't care whether Mum and Dad lived or died. But I did care about Carole and Chris, left behind in that hellhole. Now I felt guilty, as though my thoughts had tempted fate in some way. I would have done anything to bring Chris back, to give him the help he must have needed. I couldn't help thinking that I hadn't tried hard enough to give him a better life when he had come to us in Colchester. I felt I had given up too soon, and now it was too late.

Dad was utterly predictable. He strutted around, revelling in being the centre of attention, while posing as the grief-stricken father. Yet he didn't shed a tear, and he barely seemed to care that Chris was dead. He showed no genuine sorrow. When he said, 'We'll have to get in touch with the Social to see if they'll help us pay for the funeral, coz we ain't got the money to pay for it,' I flipped. I shouted at him, 'You inconsiderate bastard, your son's lying in the morgue and all you can worry about is how you're going to screw the Social to pay for his funeral.'

At that point Jen grabbed my arm, said, 'Drop it, Kim, let's go,' and led me to the door. As we left I could hear Mum shouting, 'That's my fucking son and all you're bothered about is how we're gonna fucking pay.' Then Jenny slammed the door and we walked away.

Eddie and I went to Jenny's and stayed for the evening. It was a difficult time for Eddie, he had never met any of the family before and it didn't seem to be the right time to exchange pleasantries. At about one in the morning there was nothing left for us to say or do, so we eventually returned to Canterbury, where I went into work and arranged to take a week off. The next week proved to be difficult. I cried lots, looked at old photos of Chrissie, and wandered around in a daze, hardly believing he was dead. Two days before the funeral I made my way to Jenny's, feeling the need to be in her company so we could grieve together.

Jenny

In the days before Chris's funeral I had tried to carry on as usual, but everything reminded me of Chris. I would turn on the radio and The Jam would be on, singing one of Chris's favourite songs. He loved The Jam, and his other favourite band was Madness, though he loved some of the old songs too.

I got through by keeping myself as busy as possible. I cleaned the flat from top to bottom, went to work and looked after Martine. There was plenty to do helping to organise the funeral too. I had been to see the funeral directors with Laurence and Kim and we'd made all the arrangements. Laurence had asked me and Kim to split the cost and of course we agreed, even though finding the money was a struggle. We'd never have allowed our brother to have a pauper's funeral. It was to cost £185, and Laurence paid the £100 while Kim and I split the £85. My dad had insisted that he would get Social Security to foot the bill for Chris's funeral, and Laurence, Kim and I had been horrified. No matter how tight money was, we would pay for it ourselves.

The funeral directors had given us Chris's personal effects. There seemed so little, just a few small items. Among them was a watch, which Chris had been wearing when he died. Laurence had given it to him and it seemed only right that Laurence should keep it. I handed it to him and as he looked at it his face began to collapse and he sobbed. I walked quietly away and left him with his private memories.

The funeral directors explained that we could visit Chris in the chapel of rest. Kim and I persuaded Laurence to go, thinking he might feel better if he saw Chris again, but we were wrong. After his visit to the chapel Laurence wanted to clear the memory of the dead Chris from his head and remember only the lively, happy boy he had loved.

I decided to go and say goodbye to Chris myself. Pam came to keep me company and was brilliant, as always.

When we arrived the man who greeted us smiled and said to me, 'There's no guessing who you've come to see, you're the spitting image of your brother, Christopher.' I was a little taken aback, as I'd never thought Chris and I looked alike.

The room we were shown into was cold and very quiet. Pam stood back as I made my way over to the coffin. When I saw Chris I had to clasp my hand over my mouth to stifle a scream. Despite the make-up that had been applied I could see that his face was bruised, his lip was split and he had a black eye. An autopsy had already found a large dose of barbiturates in his body, along with a thick black mass on his lungs that was the result of glue-sniffing. But there was more to the story. He'd been arrested the night before he died, and there was to be a police inquiry into what had happened.

Despite his injuries, Chris looked peaceful, with his streaked blond hair across his eyes. And to my surprise, he did look like me. Pam edged closer. 'He's a ringer for you,' she said. I stared at him, unable to take my eyes from his face. Pam said she would leave me alone for a few minutes, and left the room.

As she left, my tears began to fall. 'Why, Chris, why?' I sobbed. I remembered the last evening we had spent together. 'I'm not meant for this,' he had said. Was it life he was talking about? I would never know. I stroked his hair and leaned over to kiss his cold cheek.

Kim

I didn't want to go to see Chris in the chapel of rest, but I felt I had to. Jenny and Laurence had both been, and I wanted to see him one last time too. After he died my head was filled with images of him as he had been in Colchester when he was brought home to us after sniffing glue. He'd been high as a kite, his eyes unable to focus and with spots all over his face. Despite seeing him only days before he died, I couldn't get that earlier memory out of my head. I hoped that saying goodbye to him would help.

I walked up from Monteagle Court, through the flats on the estate. From there I could see the rooftop of the undertakers Haynes and English and the sign 'Chapel of Rest'. I knew this had been hung there to deter burglars. In this area even an undertaker's wouldn't have been out of bounds.

It was sunny and hot outside, but inside it was so cool that it felt like a completely different climate. I recognised the familiar smells from the hospital mortuary and remembered the autopsy I'd seen the day Chris died. It sent a shiver down my spine.

A tall, stooped man with his hands clasped together came forward and said, 'How may I help you?' I told him I was there to see my brother and he said, 'Ah yes, we'll get him ready to receive you.' He exited behind a curtain and returned a few moments later to beckon me through into a corridor and then another room, where he said, 'I'll leave you two alone,' and disappeared.

I stood at the door, nervous about approaching the coffin. I slowly moved forward and I looked down on Chris's beautiful face. It was coated in make-up and his hair was all brushed forward into a fringe which he never wore. I cried, 'What have they done to you, babe? This is not the way you do it.' I took out a packet of tissues and began wiping the make-up off his face, talking to him all the time as if he could hear me. 'God, you'd be so mad if you could see what they've done to you.' As I wiped away the make-up I could see he had bruises, a black eye and a cut lip. 'Oh, Chris, what are we going to do without you?' I was sobbing, great gulping sobs. All my tissues had been used and the tears had to be wiped on my blouse.

Before I said goodbye for the last time I had to rearrange his hair. He always spiked it up, and with his highlights it looked really trendy. I ran my fingers through his fringe in an effort to get it the way he liked, and as I did I realised why his hair had been plastered down. Across his forehead was a wide slit that had been stitched up. It looked like something out of a Frankenstein film.

I knew this must have been part of the autopsy, but the other injuries on his face were not and I wanted to know what had happened.

I carried on arranging his hair and I did the best I could to make him look the way he had in life. When I was ready to leave I kissed the tip of my finger and put it to his lips and then ran my finger over his cheek, took a deep breath and said, 'Bye, babe.'

I walked away, still sobbing, and as I did, thoughts of my father came into my head. 'This is your fucking fault,' I said, out loud.

11

Endings

Jenny

We buried Chris on a blazing hot summer's day, just a few days before his eighteenth birthday.

From the moment I got up, after a sleepless night, the day seemed unreal, as though I was seeing it all from a distance.

I had explained to Martine that her uncle Chris was going to heaven and that she would see him again there, one day. She was very sad, but she believed me when I told her that he would be happier in heaven. She was too young to go to the funeral, so Pam offered to look after her, and they came to see us off in the cars, which were collecting the family from Monteagle Court. It was really good of Pam, who would have liked to come to the funeral herself to say her goodbyes.

There had been no one to accompany me to the funeral, so when Liam, the guy from the pub, volunteered I was grateful.

By the time the cars arrived a crowd had gathered to see Chris off. It was an old East End tradition: as a mark of respect everyone would come out to say goodbye, whether they knew the deceased or not.

Standing a little distance from the car, with their heads bowed, was a group of young boys. They had been Chris's friends and glue-sniffing buddies. Suddenly Mum did something totally unexpected. She approached them and stared at them, one by one.

'Take a good look,' she demanded. 'That could be you – or you – or you,' she said, pointing at each one of them in turn. 'But it's not any of you. It's my boy, my baby. God help you all.' An eerie, unsettling silence fell over the crowd, as Mum turned away and walked to the car.

The car was draped in flowers. Chris had been a mad keen Arsenal football club fan, and his name was spelled out in flowers of their colours, red and white. He had a gateway of flowers to open the gates of heaven, and I had bought him a flower pillow to rest his head on while he waited.

The funeral cortège drove all around the district and everywhere we went I was amazed to see so many people come out to say goodbye to our Chris. As our car followed his, I thought about all the times we had shared. I remembered taking Chris to his first Arsenal game with John Falconer and Kim. He'd only been seven and the crowd had lifted him and passed him, over their heads, down to the front to give him a better look. How he jumped for joy when his team scored.

I remembered his cheeky smile and the first time he arrived at my house on his newly purchased second-hand moped. He'd taken off his helmet to reveal a shaved head, saying long hair made him sweat too much, and we'd both laughed. I thought about the times he'd spent with Martine and Carrine, how they had adored him, and how he had cherished them.

Now all of that was gone. Chris was gone. All I had left were those memories. I felt Liam put his arm around me. He had been so sweet, I was glad he was there. Kim was with Eddie and Laurence was with his new partner Jan, and we stood as a force together. Carole was still in shock, but with us to help her she made it through the day.

When we finally arrived for the service, Kim, Laurence, Carole and I all sat together a couple of rows back. Mum had managed to arrange a Catholic service, but with a cremation. This was unusual at that time, but, showing a streak of determination she usually kept well hidden, she had got what she wanted. Towards the end of the service came the solemn moment when the curtain was drawing round the coffin, and everyone was quiet. Suddenly Kim shouted, 'You bastard, you fucking bastard, you did this.' Everyone was startled and turned to look.

I put my arm around her. 'Kim, stop it,' I whispered.

She brushed me aside. 'It was you,' she screamed at Dad. 'You let this happen, you fucking cunt.' Kim was seething and spitting as she screamed at him.

I struggled with her again and suddenly felt Eddie next to me. 'Let's get her outside, and quick,' he said.

Outside, Kim began to cry. 'Did you see him, Jen? He turned and smiled at me, that sick fucking bastard. God forgive me, Chris,' she wailed. Eddie put his arms around her to try to console her. 'That's it,' she said, 'I'm leaving, I won't breathe the same air as that fucking prick. Jen, meet me at the Royal Standard. I can't stay here any longer.' She turned and left, with Eddie beside her.

Before I could meet Kim at the pub I had to go to Monteagle Court, because everyone had been invited back for food and drink. I hadn't expected Kim to come, so I was surprised when she arrived, though she didn't stay long.

Inside the house the front room was strewn with food. Dad had arranged a massive buffet. I felt sick. This wasn't to celebrate his son's life, he just wanted to be the centre of attention. My brother was dead, and all he could think of was entertaining. I looked at him and hated him with a passion. Mum sat quietly in the corner, with a piece of pork pie on her plate, and a large whisky in her glass. I grabbed the brandy bottle, poured a very large glassful and swallowed it in one. My legs wobbled and Liam held me up. 'Let's get out of here,' he said.

At the pub, Kim was waiting with Eddie. Soon after we got there, Laurence and Carole followed. We ordered drinks and had our own private wake in memory of Chris. We raised our glasses and honoured our beautiful little brother.

Kim

I was dreading the day of the funeral. Not only because it was our last goodbye to Chris but because I had to see the old man again. As I neared Monteagle Court I saw Dad outside the flats waiting for the hearse to arrive. He had one hand in his pocket and the other was holding a cigarette. He was wandering up and down, as if he was taking a stroll on a lazy Sunday afternoon. The only thing that could be said for him was that it was the cleanest I had ever seen him. As our car approached he grinned at us and I turned my face away. I got out of the car and walked past him without saying a word or making eye contact.

Inside the house Mum had drawn the curtains as a mark of respect. Carole was sitting on the settee. She was closer to Chris that anyone and his death had hit her very hard. There was only a year between them and they had grown up in each other's pockets, in the same way that Laurence, Jenny and I had. My heart really ached for her and I cuddled her and said, 'At least he's at peace now.' Mum was in a bad way too. Crying one minute and putting out the buffet food the next, she didn't know whether she was coming or going.

Mum introduced me to Chris's girlfriend, Tina. She was a pretty little thing who smiled and dabbed at her eyes. She spotted Carole and went over to embrace her, which led to more tears. I went over to them both and Tina started telling me what had happened the night before he died. They had been out together, drinking in a pub called the London Apprentice near the City Road. As they left a fight broke out. Chris wasn't involved, but they stood watching as it spilled into the street.

The police arrived to disband the crowd and began looking for the culprits. As Chris and Tina were walking home a police car pulled alongside them and the officers started questioning Chris. Not a lover of police, he foolishly told them to 'piss off' and they immediately attempted to arrest him. He broke free by kicking one of the officers and ran, but they eventually caught him and put him in the cells overnight. Tina went on to explain that at six the next morning Chris had phoned her in tears, saying that every hour on the hour the police had gone into his cell and hit him. He was released a couple of hours after this conversation, and later that day he was found dead. There was no evidence to corroborate this story and although we were told that there was to be a police inquiry, we never heard anything more about it. The coroner's official verdict remained that Chris had died from an overdose of barbiturates and the effects of sniffing glue.

The hearse arrived strewn with flowers. Mine were red and white carnations, in the shape of an Arsenal football shirt. There were some lovely tributes, and looking at them I realised how many people had liked Chris.

We travelled up to the crematorium in the car behind the hearse. Much to my relief, Dad sat in the front with the driver, leaving everyone else in the back. Eddie followed on behind in our car, with Liam. I kept glancing out of the window to make sure they were following; I didn't feel I could get through it without Eddie's support.

At the chapel Mum and Dad sat in the front and I sat a couple of rows behind with Jenny and the others. At the end, as the chaplain reached down to press a button and the coffin was about to disappear behind a red velvet curtain, grief got the better of me and I sobbed loudly in Eddie's arms. I looked up for a last glimpse of the coffin, to say goodbye, and at that moment Dad turned round and grinned the same gloating grin he'd given me in the courtroom ten years earlier. It was as if a red mist appeared in front of my eyes again, and I screamed, 'You did this to him, he would still be here if it wasn't for you.' I couldn't stop, I hated him so much. As far as I was concerned he'd killed Chris. I wanted to tear him apart with my bare hands. Everyone was looking, but I didn't care, I wanted them all to know what he'd done.

Jenny and Eddie each took one of my arms and almost frog-marched me out of the chapel, as Dad continued to stare and grin, and I continued to shout.

Eddie drove me and Liam back to Monteagle Court. As we went around Highbury Corner I thought of Auntie, and I asked Eddie to turn up Laycock Street so I could go past her flat. The flats I remembered so well looked sad. They were due to be demolished and some of them had been boarded up, as the occupants had already been re-housed.

We stopped at Auntie's block and I got out of the car and went up to the railings. I pressed my face against the cold steel and looked up at her window. I remembered the laughter that echoed round that tiny one-bedroom flat, the long summer holidays and the cold winters, when we'd sat around a three-bar electric fire drinking cocoa, and I whispered, 'Look after him for us, Auntie.'

When we arrived back at Monteagle Court there

were dozens of people inside the flat; even the undertakers were invited in for a sherry and a piece of pork pie. I could hear snippets of lots of different conversations about Chris. Mum was telling someone it was a lovely service, Laurence was handing over the money to the gentleman in the morning suit from Haynes and English, and Jenny was still trying to console Carole. In the middle of all this Dad was walking round with a tray of pork pies shouting for Mum to cut some more up.

I didn't want to stay another minute. I whispered to Jenny that I was leaving and would meet her in the pub, and slipped quietly out.

After swallowing two Bacardi and cokes in quick succession I ordered a third and sat down next to Eddie. Jenny and Liam soon arrived, followed shortly afterwards by Laurence, Jan and Carole. We all raised our glasses to the memory of our little brother, and Jenny called for a second toast to Auntie. We sat for a moment, each with our silent memories of two people we had loved dearly and would always miss.

Jenny

The months that followed Chris's death were painful. I remember one day boarding the bus for work and then seeing a boy I was quite sure was my little brother, running towards the bus, calling my name and asking me to tell the conductor not to ring the bell.

At night I would have dreams about him, in which he'd be talking to me and smiling. One night I sat bolt upright in my bed and looked towards the wardrobe. Chris was standing there, bathed in a bright light. I remember feeling no fear, just elated that he was there. I asked him if he was OK, and he replied that he was happy. He said he was sorry for everything and went on to ask me to try to do something to help the youngsters who continued to sniff glue. He started to wave at me, and I begged him to stay a little longer, but he said he had to go. As he faded away, tears rolled down my face.

I couldn't get the image of Chris, or his words, out of my head. I felt so strongly about his message that I wanted to do something positive to help. One Sunday I turned on Capital Radio and heard an item called the 'Sunday Soap Box', which gave people with something to say the opportunity to speak out.

This was my chance. I called the radio station and they asked me to record what I wanted to say on a cassette and send it in. I did as they asked and the very next Sunday they played my tape. I felt so pleased that I had in some way helped to spread the word about the dangers of glue-sniffing, and also paid tribute to Chris.

The next day I started a new job, back in recruitment, at the Atlas Staff Bureau in Holborn.

When I met the rest of the staff I instantly hit it off with a girl called Jackie. She had heard my speech on the radio and thought it was great. She was to become a good and lasting friend, and we had a great laugh during our time at Atlas.

I was still deep in grief and the last thing I wanted to think about was Keith. But the date of his Old Bailey trial was drawing near and we needed to prepare. Much of the case rested on Carole's shoulders: she would have to testify that Keith kidnapped and assaulted her and that he had made death threats against me. I began to worry, because Carole had been distant of late. But the time following Chris's death had been awful for all of us and I wondered whether she would be up to being grilled in court.

My fears became a reality when, two days before we were to appear in court, Carole disappeared. I drove round Hackney all night looking for her, and the police launched a fevered hunt, but there was no sign of her and no one knew where she had gone. In her absence the entire case against Keith was dramatically weakened, and the police had no option but to drop the charges against him and set him free.

I was gutted. How could Carole let us all down? And what would happen now that Keith was out again? I'd worked so hard to rebuild my life, and now I felt it was being torn away from me again.

Kim

I had to take my first-year nursing exams only days after Chris's funeral. I threw myself into working for them and passed with excellent grades. After that I put all my energy into my nursing.

When I had a couple of days off I would visit Jenny and Martine, staying overnight on their sofa. By this time Graham had bought a house in Canning Town, where he was living with Carrine and Daniel, and I was able to see them when I came up to London. All the arrangements were made through Laurence, who would collect the children and bring them over to Jenny's.

It was always wonderful to see them. They were growing up fast and looked happy and healthy, and I admired Graham for the great job he was doing with them.

As far as I knew the children accepted the situation between me and Graham completely – certainly neither of them ever said anything to me when they were small. But in later years Carrine told me that as a little girl she used to wish that Graham and I were back together. And when she was a teenager and able to talk openly about these things, it became a standing joke – and it still is – that she was convinced we would some day get back together.

Graham believed that the children should keep in

regular contact with my family as well as his, and he made sure they saw Jenny and Laurence regularly. I admired him for this, and was grateful. But one day Jenny told me that Graham was planning to take the children to see Mum and Dad. When I heard this I was worried sick that he might leave them there or, even worse, allow them to stay overnight. The thought made my stomach turn over.

Until now I had respected Graham's request not to contact him directly. But this was too important – I had to speak to him. I went to a phone box to make the call, as I didn't want to speak in front of Jenny. Although we had talked about what Dad did to Mum, we had still never spoken to one another of the abuse each of us suffered at Dad's hands and I didn't want to refer to it, even indirectly, within her hearing. And besides, it had been a couple of years since I had spoken to Graham and I was unsure of my reception and very nervous.

I dialled his work number, which I still remembered. But when he answered, nerves got the better of me and I hung up. The same thing happened a second time. Hearing his voice brought back lots of memories and feelings that I thought had gone, and I wasn't prepared for that.

I braced myself to try again. However hard it was, I needed to be sure that when he visited my parents he never let the children out of his sight or allowed Mum and Dad to take them out on trips, even to the local swings. When I thought of Dad doing something to Carrine I felt physically sick. I dialled Graham's number again, and this time when I heard his voice I blurted out, 'Hi, Graham, it's me.' There was a short pause, so I carried on. 'I know you asked me never to contact you, but I heard you were planning to take the kids to see my mum and dad.'

'Yes, we're going on Saturday,' he replied.

With my heart beating so hard I was sure it must be visible through my top, I continued, 'Well, can you do me a favour and promise me you'll never leave the children alone with them?'

'Why?' came the reply.

'Look, I don't want to go into detail, but I beg you not to leave them alone, especially with my dad. There are things I never told you, so please don't leave them alone with him.'

'You must have your reasons, so I'll agree,' Graham said.

'Thank you,' I replied, desperately relieved. Thank goodness he was such a fair-minded man. He could have been angry or used it as a chance to get back at me, but that wasn't in Graham's nature.

There was a long silence. 'How are you?' he asked me. The ice was broken. We were talking again, even if it was a little awkwardly. We chatted for a few minutes, before saying goodbye.

That day I smiled to myself, feeling happier than I had for a long time. I could stop worrying about the children's visit to Monteagle Court, and Graham and I were on speaking terms again.

The truth was, I really missed him and the children. Although I had Eddie, I couldn't help thinking that if I hadn't been so eager to run away from my problems, we might have been able to sort things out. It was too late for that now, but to be friends with Graham meant a lot to me.

Keith's court case was looming, and when I went to stay with Jenny the weekend before it I was shocked. She'd lost so much weight, she looked gaunt. Her skin was a mess and her shoulders looked like coat hangers. I knew it was because she was worried sick. She was terrified that something would go wrong and Keith would be back on the streets, and I couldn't blame her. I was worried too.

I tried to cheer her up by suggesting we take Martine, collect Carrine and Daniel and go on one of our outings. I thought I'd raise a smile by suggesting we take a packed lunch with us, as Auntie used to. But Jenny was in no mood for fun. Carole was missing. Instead of taking the children out we combed the streets looking for Carole, before coming home, putting Martine to bed, and spending the remainder of the night worrying about where on earth she was.

The following day we searched again, but without success. Carole didn't show – and with the case against him weakened, Keith walked. The following day Jenny and I bought new locks and door bolts for her flat. Just in case.

Eddie had completed his social work degree and been offered a job up in Chester. It was a great opportunity, so he accepted the job. He moved up to Chester and the plan was that I would follow him when I'd finished my nursing course, in three months' time.

I visited him whenever I could, as it was hard for Eddie to get time off from his new job. One Thursday afternoon my nursing class was told that we'd all been given the weekend off to study. Delighted at the chance to visit Eddie, I raced out of class, packed a weekend bag and started the drive to Chester.

I wanted my visit to be a surprise, so I stopped off at the motorway services and phoned Eddie, as I always did after work every evening, so that he wouldn't suspect anything. I told him I was working late and asked what he was doing for the evening. He said he would be sitting at home missing me. Just what I wanted to hear.

As I parked the car outside his flat I could see a dim light through the curtains. I was excited and couldn't wait to see the surprise on his face.

I had to ring the bell three times before I saw his

familiar figure coming down the stairs. He opened the door in his dressing-gown and the shock on his face when he saw me was tinged with fear. Instead of taking me in his arms, he asked what I was doing there and told me I couldn't go upstairs.

I pushed him aside and climbed the stairs to his first-floor flat. There in our bed was a woman with dyed pink hair and a stud in her nose. I froze. I was conscious that Eddie had entered the room and was talking, but I couldn't hear a word he was saying. The woman scrambled for her clothes, and as she did I punched her so hard she fell towards the door. I scooped up her clothes and threw them down the stairs, and as she darted after them, dressed only in knickers, I followed her, hurling abuse. Although it was Eddie I was most hurt by and angry with, she was no innocent party: the evidence that he had a partner was all over the flat.

I returned to the flat to find Eddie sitting with his head in his hands. I sat on a stool, while on the radio Sad Café sang, 'Every day hurts without you.'

I got up to leave and Eddie followed me, insisting she meant nothing to him. He had strayed because he was missing me, he explained. He was just lonely – I meant everything to him. We stood outside arguing for a long time. Eventually Eddie leaned against the wall and pleaded for me to come inside. I was tired, hungry and cold and it was now late at night. I mustered up enough strength to punch him in the face. Once I had released my anger, I started to listen to his pleas, and I found myself following him back into the flat. After hours of talking and tears I started to forgive him. Eventually we went to bed and made love, and I fell asleep wrapped in his arms.

It was only weeks until I was due to sit my final exams. I was within reach of qualifying as a psychiatric nurse. All my hopes, dreams and efforts had gone into my training, for which I'd given up so much, and that qualification was to be the proof, to everyone, that I could make something of myself. Yet I was so afraid of losing Eddie that I rang my tutor at the nursing college and asked if I could take study leave and then transfer to a hospital near Chester to take my exams. I went back to Kent to get my things and moved up to Chester the next day.

I was eventually offered a place at Denbeigh Psychiatric Hospital to complete my training and take my exams. But it was a hundred miles away, and I never did take those exams. Instead I took a job in a home for recovering alcoholics near Chester.

Looking back I wonder if, deep down, I was afraid to succeed. I knew I could do it, and yet, in the end, I didn't. Instead I gave it all up for the man who had just betrayed me.

Jenny

Several weeks passed without incident after Keith was freed. I was very happy at work, and had enrolled in night school to take the O levels I never took at Haggerston Girls. Although my teachers had said I was bright and should stay on, Dad had insisted I leave school at fifteen and get a job, so that he could have some of the money. Now I was determined to make up for what I had missed. Martine was happy and doing well in school. She was now six and in her second year. One day in December she came home eager to tell me she had got the part of the Angel Gabriel in the nativity play. She was so excited and I was delighted for her.

By this time I was earning better money and I wanted this Christmas to be a good one. Pam had invited us for dinner on Christmas Day, and on Boxing Day they would come to me. I'd bought Martine a new bike and disco roller boots and I couldn't wait to see her open them.

The night of the nativity play came round, and all the parents crowded into the assembly hall and sat on rows of small benches. Pam and I sat together to watch her youngest son Martin and Martine in their first play. As the lights dimmed and Martine appeared in a large white sheet, a broad band of tinsel on her dark hair, I felt tears fill my eyes. She opened her mouth to sing, and the voice that came out astounded even me. It was pure, clear and strong, quite astonishing in a child so young. As she sang 'Away in a Manger' you could have heard a pin drop.

On the way home, it began to snow. Martine skipped along with Martin, while Pam and I chatted about the play. 'You have a special kid there, Jen,' she remarked, and I nodded and smiled. I knew she was right.

As we turned the corner into our street I saw a man walk away from my front door. I called out and he turned and smiled at me. 'Jeanette Ponting?' he asked. He placed a large envelope in my hand. 'I'm here to deliver this,' he said, and smiled as he walked away.

Inside the flat, while Pam made tea, I opened the envelope. It was worse than I could have imagined and I felt my world cave in. Keith was taking me to court to get access to Martine. So he had found a way to get at me, after all.

I said nothing to Martine, I didn't want to upset her Christmas. She'd had a fabulous evening and was happy. As she played with Martin in her bedroom, Pam put her arm around my shoulder. 'Don't worry, Jen, he doesn't stand a chance,' she said. How I hoped she was right.

I was required to appear in court in January. In the days after Christmas, when the excitement was over and everything felt flat, I didn't know what to do with myself. I had no plans for New Year's Eve either. Pam was going to a dinner-dance, and Robert, my part-time boyfriend, hadn't been around for a while. Then, out of the blue, Kim phoned and invited me up to Chester. Eddie had gone back to see his family and she hadn't been able to go with him as she had to work some extra shifts.

I hadn't seen Kim for six months, since Chris's funeral. I couldn't wait. I packed Martine and our bags into my car – I'd swapped the old Cortina for a Vauxhall saloon – and set off. We stopped only once, for a cup of tea, and made it to Kim's in five hours.

Kim's little flat was pretty and comfortable, and we chatted for hours. We had so much to catch up on. We talked about Keith, and I told her the latest development. We both felt so disappointed and frustrated that Carole had vanished. We still had no idea where she was and we wondered if, this time, she was really lost to us.

That New Year break gave us a wonderful respite from our worries. We visited some famous landmarks in Chester and had a lovely New Year dinner at a local restaurant. Kim was thrilled to have Martine there and spoilt her. Then, all too soon, it was time to go back to London and to face the next court case.

Kim and I had talked about it for ages. Kim felt,

just as Pam had, that Keith hadn't a leg to stand on. She suggested I escape Keith by moving up to Chester, close to her. But I felt I couldn't uproot us again. Martine was settled in school and I had a great job, as well as night school. Besides, Keith would only find us again. I made the decision to stand my ground, and fight him in court.

12

Heartbreak and Happiness

Jenny

Back at home Martine and I settled back into our routine, but my mind was occupied, every minute of every day, by the coming court case. How could a man who had done the things Keith had done, be allowed access to a child? Surely, if there was any justice in the world, he would be kept away from her. But even as these thoughts went round in my head, I was aware that nothing was that simple, especially when it came to the workings of the law. When the day of the case arrived I dropped Martine at school as usual. I hadn't said anything about it to her; I still hoped I would never have to.

I walked into court a couple of hours later and saw Keith for the first time in many months. He stared at me with a look of sheer malice, confirming my suspicions that his motive for bringing this case was not to see Martine, but to get at me.

I was nervous, but then I looked at the judge and recognised him. He was the judge who had granted my numerous injunctions, and I felt very hopeful that the decision would be in my favour.

It wasn't. The judge decided that no matter what Keith had done to me, he was still Martine's father and had a right to have contact with his child. My lawyer tried to battle for me, but the decision was made and Keith was awarded reasonable access. His first visit was scheduled for the following Friday.

I was utterly crestfallen. How was I going to go home and tell my baby? In the end I kept it simple and Martine's reaction was calm for one so young. She said she didn't want to see her father, but she understood that she had no choice. We hugged each other and I told her she must be brave and promised her that he would never hurt either of us again.

The following Friday he arrived on time. I could smell alcohol on his breath, but made no comment. I refused to let him in and made him wait outside while I put Martine's coat on. I held her by the shoulders, my face level with hers. There were tears in her eyes. 'Don't cry, baby, it will all be OK,' I said, and pulled her towards me for a final hug before leading her out to Keith.

The afternoon passed very slowly as I struggled to keep busy. I had sounded more confident to Martine than I felt. Would he look after her and bring her back on time? I hoped he wouldn't dare step out of line, as the terms of the access had been agreed and he might well lose it if he messed around.

Finally the doorbell went and there was Keith with Martine. She looked happy and was carrying lots of bags. 'Daddy's bought me lots of things,' she said excitedly. I looked long and hard at Keith. 'You can't buy her,' I said. 'We'll see,' he replied with a smirk on his face.

The visits continued and Keith was a model of good behaviour. He made no aggressive moves towards me, in fact he rarely even looked at me. Martine seemed to enjoy her time with him, but after one particular day out she was quiet. I asked if she was OK, and after hesitating a bit she said, 'I like going out with Daddy, but I don't like going to his girlfriend's house. They make me wait downstairs while they go to her bedroom on business.' She was so innocent, and I was enraged.

The next time he arrived to pick her up, I asked him about what Martine had said. Unconcerned, he confirmed that he was having sex with his girl-friend while Martine waited downstairs. I was furious. I tried to discuss it with him further, but he said it was none of my business. As he walked away with our daughter, I called my soli-citor, who advised me that I could make a request to the court to have the access reversed.

I decided to go ahead. I still wanted Keith out of our lives and this was my chance. But before any-

thing happened Keith made a move of his own —
and disappeared.

The next time he was due to collect Martine he
didn't turn up. Or the time after that. Although I
had wanted Keith to leave us alone, I didn't want
this abrupt departure, and having no idea if or
when he would return. Martine had got used to
seeing him, and when she did she had enjoyed
herself. Determined to show me he could win
her over, he had showered her with sweets and
presents and given her a nice time. Now he was
gone, without a word to her, and I watched help-
lessly as she waited, with her little face pressed
against the window, for visits which didn't happen.
A few weeks passed and still he didn't phone or call
round. I tried to contact him through his mother,
but she hadn't seen him either. Eventually Martine
accepted that Daddy was gone again. I felt so sorry
for her and so angry with him for building up her
trust and then letting her down. She wasn't a toy
and I was determined he wouldn't use her any
more.

I called my solicitor, who advised me to drop the
case to have his access reversed. After all, as he
hadn't been round, it seemed pointless to trouble
the courts again. I took her advice and once again
we settled down to a life without Keith. I continued
to work and study, and Martine continued to do
well at school.

After a few months, true to form, Keith reappeared. He rang me and made promises to see Martine, but I didn't tell her, and I was glad I hadn't because he never showed up. I really didn't care any more and was just grateful that he had a new girlfriend and was leaving me and Martine alone.

Not long afterwards I took my exams, and when the results arrived I was the proudest student on the course. I achieved eight O levels, most of them with grade A. This achievement did wonderful things for my confidence and I decided then to do two A levels, in English and Art. I was really enjoying myself, having met lots of new friends, and loved the courses. But I dismissed it as an impossible dream when my English teacher asked me if I'd ever thought of writing as a profession!

During the next few months Keith started to call round again, turning up out of the blue with no warning. I found his visits unnerving and uncomfortable and refused to let him see Martine. He was furious, but I really had no feelings left for this man and was desperate to have him out of my life for ever. It seemed that every time I thought he had gone, he would turn up again like a bad penny. I was grateful that none of his visits had resulted in violence, but I knew he could blow again at any time.

With the demands of work, studying and being a single parent I was constantly exhausted. And my weight had ballooned, which upset me – too much eating on the hop and very little chance of exercise. One day a friend of a friend suggested I try a local slimming clinic. Apparently, the diet was easy and they gave you pills to suppress your appetite and an injection to combat water retention. It sounded good, so I went along. But within weeks I was hooked on the slimming pills. They gave me so much energy that I found myself doing ridiculous things like de-icing the freezer at three in the morning. I whizzed around everywhere, constantly on the go and never relaxing for a second.

As the weeks passed and I kept taking the pills I certainly became slimmer. But I was also nervous, edgy and, underneath the high of the pills, ex-hausted. Then another friend warned me about the dangers of slimming pills and asked why I didn't take speed. It was surprisingly easy to get, she told me, plus the effects lasted longer and there were fewer side-effects. So I tried it. Speed led to sulphate, a cheaper option with the same effects, and before long I was barely ever sleeping: my days were spent rushing around, and my nights – when I wasn't cleaning the house – sleepless and staring at the ceiling.

I knew what I was doing was illegal, but I reasoned that I wasn't hurting anyone and a lot of the people I knew were taking something to keep them going. But I had very little idea about the dangers. I could see that some of the others were completely manic on the pills, but I told myself I had it all under control and was only taking what I needed to get me through the demands of my life.

Then one day Martine arrived home from school while I was busy getting ready for my evening job. I was working as a barmaid again, and Martine was going to stay with friends across the road. She was eager to show me something, but I shouted at her to go away. She sobbed and ran to her bedroom and I sank down on the sofa in tears, horrified that I'd behaved so badly and hurt her. I knew it was the drugs. I thought of Chris and Auntie – what would they think of me, behaving like this? I got up and collected all the pills and emptied them down the sink. I had been stupid and silly, but it was over. I called Martine and held her close to me. She was so precious, I promised myself I would never risk hurting her like that again.

Despite the ever-present threat of Keith, I knew we had to get on with our lives. His visits had tailed off, and although there was nothing to stop him coming back and causing us misery at any time, I wasn't going to live in fear, or let him have a hold over me any longer. And life was often good; there were long spells of sheer happiness for me and Martine. At nine years old she was lovely looking and was doing well at school and in her dancing.

Her dance teacher, Ann Smith, was fond of her and knew she was something special, and she would often give Martine private singing lessons. So it was no surprise to anyone who knew her when Martine announced that she wanted to go to a performing arts school.

Around this time Keith began visiting again. It was only when his mum told me he had finished with his girlfriend that I realised why he was back. Again he started to bother me for access and again I refused, knowing that he had no real interest in Martine, or concern for her. I was surprised not to receive a lawyer's letter or summons, but nothing arrived. I got the impression that, in a warped sort of way, Keith found the whole thing very amusing. And Martine accepted it when I said it was better that she didn't see him. She had understood by this time that he didn't really care for her, and was simply playing games.

Meanwhile I had continued to see Robert from time to time, and that suited me. I really had no time in my life for anything more permanent. Besides, Martine and I were doing fine on our own. I did think sometimes that it would be nice to settle down with someone, but at 28 I had given up all hope of finding Mr Right. Until I met John McCutcheon.

Kim

I had settled down in Chester, and Eddie and I were happy, at least on the surface. I had put the incident with the other woman out of my mind, but it had hurt me so deeply that I couldn't put it out of my heart. Instead of blaming him, though, I began to look critically at myself and I wondered if my childhood had left its mark on me as an adult. I had always believed that, because I chose never to remember the abuse or talk about it, it hadn't affected me. But now I began to wonder. I realised that because I was so desperate for stability in a relationship, I wanted constant reassurance that I was loved. After seeing what my mother went through at the hands of my father, I wanted my own relationship to be perfect. I wanted to prove that fairy tales and dreams really do come true, and I needed to have complete confidence in my partner, which, in the end, put a lot of pressure on him.

Six months after moving to Chester I applied to work in a new social services home for adults with learning disabilities. I got the job and after a two-week induction period I was told I had shown so much potential that I was being promoted to senior care officer. It was shift work and very demanding, but I enjoyed it and the pay was decent.

With two salaries coming in, Eddie and I decided to buy a house together. We bought a property fifteen miles from Chester but within easy reach of both our jobs. I loved our new home and life was good; we worked hard but we could afford to enjoy the nicer things in life, like eating out, going to the theatre or dancing. During school holidays Carrine and Daniel would come to stay with us.

Carrine didn't particularly like Eddie, and there were awkward times when he would ask her to do something and she would refuse. Always the peacemaker, I would step in and smooth things over.

One holiday Carrine, who was now almost ten, asked if she could come and live with me. I was touched and pleased, but concerned about how Graham would feel. But Carrine explained that she had discussed it with him and he had told her to speak to me. Later I spoke with Eddie, who was very supportive about the idea, but suggested that if she was coming to live with us we should get married.

It wasn't the most romantic proposal in the world, but I was still pleased. I had always felt that Eddie would be my partner for life, he was a good friend as well as my boyfriend, and the idea of marriage had been in the back of both our minds. Carrine's arrival simply gave us the push we needed to go ahead and do it.

We settled for a register office wedding in early August 1984. All his office colleagues came, as well as the staff and even some residents from the home where I worked. It was a quiet affair, but lovely. I was so happy that I'd been given a second chance, with someone who was loving, supportive and smart.

My only regret was that Jenny couldn't make it. We were married on a weekday and she couldn't get away from work. I was disappointed, but I accepted that we were miles away from each other and that we both had full and busy lives.

We didn't have a honeymoon – neither of us could get time off work – but soon after the wedding Eddie came home one day with a belated wedding present for me, a Jack Russell dog called Sam. He was adorable but he ended up being more Eddie's dog than mine as it was Eddie who usually walked him.

Eddie and I had talked several times about having children of our own, and after we were married we agreed that we'd wait a few months, to get used to married life, and then begin trying for a baby. I had only briefly been on the pill, because I suffered awful side-effects, so I'd used a coil instead, which I planned to have removed.

I had suffered from heavy periods for some years. Whereas the majority of women have regular five to seven-day periods, mine often lasted twelve or fourteen days and were so heavy that I could have kept the tampon manufacturers going on my own.

A few months after our wedding I awoke one night in excruciating pain, with what I thought was the start of my period. After quietly getting out of bed, without disturbing Eddie, I crept downstairs to suffer in silence. I always prefer to be alone when I'm ill – perhaps a legacy of my childhood, when I learned to cope with suffering silently and alone.

I thought the pain would ease, but it didn't, so the next morning I went to the family planning clinic at the local hospital. When they attempted to examine me, my discomfort was so great that they decided to call in a gynaecologist. He requested tests and then announced that I was pregnant, but it appeared that, because the coil was in situ, I was naturally aborting the baby. He told me there was no chance of it surviving, and that he would have to operate immediately to remove both the coil and the foetus.

When I awoke after the operation Eddie was beside me, telling me that everything had gone OK. He said the doctor had told him there was no baby, and yet the same doctor had confirmed that a pregnancy test had been positive. I was distraught. I felt I couldn't even grieve because I didn't know whether there had been a baby or not.

Within hours I contracted an infection in my womb, which meant I had to spend nine days in hospital. I was discharged with my abdomen so swollen that, ironically, I looked eight months pregnant, and I was signed off work for the next three weeks.

I felt terribly low. I was afraid that any chance I had of having another baby had now gone, but the doctors wouldn't be able to tell me until I had recovered.

After a week of moping around at home I decided to go and visit Jenny in London. I knew she would look after me, and it would ease the pressure on Eddie, who was having to come home each lunchtime to look after me and then rush home in the evenings.

I wasn't well enough to drive, so I went by coach and Jenny picked me up from Victoria Coach Station and filled me in on all the gossip as we drove home. I spent a lovely week with her and Martine, and saw Carrine and Daniel several times too.

I was still hoping very much that Carrine could come and live with me, and when I spoke to Graham he was in favour of it. He said Carrine felt there were some things dads just didn't understand, and she was getting to an age where she needed her mum. But at the same time he felt that Daniel was better off with him.

By this time Graham was making frequent trips to Switzerland. A friend of his had moved over there and, while visiting him, Graham had met someone new. He told me he was thinking of moving there permanently. Splitting the children up was a difficult decision, but in the end we felt it was the right thing to do. So we made plans for Carrine to move in with me and Eddie in time for the new school term in September.

During the last week in August I returned home, with only ten days to prepare for Carrine's arrival. Eddie suggested painting and decorating her new bedroom as a surprise for her, so we bought a bed, a quilt cover with curtains to match, furniture and the all-important pink wallpaper. Eddie even suggested buying her a stereo. He was really making an effort and I was so glad that he was looking forward to her coming, especially as they hadn't had the easiest relationship. I loved him dearly for all he was doing – he clearly knew how much Carrine coming meant to me.

I returned to work four days before Carrine's arrival and rushed home after my early shifts to help prepare her room. I also started cleaning the house from top to bottom before dashing off to work. Several times that week I rang Eddie at home, to ask him to do something I hadn't been able to do or had forgotten. He seemed to be out an awful lot of the time, but he told me he was taking Sam for walks. I knew that Sam could run off in the park for hours on end, so I believed him.

Three days to go and I decided to get the entire washing and ironing done. While checking the pockets of Eddie's jeans I came across a piece of paper with a woman's name and a phone number on it.

I knew, the second I saw it, what was going on. I waited for Eddie to get home, and when he walked in I looked him in the eyes and said very calmly, 'How long has the affair been going on?' He didn't even try to deny it, he told me it started just after our wedding, but that he didn't love her, he had just been lonely when I worked long shifts and while I was in London. I kept very calm, though inside I was in turmoil. I walked over to the case I had already packed for him, picked it up and threw it out of the front door. Then I told him to go. As he left he pleaded with me to forgive him and give it one more chance. I slammed the door in his face.

I cried for days. At night when I crawled alone into bed I kept wondering if I should forgive him and give him one more chance. But I couldn't, because I knew deep down that after this second betrayal I could never trust him again. When I eventually convinced myself of that, I stopped crying. But I was in a state of grief, unable to eat, sleep or go to work – I had phoned in sick. No matter what I did I couldn't get rid of the ache in my heart or the feeling of being utterly alone. Again I started to ask what I had done to deserve such treatment. Was I such a bad person that someone I loved needed to go elsewhere?

I didn't have long to grieve. At the weekend Graham arrived with Carrine and Daniel. I told him Eddie was at work. I couldn't face admitting the truth when I was still feeling so raw. I hated to think that I had failed at another relationship – and after less than a year of marriage.

I always wanted to prove to Graham that I had left him for a good reason, that I would make something of my life and find someone who would really love and care for me. I was ashamed to admit to him that the person I thought cared so much had decided he preferred someone else. For some weeks I didn't tell anyone about the split. I needed to come to terms with it myself first. I told Carrine that Eddie had gone away and threw myself into settling her in. It was so wonderful to have her living with me after our years apart. It was my chance to be a real mum to her again, and I wasn't going to let my broken heart, or anything else, spoil the joy I felt at having my daughter back.

Jenny

I was sorry I couldn't get to Kim's wedding, but I was so pleased that she'd found happiness with Eddie. I never really accepted him, as I felt he was responsible for Kim not getting back with Graham, but I kept that to myself. I missed Kim and we spoke virtually every night on the phone – our bills were enormous.

I was worried sick when Kim had to go into hospital, and it was great to have her to stay while she was recovering. But after she went back to work I found it hard to get hold of her. I knew she had a demanding job in residential care work, but every time I rang her Eddie would answer and say she was working. I couldn't help thinking something wasn't right.

Martine's dancing was going from strength to strength and she enrolled in a new school in Newington Green. The teacher was a young girl called Zayni, who had attended the famous Italia Conti stage school. This was one of the schools Martine had set her sights on and it wasn't long before Martine was having private lessons in Zayni's house in Southgate every Saturday morning.

Getting her there was like something out of a farce, and I laugh when I look back on it. It was a bit of a journey from where we lived, and we chugged up there in my old banger. I wasn't too hot on directions and usually got lost on the way – telling Martine I'd taken the scenic route. The car stalled every five minutes and we'd have to get out and push to jump-start it, but we made it in the end and I'd wait while Martine danced.

The two of us often watched old musicals on our ancient television. We had no aerial, the picture was always green and the sofa we cuddled up on had collapsed and had no legs, but we didn't care.

We'd drink hot chocolate and eat biscuits, watching our green picture, and we loved every minute. Martine and I still look back on those days with affection and call them our hungry years.

Martine continued to enter dance competitions. One day, after we'd gone all the way to White City for a contest in which Martine came nowhere, I asked her if she wanted to try something else. She looked at me in total disbelief and said, 'I never want to do anything else but entertain, Mum. I'll never give up.' I knew she meant it, and that nothing I could say would change her mind, although I did step in sharpish when she developed a fascination for strippers. She saw it as a glamorous profession, but I told her I'd rather watch her with her clothes on.

Keith still turned up from time to time, though he hadn't become violent again. One night he arrived after Martine was asleep. I was tired and he was the last person I wanted to see. He started to turn on the charm, telling me I looked good. I had lost a lot of weight and maybe I did look OK, but I wasn't interested. He forced his way past me, into the flat, and took my hand to lead me to the bedroom. I had no fight in me at all and just gave in. I knew that to try to fight him would be pointless anyway, and no one would help me – every effort I'd made to get help had resulted in bitter disappointment. My family and friends were sick of hearing about him and I was just so tired of him and everything he was. As he slowly undressed me I closed my eyes and just wished for it to be all over.

As he climaxed, he held my face in his hands, and willed me to give him some kind of response, but there was none. I neither loved nor loathed him; I was emotionally drained and felt nothing at all. He had killed all feeling in me.

At first Keith became angry, but then something totally unexpected happened. His face softened and for the first time in years, I saw the face of the man I had fallen in love with all those years before. But it only made me sad.

'Forgive me,' he muttered, but I said nothing, and within minutes he was gone. I lay alone in bed and wept for all the wasted years and all the pain and misery that had been so needless.

Though I didn't know it then, this was our last sexual encounter. Keith never tried to force me into sex again. Perhaps I knew, deep down, that something final had happened, because afterwards I felt a huge sense of relief.

Some weeks later, Pam invited me to go to a dinner-dance organised by a group who called themselves the Buffalos. Things hadn't worked out with her policeman boyfriend, and she had seemed very sad for a long time, so when she asked me to go with her to the dance I agreed.

It was to be held above the Prince Edward pub near Victoria Park. When we arrived the dance had already started and the place was packed. I bumped into a few people I knew, including a guy I'd been out to dinner with once or twice whom I'd decided I didn't really like. I was standing at the bar when the evening's auction started, and a beautiful onyx ashtray went up for sale. I started to bid, but backed out as the price went up. There were only two men left bidding. One was the guy I knew, and the other was a man who stood very close to where I was standing. He bid successfully, and then approached me and offered me the ashtray. I was stunned.

'I heard you say you wanted it,' he said, in a strong Scottish accent. He had a kind face, and I smiled and thanked him. 'Are you a Buffalo?' he asked.

'No,' I replied, 'I'm a Pisces,' and we both burst out laughing.

'My name is John McCutcheon,' he said, 'what's yours?'

'I'm Jenny,' I replied. We talked for the rest of the evening and he offered to walk me home.

John was a lovely man and within months we were inseparable. He was kind, gentle and very considerate, especially where Martine was concerned. He was separated from his wife, and he too had a daughter, Isla, and saw her regularly.

John was looking for a secure and happy relationship, something I had dreamed of but thought was out of reach. We made the ideal couple. I told John about my past, including what Keith was like and how he would use Martine to hurt me. I was scared, but nothing seemed to deter John. He wanted to be with me and, as far as he was concerned, no one was going to mess anything up. I never found the courage to tell him about the sexual abuse I suffered at Keith's hands, but I felt he had guessed. He also knew that my childhood had been very grim, and although he wasn't the kind of person to make judgements, he had no time for my father.

It wasn't long before Keith found out I had met someone. Within days I was again served with papers requiring me to appear in court. He was once again applying for access to Martine. It was too much. Would this man never leave me alone? His petty vindictiveness was pathetic. I sobbed in John's arms, asking over and over again, why?

The court date arrived and I was asked by my lawyer to bring Martine. John came with me and so did Pam. When we arrived I was devastated to see the same judge who had given Keith access in the last court case. Not long after the case started, the judge peered at me and then at Martine. He halted the proceedings, saying he wished to speak to Martine alone, in his chambers. Martine was led across the courtroom and out through a large oak door. We sat and waited in silence for what seemed like an eternity.

When Martine came back, she looked straight at me and winked, then she sat down next to me and squeezed my hand. The judge began to speak.

'I'm quite amazed at your young daughter, Miss Ponting. Never has a nine-year-old child expressed herself in such a mature way to me before. She is a credit to her mother and a delightful young girl. She is both articulate and strong-minded and knows what she wants. She has witnessed a catalogue of abuse, and yet she remains kind, sweet and, above all, aware of what is right. Judgement is in favour of the defendant, and Mr Thomas George Keith Hemmings is refused access to his daughter until she is eighteen and can decide for herself. I wish you and your family the best of luck.'

He stood up and it was all over. We all hugged each other and smiled. I felt faint. I couldn't believe the years of suffering were finally at an end. I glanced at Keith. His face was like a thundercloud, but I didn't care. I was free and my baby was safe.

Kim

When Jenny told me what had happened in court I sighed with relief. It seemed that Keith was out of her life at last and I couldn't have been more pleased. Jenny could have chosen the same path as Mum, sticking with a cruel and destructive man no matter what, but she hadn't and I was proud of her. Jenny had made a success of her life, she was a great mum to Martine and she was heading in a whole new direction. Now that the hurdle of the court case was out of the way, I felt I could finally tell her about Eddie. She cried for me and in the end we were both sobbing down the phone. She promised to visit soon and ended the call with 'Oh, and when we come up there may be three of us, so be prepared. Love you.' I went to bed wondering what she meant. I thought perhaps they'd got a dog, or that she was thinking of bringing Pam with her.

Carrine had settled into her new school and was thriving. I, on the other hand, was sad, lonely and missing Eddie, although I was still sure I didn't want him back. Several weeks had now passed, and I hadn't seen or heard from him since the day he'd left, which only convinced me he didn't care. I packed up his remaining belongings and deposited them in the shed.

I had no one to talk to and, apart from the people at work, I only had a ten-year-old for company. I tried to hide my sadness from Carrine, but children have an uncanny ability to know when things aren't right. She asked if it was me she could hear crying in the night, and she did everything she could to cheer me up, even offering to use her pocket money to take me to McDonald's. I was touched, and did my best to brighten up, but I couldn't help feeling that, at 26, with two marriages behind me, I was destined to be single.

Jenny came for the promised visit, arriving with John and a very happy Martine. It was wonderful to see them together as a family. John was great, we got on well from the start. I could see he was good for Jenny and I was in awe of the easy and friendly way he handled the girls. We all had such a good time that, when they left, Carrine and I decided to pack our bags and go with them for a couple of weeks in London. It gave Carrine a chance to stay with Graham and Daniel, and I had more time with Jenny and Martine.

During that visit I suggested to Jenny that we ought to see Mum. We hadn't seen her for two years – since Chris's funeral. Jenny agreed, although reluctantly, and we visited on a day when we knew our father would be out. Mum told us she had been ill. She had been having fainting spells and after numerous tests they had diagnosed a heart condition which required a triple bypass operation. She was being admitted to hospital in a couple of days. The news saddened me.

Jenny and I went to visit her in hospital the day after the operation to see if she was OK. As we walked down the road towards the hospital we saw our father coming out and instantly we both ducked behind a car. We weren't scared of him any longer, we just didn't want to see or talk to him. We waited until he left and we went in. When Mum saw us she smiled and said, 'You've just missed yer father.' We told her it was deliberate, but it was lost on her. The good news was that she was recovering well, and even though it was only a day since the operation she was being encouraged to get up. We promised we would be back before she was discharged, but when we returned we found that Dad had told the doctors he would nurse her at home and got her released early.

It was only a few days later that Jenny and I were sitting and talking, late at night, when the phone rang. I was nearest, so I answered. All I could hear were Mum's screams for help – 'The cunt's killing me, he wants sex and he keeps hitting me, help me, Jen' – then the line went dead. Jenny had heard every word. She ran up and got John out of bed while I phoned Mum back. Dad answered the phone and I screamed at him, 'What the fuck are you doing to her? Leave her alone.'

'She's OK,' he mumbled, 'we just had a disagreement.'

I screamed at him to put her on the phone, and when he did she was sobbing. I asked if she wanted us to come and get her and she said yes, so John went to get her and brought her back to Jenny's. She was a pathetic mess, tearful, in pain and shaking. She told us that just six days after her surgery Dad had demanded sex. When she said no he had climbed on top of her and punched her in the chest, saying she would get more if she didn't give him what he wanted. We knew she was telling the truth. When we were kids if Dad had demanded something you went along with it or you suffered. But it was unbelievable, even for a vicious bully like Dad, that he would hit his frail wife just six days after major surgery.

We couldn't let her go back to him yet, so after talking to Carrine I agreed to take her home with us. Mum spent two weeks with us and was able to rest and recover. Dad came up to collect her, but I refused to have him in my home so we met him in town. As she walked away, holding on to his arm, I felt so sorry for her. I knew the life she was returning to, and I had told her to ring me if she needed to come back at any time, though even as I said it I knew she would probably never do it.

Work was hectic, and we had a residents' holiday coming up, which I was scheduled to go on. I explained to the manager that my personal circumstances had changed and that I was now a single mum. They were great about it and agreed that if I paid for Carrine and she attended the kids' club at the holiday camp, leaving me to work my shift during the day, she could go on the holiday.

Carrine was delighted and we all set off for

Butlins. The other staff members who went were great, but most of them were very young. I was the senior member of staff and I felt responsible for everyone – residents and staff as well as Carrine.

At the end of each day I would nominate one staff member to work a little later to complete the daily reports with me. One of them, Stuart, was a nineteen-year-old know-it-all with what I considered to be an arrogant attitude. He wasn't my favourite member of staff, so when it was his turn to do the reports with me I hoped to get them done quickly and get off to bed.

When we'd finished our work Stuart asked me quite openly why I didn't like him. I was honest and told him, and we ended up talking for hours. As the night went on I found myself blurting out everything, including my split with Eddie and even my loneliness. Stuart was a sympathetic listener and said that if ever I wanted to get out, or needed company, he would pop round.

I was grateful for the offer and went to bed with a very different view of him. He'd been sweet and supportive, but I was quite certain I would never take him up on his offer.

After the holiday I found myself working more and more shifts with Stuart. At the end of each shift he would leave at the same time as me, and each time he'd say, 'Do you fancy going for a drink tonight?' I always turned him down, but unbeknown to me Stuart had taken all the overtime shifts available on my duties, so that he could work with me. After three weeks of being harassed to go out with him, I eventually said yes, convincing myself it could do no harm. Besides, it would be nice to have some company; we were getting on well and I enjoyed his light-hearted attitude and sense of humour.

Over the next few weeks Stuart became a regular visitor to our house. Carrine adored him and he treated her like a kid sister. One night after watching a video and sending Carrine off to bed we put some music on and sat and talked. That night I began to feel differently about Stuart. He was sweet and good-looking, and I was flattered that he liked me so much. Since the holiday I'd seen him in a very different light. But I was still very raw from the break-up with Eddie and didn't want to get into something that wouldn't last, let alone with a younger man who was my junior at work. So I decided to hide my feelings and simply stay friends with Stuart.

13

Good Times

Jenny

For over ten years Keith had dominated my life, injuring me, abusing me, terrorising me and forcing me to move home and go to court to try to escape him. Now, at last, I was free. Not only had Keith been refused access to Martine, but now we had John to protect us. He had promised me that he would never let Keith touch me or Martine again, and I felt safe in a way that hadn't been possible before.

John was a wonderful man and I loved him almost instantly. He was strong and calm, and nothing seemed to worry or intimidate him. Martine adored him almost from the very beginning too. Of course she was still wary of men, but John had a natural ability with children. He spoke to her with tenderness and love and never excluded her from anything we were doing. He stayed with us more and more often and eventually, after a few months, he moved in with us – but only after we had talked everything over with Martine to make sure she was happy. From then on John always told her of his plans for us as a family, and he was thrilled when one day she called him Dad.

Life had changed beyond recognition, yet at the same time all the years of abuse had left me bruised and, I suppose, damaged in many ways. Despite having John there to protect and love me, my sleep was still full of the nightmares of the past. If Keith didn't haunt my dreams, then my father did.

It was almost as though I felt I didn't deserve the happiness I'd found – I often felt afraid that everything would be taken away from me. John was strong and reassured me frequently, but I would still jump out of my skin if he moved suddenly; and if the phone went or there was an unexpected knock on the door, my face would drain of colour and I would start to tremble.

John did everything to try to help me forget. At night when the dreams became too real, he was there to hold me and comfort me. But there were times when even he couldn't take away the terror. After one particularly bad night, John said we ought to get away for a few days, and I suggested making a trip to Chester to introduce John to Kim for the first time.

I hoped our trip might cheer Kim up. I had been devastated to hear about Eddie leaving. I was always afraid that he would hurt her, but had stayed silent, hoping I was wrong. There was something about him that I had never liked, but Kim was old enough to make her own choices. In the end he wounded her very deeply, and I hated knowing how unhappy she was.

A few days before our trip John proposed to me. I was stunned, and a little afraid too. I loved him dearly, but did I really know what true love was now, and was my love for him deep enough? I knew he loved me completely, and I felt I couldn't let this chance for happiness pass me by, whatever my fears. With John's support I would deal with them.

I didn't say yes until we had talked to Martine. I knew John would love and cherish both of us, but how would she feel about it? John told her he would love to be her dad and Martine was thrilled. I was so happy for her as well as for me. She needed a real father and had found him in John. We set off for Chester in a hired car – the old banger would never have made it. John hadn't passed his test, so I drove while John kept Martine happy playing games.

When Kim came out to greet us she looked at John with a big smile on her face. Over dinner they chatted and I could see he had Kim's approval. Afterwards John went out for a walk, leaving me to catch up with Kim, while Martine and Carrine went off to do girlie things in the bedroom. Kim told me in more detail what had happened with

Eddie. I was so mad at him and felt so protective towards her. She was my younger sister and I'd wanted to protect her since we were little, but at that moment I knew nothing I could say would make her feel any better.

Kim was eager to hear about how I met John and the plans I had. She was stunned when I told her that we were going to get married. I had kept quiet about it as I wanted her to be the first to know, and to tell her in person. She was so excited I thought she would burst.

John was marvellous that weekend as he followed us around the shops in Chester, looking for wedding stuff. It was exciting for all of us. Something lovely was going to happen in the family, and no one was going to burst my bubble of happiness. It was sad to leave Chester, but we had all had a great time and we had lots of plans to make for the wedding and the future.

When John and I arrived home, everything went full steam ahead. John got his divorce finalised.

Then one night the phone went and John answered. He handed the receiver to me and I was shocked to hear Robert Walker on the line. I hadn't seen Robert in a long time, and I told him all about John and our plans to marry. He said he was pleased for me, and hoped I would be happy. He told me he had loved me for a long time, and wished things could have been different. That made me sad. Robert had been in my life for many years and I was going to miss him.

By this time I was working at the Woolwich Building Society in Victoria. All the girls were happy that I'd met someone, and we invited them all to the wedding. It was turning into a bigger wedding by the minute, as the numbers grew, and John and I were worried about the cost – until an extraordinary piece of luck solved everything. Each month the Woolwich had a lottery in which each member of staff had a number. One day I was told that my number had come up – and I had won fifteen hundred pounds.

The wedding had been set for 12 October 1985 at the Methodist Church at Stoke Newington. Just like Kim, I had decided that there was no way that my father would give me away. This was my special day, and although I had to have him there because of my mother, I refused to let him walk me up the aisle.

Once again, Laurence stepped in and agreed to give me away. He liked John enormously and was delighted that, after the years of misery with Keith, I was marrying such a good man. Throughout the Keith years Laurence had done what he could, visiting me and trying to make sure I was OK. There were many occasions when he wanted to step in, but he knew that Keith would take revenge on me for any action that Laurence took, so reluctantly he had remained on the sidelines. In the meantime Laurence had married his girlfriend, Jan, and we were all delighted that they were expecting a baby.

John wanted to stick to his Scottish traditions, so he wore a kilt, as did Laurence and Steve, John's close friend and best man. I had travelled to Chester to spend another weekend with Kim, but this time on my own. I wanted to find my wedding dress, and I was thrilled to find the perfect one in a tiny wedding boutique in Ellesmere Port. It was white and very frilly – in the photographs it looks very dated now, but at the time I loved it.

Kim also had another surprise in store for me after I returned home. She phoned me to see if she could bring someone with her to the wedding. Was it a new man, I asked. I was told to wait and see. That afternoon, Kim appeared with a good-looking, tanned, blond young man who she announced was her friend Stuart. I was gobsmacked and winked at Kim. She looked so happy and I was overjoyed for her. The wedding day was going to be great.

The wedding party was huge. In the end we had four hundred guests and all my family and friends were there. Martine, Isla, Kim and my old flatmate Sylvia were among the seven bridesmaids, and everyone partied until the early hours in a hall in Mare Street, Hackney, which was big enough to house our vast number of guests.

Some weeks before the wedding, I had been shopping with John and had wandered off down the aisles looking for something. Suddenly I felt a hand on my shoulder. I knew instantly that it was Keith and turned to see his usual smirk.

'Getting married to that Scotsman, are ya?' he asked. I told him to go away, but he hadn't finished. 'He won't replace me as Martine's father and don't expect any of my family at the wedding. They're out of bounds to you,' he said. Again I told him to go away and leave me alone. At that point he said something that I will never forgive him for as long as I live. 'What family have you got? Carole hates ya and yer brother was a junkie who's dead and burnt. How's that make you feel? Don't try and take my family.' I was so angry that tears of pure hatred filled my eyes. As always there was nothing he wouldn't do or say to hurt me. At that point John came marching down the aisle and told him to clear off. He took my arm and led me away.

It was to be many years before I saw Keith again, but his callous remarks hurt me so badly that I never forgot them. The truth was that I hadn't heard from Carole in a long time, but she certainly had no reason to hate me. I had heard that she was living with someone and had a daughter, and I hoped she was happy. I invited her to the wedding, but I wasn't surprised when she didn't come.

It was Keith's dig about Chris that really wounded me. But he wasn't going to intimidate me again. I invited his mother, his sister Sandra and her daughter Yasmin to the wedding, and they all came. They had always been good to me and to Martine, and I wasn't going to let him sever my relationship with them. Sandra even offered to have Martine while we went on honeymoon to Torquay, where we stayed with Sylvia and her family and had a wonderful week.

While I had been falling in love with John and planning a future, things had changed for some of my closest friends too. Pam had met another man and had given birth to a baby boy, Ricky, while Sherri, my old schoolfriend and travelling companion, had married a vet and was living in Forrest Gate.

Meanwhile a letter had arrived with an offer concerning our flat, which was rented from a housing association. They would pay us a sum to move out, and it would be enough for a deposit on a home of our own. The thought of owning my own home was unbelievable, but suddenly it had become a real possibility.

In the months after the wedding we settled happily into family life. Martine decided she wanted to become a McCutcheon, but for John to adopt Martine and give her his name, Keith would have to give permission, and we knew he would never do that. However, her school and everyone else, including the family allowance people and even the passport office, agreed to let her be called McCutcheon. To this day Martine has two names in her passport.

I had been thinking long and hard about her education. It was obvious to everyone what she wanted to do, and I was determined that she should have her chance. She had been in every play at primary school and had entered the Metropolitan Police Disco Dance Championships for three years running and won each time. She had dedicated every Saturday for the past eighteen months to working with Zayni on her dancing and singing, and she was now ready to audition for London's two major stage schools, the Arts Educational School and the Italia Conti Academy. Both were supported by the Inner London Education Authority (ILEA), which paid the fees for four scholarship places in each school every year.

Martine was convinced she could win a place, but I wasn't too sure. I knew she had real talent, but also that there would be hundreds of hopefuls trying for those few assisted places. Martine had a tough job on her hands. Looking back, I can only admire her resilience. For her, failure wasn't an option. For the auditions she had to perform ballet, tap and modern dances, followed by a piece of drama and a song, and she worked long into the evenings after school, practising her routines to get them perfect.

The two auditions were held in April 1987, only a few days apart. First was the one at the Arts Educational School, for which we had to travel to west London. I left Martine at the door and went to wander around the shops while she auditioned. I was terrified for her, but she was confident and happy. The Italia Conti school came next. A world-famous stage school, it was in central London, in the Barbican, which was a much easier journey for us. Again I paced the pavements before going into the school's small cafeteria to wait with the other anxious mothers. Martine came out of her audition glowing, and on the journey home she told me how much she loved the school. It was an all-round performing arts school and was definitely her first choice.

A week later the letter arrived from Italia Conti. Martine was in. She had passed all her auditions and was among the top five candidates in every category. However, the ILEA had allocated the four scholarship places and Martine had not been given one. I couldn't understand why, after she had done so well. Martine sobbed with disappointment, but both John and I agreed that, somehow, Martine would have her dream and go to the school. We would just have to find the money for the fees.

wanted and the most important person in my partner's life. Was I striving for the impossible?

Stuart had become a regular visitor to my house. We got on so well, we talked for hours and I found him compassionate, caring and witty. We'd laugh at the same things and liked the same music and pastimes. Football was a priority, even if I was an Arsenal fan and he supported Manchester United. He also loved horse racing and promised he'd take me to the Chester race meeting the following year.

As we became closer he would sometimes stay over, and even share my bed, but there was no sexual contact between us. I insisted we keep things platonic and he never pushed me. I felt comfortable and relaxed with him, and in my heart of hearts I knew I felt more for him than just friendship. But I didn't want to do anything to spoil the closeness we had, so I left things as they were and kept my feelings under wraps.

Jenny's big day was coming round and I was to be maid of honour. Stuart had said that he'd love to come to the wedding with me, and I was glad that I didn't have to go alone. I rang Jenny four days before and asked if I could bring a guest and she agreed. We turned up at her house the day before the wedding and I introduced her to Stuart. Jenny turned to me and winked. She could see I was happy to be in his company. That night Stuart went out with the men and I went with the girls. Later he told me that he was the butt of their jokes for most of the evening, firstly because he was so young, and secondly because he was from 'up North' and had an accent, but he took it well.

He also told me that the stag party had walked into a pub to find Keith sitting there. An argument started, threats were exchanged and John had to be pulled from the pub, but everyone had made a pact that nothing would be said to Jenny about the incident until long after the wedding.

On the day of the wedding we all rushed around helping to get things sorted. There was the usual wedding chaos, but I kept reassuring Jenny, who was getting ready, that everything was fine. Stuart was asked to carry the cake out to the car and as he did he dropped the top tier. Martine screamed, 'I'm telling Mum,' but we hushed her and rescued the cake as best we could, although for the rest of the day it resembled the leaning tower of Pisa. To top it all, the bridesmaids' car broke down on the way to pick us up. In a last-minute bid to ensure we all got there on time I got all the bridesmaids into my car, hoops and all, and drove them to the church myself. I ended up parking about a mile away and all seven of us, in our long dresses, had to run to the church along the busy main road. As we reached the zebra crossing the bride's car drew up to let us cross. We all waved at Jenny, and the look of confusion on her face was a picture.

That day I got my first sign of affection from Stuart. As we stood outside the church posing for group photos he reached out and held my hand, and as I looked at him he squeezed it gently and smiled. I still wasn't prepared to show him my true feelings, but I began to feel that it would be only a matter of time.

Jenny looked blissfully happy. She had waited a long time and I was so glad that she had eventually found a really good man.

A couple of months after Jenny's wedding Graham told me he'd like to take Carrine and Daniel to Switzerland for Christmas, to spend it with his new girlfriend and the friend who lived there. I agreed, and at work I offered to do shifts on Christmas Eve and Christmas Day to keep myself occupied.

One evening Stuart mentioned the Cheltenham races on Boxing Day and I suggested we go. Jenny was away in Scotland that Christmas with John's family, so I rang Laurence and asked if we could come down on Christmas night and stay with him and Jan, so that we would have a shorter journey to the meeting the next day. Everything was arranged.

When we finished our shifts on Christmas Day, Stuart went home to his family to have dinner and exchange gifts, while I went home to an empty house. It wasn't until I was sitting watching the Queen's speech, with my beans on toast on my lap, that it dawned on me I was alone for Christmas.

I suddenly burst into tears and couldn't stop. I thought of all the Christmases I'd lived through as a child, which ended in tears, fights and arguments. Here I was, an adult, and still in tears on Christmas Day. I felt so sorry for myself that the crying went on and on. I cried over being away from my children, the break-up with Eddie and my loneliness. I had bottled up all my feelings for so long that, once I'd started, I cried for everything. When the tears wouldn't come any more I began to feel better and I dried my eyes, washed my face and packed my case to go to London.

I had arranged to pick Stuart up late in the evening so that we could drive through the night. Once we got on the road we began chatting and laughing as usual. But as we were driving along the M54, Stuart turned to me and said, 'I think I love you.' I was so shocked I couldn't concentrate on driving. I pulled on to the hard shoulder, stopped the car and just looked at him. I asked him to repeat what he had said, and when he did he looked straight into my eyes. We just hugged and kissed one another, and I told him I felt the same way.

Laurence had arranged to leave a key outside for us, so that we could slip in quietly. We arrived in the early hours and that night we made love for the first time. We never made it to the race meeting, but neither of us even noticed.

From then on our relationship went from

strength to strength. The only thing that worried me was the seven-year age difference and the fact that I had two children. Stuart told me over and over again that it wasn't a problem to him and that we shouldn't worry about what anyone else thought. And in the end he convinced me.

Jenny

If Martine was to go to her preferred school, I needed to earn extra money, so I decided to go back into recruitment, which would pay more than my current job. John had taken on extra work at the furniture factory where he was already doing day-shifts, doing overtime as well as home work. We had also been offered a mortgage and had started looking for our own home.

We saved every penny we could, but we still couldn't manage the whole of the fees for Martine's school. So I took on a pub job in the evenings to help raise the cash. John wasn't happy about this – he wanted to be able to provide for us and felt bad about me having to do two jobs – but we both knew there was no other way.

We were both very tired. Martine knew how hard we were working and she offered to do a paper round or any job she could to help out, but we insisted she concentrate on school. But although we did our best to tell her not to worry and that everything would be fine, we were worried ourselves, and far from sure that it would.

Every day when the post arrived, there were more rejection letters from charities we had applied to. Then one morning I opened yet another letter, expecting it to be the same as all the others. But this one was from a charity called the Reeves Foundation, who said they might be able to help. I was so excited that I ran to tell John and Martine. It wasn't definite, but if we met all the criteria, the letter said, they would put it to their donations panel for consideration.

We filled in all their questionnaires and forms and sent them back. Weeks passed and we heard nothing. Martine was due to start at Italia Conti in just two weeks' time and although John and I had managed to put enough money away for the first term, we had no idea what we'd do after that. By this time we had found a property to buy in Forrest Gate, near Stratford, and the final paperwork was going through. Any money we had left had to be used for the completion of the purchase.

Martine and I organised everything she would need for her new school and I said nothing to her about the money. But she was bright and she knew that without a scholarship she would have to change to the local secondary school in Stratford. I think all of us crossed every finger and every toe, in the hope that luck would come our way.

One day I was sitting at my desk as usual in the Alfred Marks office in the City. It was a hectic Friday and I was constantly on the phone, organising the temporary staff for a whole list of employers for the following week. Diane Bradbury, my area manager, was helping out and I could hear her asking someone to hold the line. 'Jen, it's the Reeves Foundation for you,' she said. This was the call I had been waiting for. Horribly nervous, I picked up the phone. 'Good news, Mrs McCutcheon,' the voice on the other end said. 'Your daughter is to be given the full four-year scholarship. Keep us updated on her progress and wish her the best of luck!' I put the phone down in a daze. All our hard work had paid off and Martine was to have her dream. I phoned John to tell him the good news.

There was a real party atmosphere at home that night. Martine was so excited, and John and I were the happiest parents in the world. Martine had her new school and we had our new house. Everything was going our way at last. For the first time in years I felt truly happy and content. I had my beautiful girl and my loving husband, and a new home to start our family life in.

A few weeks later we moved to Stratford. The whole move was a nightmare; it rained all day and the removal men were late. I had waited for them while John and some friends had gone ahead with the lighter boxes in a rental van.

When the movers had finally arrived and taken all the furniture, and I was left in the empty flat to make a final inspection, I reflected on my years in Greenwood Road.

As I wandered around the empty rooms, I thought of when we first arrived here. Martine was so young, and I had hoped for good memories in this place, but instead I could only hear my screams and recall the agony and pain I suffered here. I tried to remember the good times too, and thought of Martine's birthday parties and the smell of her cake cooking. I remembered how Pam and I had sat here talking over coffee and how we had made plans to try and escape Hackney, and I smiled.

Then I entered my old bedroom and I remembered the night of terror I had experienced with Keith, and how vivid the memories and the mental scars still were, even after all this time.

I remembered Chris and his familiar knock on the door, and the day the phone rang and my father told me he was dead. As I looked around for the last time, I felt the sobs well up and I began to cry.

So much had happened in this flat. It reminded me of all the nightmares of my father and Keith, those I had loved and lost, and of friends whose lives had changed as much as mine. I wiped the tears from my face and walked out of the front door. All this was behind me now, and I had my new husband and my wonderful daughter. Surely now I could start to live my life in peace and happiness.

Kim

Stuart and I spent so much time together through the early part of the following year that in the end he suggested moving in with me and Carrine and paying rent to help with the mortgage and the bills.

I talked to Carrine and we both agreed it was what we wanted. She was really fond of Stuart, and I had been struggling to cover the costs, so the financial help would be welcome. I was nervous about making such a big commitment after two broken marriages. There were moments when I was afraid things might all go wrong again. But it felt right, I knew I loved Stuart, and I wanted us to be together.

From the start it went well. With two salaries coming in we were able to go on holidays and redecorate the house, and the three of us had a lovely time together.

Meanwhile Graham was making plans to move to Switzerland permanently, to live with his girl-friend. But he didn't feel it was right to take Daniel away from his sister and mother and interrupt his education. I also felt very aware that Graham had given the last nine years to his children and needed the chance to have this new relationship. He had been a good dad and brought the children up well. I was only too pleased that Daniel should come to live with me and Stuart, and Carrine couldn't wait.

Daniel started at the local school in September, for his final year at primary school. At the end of the first term Daniel's teacher phoned and asked me to come in and see her. She explained that Daniel was well behind his peers and she was concerned about his ability to learn. He was ten, yet his abilities were those of a seven-year-old.

I wasn't surprised by what she said. Graham had mentioned in the past that Daniel seemed to be struggling with schoolwork, and Stuart and I had already realised, from things we'd noticed since he'd come to us, that Daniel had difficulty learning.

The teacher told me she was concerned that Daniel wouldn't be able to cope in secondary school and asked me to consider sending him to a special school. At the moment, she explained, he felt like a failure because he was so behind. But in the right environment he would be helped to learn and to catch up and his self-esteem would improve. After discussing it with Graham and with Stuart, I agreed that we should try the local special school from the following term.

Life seemed to be ticking along nicely. Stuart and I were getting on well, and I loved having both my children with me. And it meant a lot to me that Jenny was at last happily married and settled.

When Christmas came around we decided to invite Jenny, John and Martine up to stay with us. Carrine and David were coming to visit, as usual. Space was limited but we squeezed in. Daniel had his own room, Martine shared Carrine's, and we gave ours to Jenny and John and moved to the sofa-bed in the lounge. There was great excitement because Jenny and I had always made Christmas extra special for our children; we did our utmost to ensure they had a lovely time and never had to experience what we had been through as children.

The night before Christmas, after everyone was in bed, Stuart and I dozed off with the tree lights still glowing. Suddenly we were woken by a knock at the door. Stumbling out of bed I saw it was two thirty. I wondered who on earth would call at that time.

I went to the door with Stuart behind me and through the glass panel I could see a figure leaning on the door. I opened it to see Eddie standing there, so drunk that he was holding on to the door to prevent himself from falling. I hadn't seen him for almost a year and a half. I told Stuart I would deal with it.

I asked Eddie what he wanted. He shrugged and said he had never wanted to hurt me and that he truly loved me. I told him he was sixteen months too late with the apology, and I was now happy with Stuart. He seemed to accept what I was saying, but he began talking in riddles and I had no idea what he was talking about. I watched him trying to form a sentence and I thought to myself: I really cried for this man, I suffered so much pain and heartache, and here he is now – on Christmas Eve – telling me that he did really love me. I knew then that I really didn't love Eddie any more. I was over him, and I felt sorry for the woman he had left me for.

I asked how he had got to us, and he said he had driven. I was amazed that he had managed to get into the car, let alone drive it, in the state he was in. He said he shouldn't have come and he was leaving, but I told him to come in and have some coffee. I managed to get him into the house and make him some strong black coffee. Stuart didn't like him being there, but he agreed that we couldn't let him drive in the state he was in. I said I would take him home and went to dress in the bathroom, but when I got back downstairs Eddie had gone, and I could just see his tail-lights weaving their way erratically down the road.

I was told later by a mutual friend that further down the road Eddie had been stopped by the police. He was breath-tested and kept overnight in the cells, and later lost his licence. I thanked God that he caused no harm to anyone else or to himself, especially on such a night. I didn't hear from Eddie again until I bumped into him many years later.

Stuart and I had discussed the possibility of marriage and children. He was young and I knew he would want children of his own, and I liked the idea of having another child. Despite the miscarriage caused by the coil, the doctors had eventually said I should be able to have more children, so I was hopeful.

We weren't officially trying for a baby, but I wasn't using contraception and I knew that if I found I was pregnant we'd both be happy. Then one evening, while watching TV, I began to get cramps. My periods were very erratic and I hadn't had one for a while, so I thought that was what it was. But the pains went on and became more intense. Over the course of an hour they came every ten minutes, then every five and then two. Suddenly I needed to go to the loo. I thought I must have food poisoning. As I sat clutching my tummy I thought, 'God, it feels like contractions.'

Still the penny refused to drop. Half an hour later, still perched on the loo, I decided to run a hot bath and soak, hoping that would ease the pain. As I lowered myself into the bath I felt the urge to push and suddenly I understood. I was having a miscarriage.

I called Stuart. I was sobbing and there was blood everywhere, and at first he couldn't quite work out what had happened. When I explained, he comforted and reassured me in a way no one else ever had.

Once I'd got out of the bath I telephoned our doctor and explained what had happened. She treated it all as if it was a daily occurrence, which it may have been for her, but it certainly wasn't for me. I went to bed, but during the night I awoke to excruciating pains and after pacing around until the next morning I went straight to the family planning clinic.

After numerous tests a consultant explained that while it was not impossible for me to conceive again, my chances were slim. Apparently my Fallopian tubes were damaged. I wondered whether this stemmed from the miscarriage I had suffered with the coil, but they couldn't tell me. It was devastating news, as until now I had hoped against hope that I could still have another child.

There was one last chance and I clung to it. The doctors said they would put me on to the fertility programme, but pointed out that married couples took priority. It was the push we both needed, and Stuart and I set about planning our wedding. As it was Stuart's first time, and I had only been married before in register offices, we set our hearts on a big day.

14

A Special Boy

Kim

Stuart and I were married in a beautiful church on the River Dee, in Chester, on 4 August 1990. It was a grand affair with vintage cars, top hats and floating dresses. It was my first white wedding and I was thrilled. I was wearing a beautiful ivory wedding gown, and I felt like a princess. All our family and friends came, and I had even managed to arrange for Mum to come without Dad. I'd telephoned her and invited her up to stay, and although she was hesitant she agreed to come for the weekend and made an excuse to Dad. I had kept the wedding secret, knowing that if Dad found out he'd never have let Mum come without him. Jenny collected Mum and then bathed her and took her shopping for a new suit, before driving her up to us.

I was leaving from our house and Stuart was leaving from his parents'. Although I always felt that Stuart's parents would have liked him to marry someone his own age, they never excluded me or my children from their family.

Carrine, Martine and Laurence's daughter Danielle were all bridesmaids. Danielle had been born soon after Jenny's wedding in 1985, but sadly Laurence and Jan's marriage had broken up soon after. My close friend, another Jenny, was among the bridesmaids too. She was a single mum with a young daughter, Sarah. We'd met at work and got on brilliantly from the start.

Once we were married, Stuart and I were no longer allowed to work together. While Stuart stayed at the care home, I found a new job as a day care officer in a centre for adults with learning disabilities. My job was in a nearby town, and after a few months Stuart managed to change jobs and move to a more senior role in another residential home, close to the centre where I worked.

I was now employed from nine till five Monday to Friday, while Stuart continued to work shifts. It meant that we had a lot less time together, but we made the most of the time we had, and he was able to swap shifts from time to time which gave us some freedom to plan ahead.

Jenny kept me abreast of all her family's news and we managed to visit one another from time to time. The girls also came to stay with each other – Carrine and Martine got on really well and loved having holidays together. When Martine came to us

I'd know we were in for a hard week – she was incredibly extrovert and she often scared Carrine's friends by belting out songs from various musicals for them. She sang for us too, and on more than one occasion I woke early on a Sunday morning to find Martine sitting at the bottom of our bed. As soon as I opened my eyes she would begin singing, her favourite at that time being a Barbra Streisand number, 'Evergreen'. Stuart would disappear under the covers groaning, 'Shut that kid up,' and I'd usher her out of the bedroom while, in fits of laughter, she'd belt out another song. She sang 'Evergreen' so often that it became a standing joke between her and Stuart: she would start to sing the first few words and he'd throw a cushion at her or run from the room, begging her to stop.

In the meantime I had started fertility treatment. First I was given drugs, but when they didn't work I was referred to a specialist who suggested we try a method known as GIFT. This involved twice daily injections through my ovulating period, while at the same time Stuart had to produce samples at particular times of the day, which were then introduced into my womb. This arduous process was uncomfortable and time-consuming and robbed us both of our dignity. Each month we would go through it again before waiting to see whether it had worked. Each month was another failure, and when my period arrived I would become irritable and short-tempered, snapping at the children for the slightest thing. Then I'd sink into myself, tearful and angry that I hadn't managed to conceive.

No matter what Stuart or anyone else said to console me, I felt that I was being cheated of happiness. I knew Stuart desperately wanted a child of his own, and I was afraid that if I couldn't give him a child, maybe he'd go elsewhere.

Jenny

Life was good and we had all settled well into our new house in Forest Gate. John had been his usual wonderful self, letting me go on a much-needed holiday, a cruise to East Africa with Pam, while he stayed at home decorating and keeping an eye on Martine.

Before the holiday I'd been feeling unwell – nothing specific, just very run down. The break did me good, but once I was back in the routine of work it wasn't long before I felt ill again. My job at the agency was high-pressure and over the next few months I found myself falling ill on a regular basis for no apparent reason. I was tired and lethargic, and it took a huge effort to get out of bed at the start of each day. On top of this, at only thirty years old, my periods suddenly stopped. All the symptoms of menstruating were there, but there was no release for the stomach cramps and I spent weeks in agony. For months this continued, until eventually the doctor referred me to a specialist. It was a relief to know that I would finally have an idea of what was going on – and some help.

I was totally unprepared for the specialist's diagnosis. He told me I should consider myself fortunate that I didn't have to put up with periods on a regular basis, unlike other women who suffered long-term bleeding. Shocked by this callous response, I stood my ground and refused to be pushed aside. I demanded tests and treatment. Something was wrong and I needed to know what it was. Once again I was referred, this time to a fertility clinic.

There was a long waiting list, but eventually my appointment arrived. Fortunately I was seen by the top consultant there, who was sweet and lovely as I poured out my story. He asked me if I wanted more children and I told him of my recent marriage and that I'd like to have the choice. He put me on fertility drugs in the hope of kick-starting my periods. However, weeks and months passed and, despite the drugs and nasal sprays I took daily, nothing happened. Eventually I was admitted to hospital for a routine investigation. Soon after I came round from the anaesthetic the consultant came in to speak to me. He told me, gently, that it was unlikely I would be able to have more children.

There was something wrong with the lining of my womb, and I was advised to try and carry on with my life. After all, I did have one child.

Meanwhile, up in Chester, Kim was experiencing a similar trauma, and she too was on the treadmill of fertility treatment. Kim was suffering from periods that lasted for weeks and she had lost weight, was anaemic and looked ashen.

We spoke often on the phone about our various treatments. Kim had decided not to give in and was undergoing GIFT, whereas I had accepted that fate had destined me to have only one child.

I had been advised by the hospital to finish the course of drugs I had been given, so I continued to take them. John knew I was upset and did his best to support me. Although he would have liked another child, he said he was happy for us to be together with the two girls we had. But for me it was harder. I felt that the choice had been taken away from me too early and I couldn't help but wonder if all I had been through with Martine's father had affected my fertility.

To help me feel better about it all, John took me out for a romantic candle-lit dinner. Later, when we returned home, he put on some soft music and we opened another bottle of wine. It was red Bull's Blood and quite strong. We made love on the living-room floor and as he held me, I thought how sad it was that I couldn't give him a child. I knew he wanted to be a father again, but he loved me enough to accept things as they were.

Since our move to our new house, John had changed jobs. Laurence had always wanted to be his own boss and had finally achieved it with Vala Services, his own industrial cleaning company. John, who had finally passed his driving test at the third go, was now working for Laurence as an area manager, on a better salary, supervising the window cleaning rounds. It was a complete change of career for him.

My work had continued to be busy, and all the hospital treatment hadn't helped my health, as I still felt ill. So I decided to leave and look for something more local. It was a hard decision as I loved my job, but it was good to think I would no longer have to make the long journey into the City each day.

I found a job as a cashier with the local council. The office was nearby, the hours were flexible, and the people I worked with were all nice, so I soon settled in. Martine was doing very well at her new school and had even landed her first few jobs. Because of her dark looks, she was used for many adverts in the Middle East, and when an American company came to the school looking for children for their Cool Aid campaign, Martine was one of the ones chosen. She also had lots of modelling jobs for Habitat, Tammy Girl and various catalogues.

In fact she never stopped working! I was especially proud of her when one day she came home to announce that she had won a part in a children's TV drama. The show was called *Bluebirds* and she was working with Barbara Windsor, Isabelle Lucas and Lance Percival.

Just as filming was to start on Martine's show, she developed a high temperature and a rash. I took her straight to the doctor, who diagnosed shingles. I was upset, especially as this is normally an adult condition. The doctor advised rest, but Martine insisted on going ahead and filming the show. It was only later we realised that pushing herself so hard had weakened Martine's health. In the following months she constantly picked up coughs and colds, but her determination to work through any health problems meant that she hardly missed a day of school.

By early 1991 I was finding it increasingly difficult to get up in the mornings. I felt exhausted all the time and I knew something wasn't right, so I called the fertility clinic and spoke to the senior nurse there. She advised me to come down and see the consultant. I was swollen and uncomfortable and I had started bleeding – I had no idea what was going on. I was sent for a scan immediately, and nearly fell on the floor when they announced I was pregnant.

Neither John nor I could believe it. After six

years together we were finally going to have a baby. We were ecstatic. It was explained to me that I was in for a difficult pregnancy, and would need plenty of rest if I was to carry the baby to full term. However, I was allowed to go on working, as long as I was careful, and with the help of the people at work and flexi-time, I managed to hold on to my job.

I knew money would be tight once I had to give up work, so when Martine's school asked if we could take a pupil as a boarder, we readily agreed. Gemma's family lived too far away for her to travel to school each day, so she stayed with us during the week. She was a little older than Martine, but they seemed to get on fine. It was good for Martine to have someone to travel to school with, and Gemma was no trouble and fitted in well with the family.

Despite a few brief hospital stays, everything seemed all right until late in the pregnancy when I started to bleed again. John took me to the hospital and I was admitted. Luckily Martine had gone on holiday with Laurence and his girlfriend Jo, whom he had met after separating from Jan. She was a lovely girl with two young children, both of whom got on with Martine very well. Gemma was with her parents for the weekend, so John was able to stay with me.

The diagnosis was not good. The baby wasn't moving and they needed to induce me. But two attempts at induction failed – I still wasn't in labour. John had called Kim to say how worried he was; he knew I was terrified that something awful was going to happen. Kim immediately got into the car and came down to help.

The following day, Sunday 9 June, Kim arrived at the hospital. I was attached to all kinds of machines and was in floods of tears and very frightened for my baby. Kim tried to reassure me and then went to see the doctor and demanded action. After yet another examination the doctor explained that the baby was now in distress and they would have to perform an emergency Caesarean.

Kim and John came down to the operating theatre with me. I wasn't conscious during the birth, but I awoke shortly afterwards and a bundle was placed in my arms. My son had been born – six weeks premature, but healthy. He was beautiful, with soft, blond, downy hair and blue eyes. He weighed 5lb 13oz and looked tiny but perfect. I watched as John scooped the baby from me and held him close. He smiled at me with tears in his eyes. 'Let's call him Laurence John – LJ for short.' I was pleased with the name. John and Laurence had become close through working together, and Laurence was delighted that his nephew was named after him.

After a spell in special care, LJ began to thrive.

He was a long, skinny baby, and gorgeous, but I was alarmed when I noticed a small hole in his back. We were all terrified it was something serious and alerted the doctors, but after an X-ray we were relieved to discover that LJ had inherited the family blind dimple! Not all of us have it, but Carrine has, and so do Kim and I. Those who know us intimately have often told us it's very cute!

While LJ was still in special care I was sent home, but my scar was infected and just would not heal, so I had to rest a lot. I was hugely grateful that Kim was able to stay on and help. LJ wasn't feeding well and needed to be fed through a drip, so I would express milk and Kim or John would go up to the special care unit to take it to him.

When the moment came to bring him home, after twelve long days, we were all very happy. Martine was fifteen by then, but she fell in love with her little brother and a deep bond formed between them which remains to this day.

As I sat one afternoon looking at my boy, I gazed at Kim who was fussing over his clothes and generally tidying away. I said quietly to her, 'Give him a cuddle, Kim,' and she picked him up. The tears began to roll down her face. We sat together and hugged each other. Kim was suffering, and although we said very little, I felt her despair.

Kim

For a while Jenny was experiencing fertility problems too, the difference being that she had no periods, while mine wouldn't stop. We were able to compare treatments and chat over the phone about the nightmare of hospital visits and endless waiting. As always, we didn't say a lot about our feelings, but we both knew what it was like to long for a baby and fear that you might never have one, and the silent sympathy was always there, holding us close to one another.

Then Jenny became pregnant. I was so happy for her, and so glad that she and John had this joy to share. But I couldn't help feeling envious too. After all I'd been through, why couldn't I have succeeded as well?

When John rang to say that Jenny's baby was being induced early, I leapt into the car and headed for Essex, knowing how worried she must be. Thankfully all went well in the end, and when Jenny came home I stayed on for a while to help her recover. LJ was the most adorable baby, and I fell in love with him straight away. Holding him for the first time was wonderful – and heartbreaking. It made me realise just how badly I wanted a baby, not only for Stuart but for me as well. I was convinced that it would make our lives complete.

The fertility treatment ground on and took its

toll on both of us. Stuart never complained, but I knew it was getting him down. And I felt a little less hopeful with every month that passed. After several attempts at GIFT had failed, the doctors suggested our last option was to try IVF. We couldn't afford to have it privately, and although we were accepted for NHS treatment, there was a long waiting list.

With our plans to have a family in limbo, we immersed ourselves in our work. We were both doing very well and becoming recognised as experienced people in the field of learning disability. One day I saw an advert for a post as manager of a new project opening in the Wirral. Although I didn't have a wealth of experience in management I decided to apply for the post. I knew it would mean long hours and dedication, but I felt it was what I needed.

The interview was nerve-wracking, but to my delight I got the job. I was to manage one of four new homes for adults with learning disabilities. It was really exciting as we were fortunate enough to be employed before the homes were refurbished, so we were able to bond as a management team and be involved in the design and décor of the houses. I was so happy in my new role and full of enthusiasm that I never noticed the time, and each day I would end up working later than I was scheduled to, simply because I wanted to be a good manager and succeed in my new role.

Despite the strain of longing for a baby, only to have our hopes dashed again every month, Stuart and I remained strong together and I never doubted his love for me. Every month, when disappointment came yet again, I reassured myself that at least we had each other.

To cheer us up and fill the gap in our lives we decided to get a dog, and I went off to the dog rescue home to choose one. Stuart gave me specific instructions not to get a large or small dog but something in between. As I walked along the cages stopping at each one, I found my heart going out to every one of the dogs. The warden came with me, explaining each dog's story. We came to the last cage, in which there was a mass of hair and, peering out of it, two big brown eyes. 'This one was picked up in a motorway tunnel,' the warden said. 'We've just prosecuted the owner for cruelty. The dog is due to be put down tomorrow unless we can find someone to have him.' As the warden spoke, the dog fixed his eyes on me, and when I spoke he tipped his head to one side and wagged his tail. How could I say no?

Twenty-five pounds and ten minutes later I was the proud owner of a bearded collie Irish wolfhound cross. He sat in the back of the car, sticking his head out of the window and loving every minute of the journey. It was almost as if he sensed that he had been given another chance. I'll never forget

Stuart's face when an enormous ball of hair bounded out of the car towards him. We named him Shaggy and he settled down well as the fifth member of our family. The children really loved him and he had a wonderful temperament – soppy, fun and so intelligent. He received Christmas and birthday presents every year and knew instinctively which were his under the tree, despite the fact that they weren't pet toys that would be given away by smell.

Down in London Martine was going from strength to strength with her career, and when she was in a new production we would all go to London to support her. We were incredibly proud of her and got very excited every time she won a part.

Meanwhile Carrine was doing very well at school and decided to stay on for A levels. She had a passion for France and anything French, so we decided she should spend three months with Graham, who was living in a French-speaking area of Switzerland. I knew I'd miss her badly, but it was a wonderful opportunity for her to practise her language skills every day, before settling in to her A level course.

Daniel was doing well at school, but because his school catered for severely disabled children I felt concerned that he wasn't being encouraged to fulfil his potential. I asked whether he could join some lessons in the local comprehensive, but was told that he wouldn't be able to cope. I had to accept this, but it was disappointing. At home Daniel was a happy teenager who never got into any trouble. Our only worry was that he could be lazy and needed a prod to get going, but as teenage problems go we felt this was low on the scale. Our main concern was what he would do with his life and whether he would be able to find a job he could be good at and enjoy.

Jenny

In the months following LJ's birth money became a real problem. It was the recession, with prices and interest rates spiralling, and despite all our efforts things were going from bad to worse. I had hoped to carry on working, but it proved impossible. Pam, who worked as a childminder, had offered to have LJ while I returned to my job, but she had injured her back and she was forced to give up childminding. Without Pam, I was lost. She had adored LJ from day one and I had felt I could leave him with her, knowing he was safe and loved. But I couldn't face leaving him with a stranger, so I had no alternative but to give up work.

With only John's salary coming in, debts were piling up and we were finding it hard to cope. When Gemma had finished school and left us we took in other pupils from the school, which helped, but money was still scarce. I tried to get other work, but nothing fitted in with the family. We knew we were close to losing the house. One evening, as John and I sat discussing what to do, Martine overheard our conversation and came in to offer us what savings she had. I was choked by her generosity. She was so young and yet, when the family was in trouble, she wanted to help.

After *Bluebirds* Martine had continued to work. She had co-starred with Denise Van Outen in *Stop the World, I Want to Get Off* and had also had a juvenile lead in *Bernadette, the People's Musical*. All this work meant hours spent rehearsing, on top of her schoolwork, but she never complained and was willing to give us all she had. She was paid for the jobs she did, though the money was not great, and we saved it for her. She would gladly have handed it over, but we wanted her to have a nest-egg and wouldn't have touched it, even if it had been enough to bail us out.

Nothing short of a miracle would help us, so with heavy hearts we went to the building society to explain our situation. Repossessions were happening every day, and we knew that if we couldn't keep up the mortgage payments it wouldn't be long before we lost our house. We decided to hand the keys over and move out before that happened. The building society manager was sympathetic, but there was little they could do.

Laurence did his best to help, as he always did. He helped us to clear some of the debts and found us a house to rent in Rainham in Essex. It was very small in comparison to the house we'd left, but we were grateful. It also needed some work, but we were happy to do it. The biggest problem was that we were a long way from Martine's school and the local transport wasn't good. It meant getting up very early and a long journey for her, but she cheerfully put up with it.

Soon after we moved, Martine got a Saturday job in Romford, working in Miss Selfridge. When she was paid, she would hand her money to me, insisting that I should have it. She never once moaned or complained. Martine continued to find stage work and we were all delighted when she won her second television part, in ITV's hugely popular police soap, *The Bill*.

Most of Martine's jobs were organised through the school, which sent pupils to auditions whenever they thought a role might be suitable. But Martine also looked for work in the *Stage and Television* newspaper, where there were dozens of ads. And it was through one of these ads that the group Milan was formed. Martine had seen the advertisement from someone looking for a new girl group to promote, and she went along with her two friends Claudia and Dionne. Within weeks they were offered a record deal by Polydor, and Martine was wild with excitement.

With John at work and Martine at school or rehearsing, I found it hard being at home with LJ all day. In an effort to make new friends I started to venture out with him to mother and toddler groups. But I found that most of the mothers already knew one another and I often went home feeling quite lonely. So I was glad when a new mum appeared in the group one day. She was very friendly and explained that it was her first time out in ten days because her daughter had caught rubella, or German measles, and had only just fully recovered.

LJ was thriving and very bright. At eighteen months he had an amazing vocabulary and an uncanny ability to repeat words. His hair had grown into a mass of blond curls and he was a chubby and happy little boy. Everyone loved him, especially Martine, who couldn't wait to get home each day to see him.

He was due to have his first measles, mumps and rubella (MMR) jab. This hadn't existed when Martine was a toddler and she had caught both measles and mumps and recovered well. But this new jab sounded like a good thing, so I thought nothing of it as I took him to the clinic; it was just another routine vaccination.

I remember the day as if it was yesterday. As we waited in the clinic, LJ was his usual chatty self. When we entered the room, the doctor was looking at her notes, and without looking up she asked me to roll up LJ's sleeve. When she did look up at us she remarked on LJ's ability to speak so well. LJ made no move as the injection went in, but as the doctor took the needle out, I saw his little lip drop. 'Hurt, Mummy,' he said, and I cuddled him close.

On the short journey home, LJ fell asleep. When we reached home, I scooped him out of the buggy and I remember thinking he was a little limp. I laid him on the sofa to sleep, but I noticed that he was restless, even in his sleep. After a cup of coffee, I went to check on him and realised immediately that he had a temperature. I tried to rouse him from his fretful sleep, but couldn't. I shook him gently, calling his name, but as he opened his eyes there was nothing but the whites of his eyes and he began to choke.

I realised that he was fitting because of his high fever, and I knew I had to bring his temperature down. I rushed him upstairs, ran some lukewarm water in the bath and began to bathe him. As I dried him and rocked him in my arms, I phoned John, frantic that LJ was going to die.

It took John just thirty minutes to get home. I felt so relieved when he came in. He took charge immediately, and as LJ went into another fit, he shouted at me to call for the doctor. An hour passed, and still no one came. LJ had fitted twice more. John then passed LJ to me and said that we were going to go to the hospital. With our baby stripped to the waist and wrapped in wet towels, we made our way to casualty.

A nurse came straight over and took LJ from my arms, and I broke down and sobbed. John and I followed the nurse through to the cubicle, where a doctor arrived almost immediately. Eventually the fits were stopped and LJ was transferred to the children's ward, where blood tests revealed that he had the rubella virus, and the injection had over-loaded his system. I realised that he might well have caught rubella from the little girl we'd met at the mother and toddler group, though we could never know for sure. He hadn't shown any symptoms before I took him for the vaccination, so the disease must still have been developing in his system.

LJ remained in hospital for a further week. I spent most the time there with him and John came after work, but Martine was only able to visit a couple of times and missed him terribly. We were so happy to have him home, and relieved that he was better. But it was immediately apparent that LJ had changed. Gone was the bright, happy little boy we knew. The new LJ couldn't speak and took little interest in anything going on around him.

I had realised in hospital that he wasn't the same, but had hoped that once he got home he would revert to his chatty, inquisitive ways. But it was clear that LJ now had a multitude of problems. As well as his lack of speech, he found it hard to feed himself or to grab things. His walking was unsteady, and he cried continuously. He was clumsy and bumped into everything, and his fits continued, day and night. John and I had to take turns to watch him, never knowing when a fit would occur, and we were exhausted. We needed a diagnosis – and help.

We went everywhere with our son to try to find out what had happened, seeing one specialist after another. But no one was able to give us any answers. It was heartbreaking, as month after month passed and LJ didn't speak a word or manage even simple tasks for himself. We knew that the vaccination had caused his problems, but no one in the medical establishment was ever going to admit that.

Our finances became more stable and we hoped soon to be able to buy another house. We chose to move to Brentwood in Essex – renting for the time being – because we found a nursery in the area that offered places to children with special needs. There wasn't a place for LJ yet, but we hoped he would be able to go there in time.

Meanwhile we had been referred to a speech therapist. After she had worked with LJ for some months she called me aside to talk to me about his progress. She started off by apologising, and I knew then that it would be bad news. She explained that

LJ was simply not responding and she believed he would never speak. Devastated, I made my way home to tell John.

I'll never forget John's face as I told him the news. Tears filled his eyes and he turned away from me. 'My son *will* speak, and I'll hear no more from these so-called specialists,' he said. As I sat and cried I remembered the last words LJ had spoken to me: 'Hurt, Mummy.' Would those really be the last words I would ever hear from him?

Over the next few months John and I did everything we could to encourage LJ to talk. The nursery hadn't been able to offer him a place, so he was still at home with me all day, and much as I loved him, it was painful to see how little progress he made. His walking was still unsteady, he was always bumping into things and had little co-ordination.

Martine, meanwhile, had left school and was concentrating full-time on the group. Milan were now on tour around the country, supporting the highly successful band East 17 and trying to make a name for themselves. Martine came home whenever she could, usually exhausted, but however tired she was she always had time for LJ and would cuddle him and play with him.

Despite all our efforts John and I couldn't get LJ into the special nursery we had hoped for. I had tried other local nurseries, but LJ wouldn't settle, and we knew we had to find an alternative for him.

A Special Boy

He needed to be with other children and we had heard of yet another special needs nursery in Harold Hill, Essex. So, after talking it through for some weeks, we decided to move again in the summer of 1995.

After renting for some time we were keen to buy a house. We didn't have much money to spend, but Laurence helped us to buy a run-down three-bedroom house in Barnsley Road, in Harold Hill. It needed complete renovation, which meant several weeks with no toilet or bathroom. But we managed, and what was more important, LJ had been accepted at the Meads Nursery for children with special needs.

LJ loved our new house, and in the summer before he started at the nursery, he befriended a little boy called Jamie, who lived across the road. That summer proved to be the turning-point for LJ, who had just turned five. One morning, as I was getting him dressed, he looked at me with his cornflower-blue eyes and his lips started to move. With an obvious struggle the sounds came. 'Try, Mummy, me try.' I tried not to let him see my excitement. 'Again, LJ,' I prompted, and he smiled and repeated 'Mummy'. I hugged him and then ran to phone John. When Martine came home I told her and I can still see the smile on her face. She had never doubted that LJ would talk again.

After that LJ went from strength to strength. He

still had many obstacles to overcome, but he had spoken, and with the support of his family and the nursery I knew he would improve.

After the tour Martine decided to leave the group. Things hadn't taken off for Milan in the way they'd hoped, so she decided to find a new agent and look for more acting work. In the meantime, at the age of nineteen, she had met a man. Gareth was a lovely guy and it was obvious to all of us, as soon as she brought him home, that they were in love.

Martine found an agent she liked and started auditioning again, but for a time nothing materialised, so while she waited for her career to take off she set out to find other work. Selling knickers wasn't exactly what she'd had in mind as a career, but she needed work, and when Knickerbox in Lakeside offered her a job she took it.

Around the same time she had been to the BBC to audition for a small part in the TV soap, *East-Enders*. Martine was convinced that if she should get a part in such a popular show, it could really help her career. The other girls at Knickerbox scoffed and teased her about it, but they didn't know Martine. A few days after her audition she was called back to see the producers again.

She gave it her best shot. A few days later she came down with a heavy cold and went to see the doctor. Whilst she was out, her agent called. Martine had won the part of Tiffany Raymond in the show. He asked me to get her to call him as soon as possible.

I was so excited I was almost bursting. As I looked out of the window, I could see Martine making her way back. She looked despondent and cold, huddled against the wind, and my heart went out to her. As she came through the front door, I casually told her to call her agent. She looked at me and narrowed her eyes. 'Do you know something I don't?' she asked. Trying not to grin, I told her to pick up the phone. As she replaced the receiver, she looked at me in astonishment. 'Oh my God, Mum,' she said, and we hugged each other.

A few weeks later she began work, which meant travelling to Elstree, in Hertfordshire, where the show was filmed. She got on really well with the rest of the cast and loved her part. Initially Martine was signed up for only a handful of episodes. We couldn't wait to see her first appearance and crowded round the television to watch her. As we spotted her in a party scene, where she was introduced as Tiffany Raymond, Bianca's friend, we all cheered and LJ ran to the TV and shouted, 'It's Martsie, Mummy!' Afterwards we opened a bottle of champagne and toasted our lovely girl!

Martine was an instant hit and the fan mail started to pour in shortly afterwards. By the end of that year her face had begun appearing on magazine covers and she was in constant demand. We had known that *EastEnders* would be good for her career, but we had no idea what a huge difference it would make. At just nineteen her dreams had come true and she was a star. She was also very happy with Gareth, who gave her steady and loving support.

LJ had settled into his nursery and his speech was steadily improving. We were delighted with the progress he was making. Then we were told that he had improved so much that he would be able to join a mainstream school, with some extra help. However I felt strongly that he wasn't ready. After a number of meetings and some persuasion on my part, it was agreed that for the time being LJ would stay in a special needs class for older children.

Christmas was coming and we decided to make it really special. Carrine and Daniel were in Switzerland, so we invited Kim and Stuart to spend it with us, and Laurence agreed to come too. He'd been having a difficult time, as he'd argued with his long-term girlfriend, Jo, and Danielle was with her mother in Wales. We were all keen to enjoy a traditional family Christmas together.

in bed, I sat alone on the sofa, deep in thought about the old days. As always at this time of year, I couldn't help but remember the horrific Christmases we suffered as kids. Martine came in and found me there, and she snuggled up next to me and asked if I was all right. I had tears in my eyes and I could see her concern, but I told her I was crying because I was happy. She hugged me and said nothing more, but she knew that I was lying.

It was a special moment, that Christmas hug with my girl. I knew that she would soon be leaving home. She had to make her own way in life, and I was proud that she was so capable and independent. But I was going to miss her so much.

She was also perceptive. Martine had rightly guessed that I was troubled by something more than Christmas memories. Things were not right between me and John, we'd hit a very rocky patch and I didn't know whether our marriage would survive. For several months John had been under pressure at work. Laurence was thinking of selling the company, and John was worried about whether he would still have a job. We also worked very different hours. John would be in bed by nine and up for three thirty in the morning to get to work, while I went to bed late, so we had become like ships that passed in the night, rarely seeing each other and hardly speaking. I also felt that John now assumed I would always be there – Jenny the wife,

John's daughter Isla, with her boyfriend Chris. We had a real party, and as the festivities drew to a close, I made my excuses and went to bed, exhausted but content. Lying in bed I could hear everyone downstairs, still laughing and joking, and despite the happiness of the day I started to cry softly, and then sob. I had a great husband and a wonderful family, but still there was an emptiness inside me that I was afraid would always be there.

After our big Christmas, we decided to spend New Year's Eve quietly at home. Kim and Stuart had already made their way back to Chester, and Martine was out with Gareth and their friends, so John and I put LJ to bed and then saw in the new year in front of the television. There were lots of 'Happy New Year' calls from family and friends, before we made our way to bed. As John kissed me goodnight, I thought of the year ahead. I was going to be forty, and I wondered where the time had gone and what I had done with my life. The prospect of hitting this milestone should have been joyful, but it filled me with despair. Although on the surface my life looked good, I felt I had spent so much of it in the shadows, too scared to try and be different or do anything different. And suddenly I was afraid it was too late. Forty seemed so old. my daughter was already grown-up. Was I destined to lead a flat and uninteresting life for ever, working so hard and looking after the family but never doing anything for me? I felt selfish thinking these thoughts, but I couldn't help it. I wanted to believe there was something more – but what?

Over the next few days I began to feel really depressed. I did my best to hide it and carry on as normal, until a call from Kim knocked me sideways. Through heart-rending sobs, she told me Stuart was leaving her for another woman. The affair had started before Christmas and she felt heartbroken. I told her to come down to us immediately.

When Kim arrived, she looked exhausted, her eyes red and swollen from crying. Over a cup of tea, she told me what had happened. As she talked I remembered Boxing Day, when John had told me he'd seen Stuart in the phone box. Suddenly it made sense. He must have been calling his mistress. Horrified, I could only hope that, with our love and support, Kim would come through this latest betrayal.

Kim

Jenny and John went out of their way to make sure everyone had a good time at Christmas, and we did. Like us, Stuart felt Christmas was a family time and he was a little upset about not being with his own family on Christmas Day. But he made an effort and joined in and I didn't notice anything out of the ordinary.

We drove home a day or two after Christmas, keen to see Carrine and Daniel, who were due back from Switzerland. We met them at the airport and headed home to give them their presents and hear all about their holiday.

We had agreed to see in the new year with Stuart's family, who lived a few miles from us, and we spent the evening in the local village pub, before gathering round the village green to sing 'Auld Lang Syne'. On the stroke of midnight, as everyone kissed and hugged, I was a little hurt when Stuart turned to greet his family before kissing me. But I dismissed it as a small thing that didn't really matter.

After the holidays we both went back to work. It was tough getting back into working shifts, and I was looking forward to my first day off. We always tried to work the same shifts and have the same rest days, so Stuart was off too. Normally we'd lie in on a day off, so I was surprised when I woke to see Stuart up and dressed and sitting on the side of the bed.

'I'm going to my mum's for a few days,' he said. I was still sleepy and at first I didn't take in what he was saying. But when he went on to say that he needed time to think, the effect was like a cold shower. I knew, instantly, that he was telling me our marriage was over. I began to ask questions, but he would only say that he loved me, but was no longer sure about what he wanted.

He asked me to leave him alone, and I did. For the next three days I didn't contact him. It was a terribly hard time. Too upset to function normally, I took sick leave and stopped eating, drinking or going out. Instead I agonised over why Stuart had gone. Was there someone else? I dreaded another betrayal. Or was it because we couldn't have a child? I simply had no idea.

On the fourth day Stuart telephoned to see how I was. I told him I missed him and that I wanted to see him and he agreed to come round. I was a nervous wreck, like a schoolgirl on a first date, and I had an awful taste in my mouth that wouldn't go away, no matter how many times I cleaned my teeth.

Stuart arrived looking thinner and very troubled. I wanted him to throw his arms around me and tell me it was all a joke, but I knew that wasn't going to happen. He explained that he was going away for the weekend, he didn't know where yet, but he needed time to think things through. I accepted this, believing that we still had a chance, and that with time to think he might come home. I still didn't understand what the problem was. It wasn't as if we had been fighting or falling out – we were still very close.

He wouldn't give me any explanation. He assured me there was no one else, and that he just needed time to think, he said he loved me and that he would sort himself out over the weekend and be back home on Monday. I clung to his every word. I desperately loved him and believed he was being honest with me, though it was hard to make sense of it. But Stuart didn't come home on Monday, and it wasn't long before I found out, from his brother's wife, that Stuart had gone away that weekend with another woman. I knew instantly that it was a girl he worked with. I'd always felt uneasy around her, and now my worst fears had come true.

Stuart never came home again. Our marriage was over and I had lost the man I thought was my soul-mate. But what made the hurt so much worse was his deception. If he'd shown me respect and been honest it would have been a little easier. I wouldn't have had to spend day after day in agony, wondering what was wrong and whether he would return.

After he left, I hoped that Stuart would never feel the pain he had caused me. But, if I'm honest, I couldn't bring myself to wish him happiness.

Jenny

The day after Kim arrived to tell us her marriage was over, Gareth came round with the Christmas video. We decided to watch it anyway, and surprisingly it was to have a more profound effect on me than on Kim. While she braced herself to watch her last Christmas with Stuart, I was transfixed by the image of a fat, comfy woman, carrying assorted trays of food, and going around unnoticed and unanswered. She looked tired and old, and appeared to be a nonentity.

For days I was shocked by this image of myself. I had lost my identity and had really let myself go, and I knew I had to do something about it. Martine knew how I was feeling, and she not only encouraged me to start dieting but even organised a facial for me at the local beauty salon to kick-start the transition to the new me.

Laurence had sold his industrial cleaning business and set up a new company, offering scuba-diving lessons. John was contented, having transferred to the new company as an area manager, and his routine never changed. So when Laurence offered me a part-time job, I decided to take it.

Being back at work gave me a new lease of life. I was in the office, doing all the bookings and administration, and I loved it. The only problem was that John wasn't happy about me being back at work. Although he encouraged me, I think that at heart he would have preferred me to stay at home while he worked. And as soon as I began the job he could see a change in me; I had something to talk about and I took pride in my appearance, something I hadn't done for quite a while.

LJ was doing well in his nursery and we were optimistic. He was still behind the others, but was learning and developing at such a good rate that John and I hoped that in time he might catch up with his age group. We still had no diagnosis of what was wrong with him, so when we eventually got an appointment with the top specialist in our area, we hoped to get some answers. I was optimistic, although LJ was never good in confined spaces and I would have preferred him to be assessed in familiar surroundings.

I told the specialist all that had happened to LJ, right from the very beginning. After nearly two hours of discussions and tests I asked if she could tell me what was wrong with my son.

She stood by the window with her back to me as she told me that LJ was dyslexic and dyspraxic. The dyslexia meant he would struggle with reading and writing, and the dyspraxia caused him problems with co-ordination, making him clumsy and disorientated. He also had speech and language problems and would always need to be in a special needs environment for his education. She paused and said, 'Mrs McCutcheon, I believe your son was MMR damaged, but I'm afraid you will never hear me say that again.' She was telling me that it would never go on the record. She went on to say that I was lucky that LJ hadn't suffered any worse damage.

I felt let down and angry. My son had been damaged by a routine vaccination, but I could never prove it. Well, I was going to do my best at least to prove the specialist's predictions about his potential wrong.

LJ became my world and John's too. We bought toys that we thought would help his progress, we fed him a healthy diet, and we took him on outings to places we thought might stimulate him. Trains were his main obsession and we spent many weekends travelling on different railways.

The nursery had proved a godsend, and the staff there not only helped with his education but treated him with love and kindness – and supported us too. We wished he could stay there for ever, but although he was allowed to stay on for an extra term, the time came when he had to move on to primary school. We had decided that he would go to the local school, rather than a special school, and receive extra tuition to help him cope. We were nervous, but in his grey shorts, white shirt and green jumper he looked very grown-up and handsome on his first day. And our decision proved to be the right one. LJ flourished in a normal school and, with the extra help, did even better than we had dared to hope.

Meanwhile my fortieth birthday was due in March, and Martine wanted me to celebrate in style. She had decided to throw a big party and invited everybody we knew. She'd even managed to track down some old schoolfriends of mine and invited a few of the cast of *EastEnders*.

When the night arrived I was excited and nervous. Martine had arranged for a limousine to take us to the party, and as it waited outside, I applied my last bit of make-up and then stood back to look at myself in the mirror.

'You look great, Mum, I'm so proud of you,' Martine said, hugging me. 'Let's see what Dad makes of the new you.' I had been dieting and exercising for two and a half months, since the New Year, and it had worked. Although I still didn't have the figure I wanted, I looked so much better than I had on the Christmas tape. I was proud of myself and I had treated myself to a new dress that really showed off my hard work. As I walked down the stairs, and into the front room, John was waiting, holding LJ's hand and looking agitated. Without even glancing at me, he said, 'Hurry up, the car's waiting, we haven't got all night.'

Crestfallen, I said nothing, but I saw the shock on Martine's face. She was as hurt and disappointed as I was that John hadn't even noticed how I looked.

The thing was that John was so wrapped up in LJ, he became his life. I felt that to John I was just his wife and the children's mum. I would never be Jenny in my own right with him.

I couldn't help feeling upset, but I decided not to let it ruin the night and I ended up having a really wonderful time. I was given lots of surprises and glowing comments about the way I looked, and as the champagne flowed I felt touched and grateful that I had so many loyal, loving friends. Gareth provided the music for the night, playing all the Seventies classics, and we danced and partied on into the small hours as I caught up with friends I hadn't seen in years.

That party was something I will always remember, not least because my daughter, at only twenty years old, threw it for me. For Martine, things were going from strength to strength. She had achieved so much in such a short space of time, yet she was still the unaffected, loving daughter she had always been. Now an *EastEnders* regular and beginning to be recognised everywhere she went, she was earning enough to buy her own home. She'd even passed her driving test, and I knew she was ready to live independently. I was proud and happy for her, but I knew I'd miss her terribly.

Martine chose a house in Brentwood, Essex, just twenty minutes' drive from where we lived. She moved in soon after my birthday party and although she wasn't far away I felt as if I had lost my right arm. I missed her voice in the mornings and her shoulder to cry on when things went wrong. She was not only my daughter, she'd become my best friend, and despite visiting her often, I found it hard to adjust to life without her.

In fact, life for me was changing in all sorts of ways. I felt restless and I knew I wanted something more, though I wasn't sure what. When Martine bought me a new computer, I decided to start writing. I spent hours pouring out the story of my childhood. Writing was my escape, and although it didn't occur to me that I might ever be published, the memories I put down then were to become my first book, *Behind Closed Doors*, which would be a bestseller eight years later.

As well as my own personal writing, I took on the job of running Martine's newly launched fan club, which meant answering letters from fans and sending out newsletters. All this, on top of my job and looking after LJ, meant that I had very little time to spend with John, and the distance between us was growing.

I had also found a hobby. I decided to learn to scuba-dive, and to my amazement I found it was fabulous fun. It opened up a new world for me; when I was diving I felt I had freedom and a life away from John in which I counted as a person in my own right. To discover that I could be good at something as different and exciting as scuba-diving was the turning-point for me, and there came a time when I knew that I couldn't spend the rest of my life with John and that our marriage was over.

Telling John that I was no longer in love with him, however, was to prove the hardest thing I have ever done in my life. He knew that I was unhappy, but he wasn't prepared for me leaving him. So when I told him that I wanted to go, he was shocked and deeply upset.

Neither of us wanted to be the one to leave our home or LJ, and we had long discussions about what to do. In the end we agreed that LJ would stay with his father at home and I would be the one to leave and to have LJ at weekends. I felt that as the one who was ending the marriage, it was right that I should go. And as I had no home of my own, it was better for LJ to stay with John, which would mean he could stay in the same home and at the same school. John was a wonderful father who was incredibly close to LJ, and I knew he would care for him just as well as I could.

Laurence had offered to put me up. He was living in Hornchurch and he offered me his spare room while I decided what to do. Martine had offered too, but she was young and having fun and I didn't want to cramp her style, so I gratefully accepted Laurence's offer.

I moved out of our family home with nothing more than my clothes and a few personal items. I drove the car to the top of the road, parked, and began to sob uncontrollably. I felt guilt, despair and total isolation. I had given up everything, just as I had before with John Falconer. I'd even left behind the son I idolised. What on earth was I going to do?

As so often before in times of need, I called Kim. She knew how unhappy I had been, and was totally supportive. She knew I loved John, but she also knew that I didn't love him enough. Everyone had said how wonderful Graham was when Kim left him, and now the same was being said about John, so she knew just how I felt. Friends told me what a fabulous husband and father he was, how hard he worked and how he had changed my life after Keith. All of this was true, but it wasn't enough to keep me there. John and I had drifted apart and I could no longer pretend otherwise. I willed myself to want to stay, and even go back, but I couldn't.

Something had died in me and I knew that being married to John would never make me truly happy. John deserved better than to be with someone who didn't want to be there. And my happiness lay somewhere else, but I had no idea where.

Kim

Although initially I was shocked when Jenny rang to say she'd left John, I wasn't surprised. I had known for a while that she wasn't happy. She fought long and hard to keep the marriage together, and in the end it had become too much. She had been doing for years what she thought was best for John, Martine and LJ, and now at last she had to do what was right for herself. As we talked I felt that only now did she truly understand how torn I had felt when I had walked out on Graham and the children. But while I was grateful to have that understanding, I was sorry that it had come at such a price for her.

Meanwhile I was going through struggles of my own. After Stuart had left I felt lost and alone for weeks. I was also worried about Daniel.

Carrine's life was blossoming and I was so glad. She had found a job she loved, as a nursery nurse, and was dating a young man she really liked. Things looked serious between them, and I felt it would only be a matter of time before Carrine wanted to set up home with him. I had first met Howard three weeks before Christmas, when Stuart was still around. He had come round to watch a video and had brought some cherryade which he knocked over on our new blue carpet. I'm sure it was just nerves, but at the time I wasn't very impressed. But he and Carrine grew very close and I soon realised that he was a nice, responsible boy who would look after her.

But Daniel was another matter. He turned eighteen the same day that Jenny had her fortieth and we went down for the party, which was wonderful. But Daniel couldn't expect the glowing future that

lay ahead for Martine and Carrine. He had left
school and had got his first job as a glass fitter in a
local double-glazing firm, but soon lost it because
he was unreliable. No matter how hard I tried to
teach him to get up and out of the house on time, he
couldn't seem to manage it. This was part of his
condition, he couldn't help it, but it made life very
difficult, for him and for everyone around him.

There had never been any kind of formal diagnosis of what was wrong with Daniel, so at first it
was hard for me to understand his lack of drive,
ambition and self-esteem. But over time, as I
worked in the field of mental health care and
saw many different conditions, I began to recognise
that he was displaying some of the traits and
behaviour of mild autism. I found this very hard
to accept, especially because I knew there was
nothing that could be done about it. I was also
reluctant to give him an excuse for his behaviour, as
I wanted him to try as hard as he could to manage
his life for himself. But the truth was that after he
left school and lost his first job he became depen-
dent on me for everything. It was almost impossible
for him to find a job, and it was difficult to see how
he would manage in the future. I would come home
from work tired, and still feeling very low, and
would then spend the evening cleaning up after
Daniel, feeding him and reminding him to do
everything from having a bath to walking the

dog. He was very hard work and I began to resent him. I even started to blame him for my marriage break-up, which I knew wasn't fair. It hadn't been Daniel's fault at all, but my morale was so low that for a while I couldn't see clearly.

One night I telephoned Graham in floods of tears and asked if Daniel could move to Switzerland for a while to live with him. We talked for ages and he agreed to have Daniel. Perhaps he would have more success in helping him to build a life of his own.

A couple of weeks later I put Daniel on a plane. I loved him dearly and I knew I would miss him, but I also needed a bit of space to sort out my life. And Daniel was excited at the prospect of living with his dad. I promised to ring often and to see him soon, hugged him tightly and waved him goodbye, hoping I'd done the right thing.

Without Daniel to look after I had more time on my hands, but while I was less exhausted, I was as miserable as ever. I heard rumours that Stuart was happy in his new relationship, and the more I heard the worse I felt. I had to do something to escape the heartbreak, so I made the decision to move back to London. Carrine was very settled with her job and her boyfriend and wanted to stay, so we agreed that she would remain in the house until it was sold and then find a place to rent.

I managed to get a job with a London branch of the same company, which was a great relief. But the move was still quite traumatic for me. I had to leave everything I had known for the past twelve years, but hardest of all, I had to leave my daughter. Carrine and I were so close, I was going to be lost without her.

On the day I left I bundled most of my belongings into the car, along with Shaggy. Jenny had moved on and Laurence, ever the solid presence in our lives at times of need, had offered to put me up. I was determined to make a fresh start. But at 38, with my kids already grown up and three marriages behind me, the prospect was daunting.

As I unpacked my belongings in Laurence's spare room I looked out of the window into the dark night. I stared at the stars and thought back to my childhood. If I had known then what I know now, I thought, would I have done anything differently? In the end, despite all the heartache, I knew I probably wouldn't. I had two lovely children and a wealth of experience behind me, and I assured myself that I was a good person and everything would be all right. But I wondered whether I would ever find that special someone I longed for. Perhaps it was too late.

The nearest I'd come was Shaggy. As silly as it seems, I felt he knew my ups and downs better than anyone. When I was sad he would rest his head on my knee and gaze up, as if to say, 'It'll be all right, Mum.' At the end of a long day I'd come home and there he would be, excited to see me and so full of beans that I had no time to wallow. Off we'd go for a long walk, which always made us both feel a lot better.

Jenny

I had thought long and hard about what I would do next. One possibility for me, having worked in so many pubs as a barmaid, was running my own pub. I loved the idea and put it to my old friend Pam that we should take on the project together. She leaped at the chance.

Not long after I had come to stay at Laurence's a pub came up for rent. I got the licence and I moved into the upstairs rooms, whilst Pam stayed at her house and came in on a daily basis. We really wanted to make a success of it and we did. I had LJ during the day and every weekend, and worked my shifts in the pub at night. With Pam covering the pub during the day, it worked well.

A few months after I had left, John told me he had met someone else and I was glad for him. He was a good man and I hoped he'd found someone who would love him and bring him the happiness he deserved. Not long after we took over the pub, Pam also met someone new. She wanted to grab this chance of a new relationship, and she told me she felt the pub would now be too much for her. I understood, but I was terribly disappointed. What had started out as a joint venture with high hopes, was now firmly on my shoulders alone.

Unsure about what to do in the long term, I carried on running the pub, doing as many shifts as I could manage and taking on a barmaid to help out.

I was so preoccupied with running the pub and fitting everything else into my life that it took me a while to notice the young man who often waited behind at closing time to help me clear up. His name was Alan Tomlin and he was one of the regulars. After clearing up we often ended up sitting and talking over a last drink – though Alan wasn't a drinker and stuck to orange juice.

He was young and handsome, with dark hair and a warm smile. But although I liked him very much, I didn't go any further than that. Elaine, the barmaid, would often say, 'I think Alan really likes you,' but I dismissed it. He was too young and couldn't really be interested in me.

By the early summer of 1997 so much had changed. I was running the pub, Kim had moved to London and Martine was on her own too – things hadn't worked out for her and Gareth, and she'd been through a few painful months. All three of the couples who had been in our Christmas video were no longer together.

Martine was due to turn twenty-one in May and

she'd organised a huge party at a venue near Tower Hill in London. It gave her something to look forward to after her break-up with Gareth, and I was looking forward to it too.

There were dozens of people there and we all had a wonderful time. Alan had been invited with a few of his friends, as Martine had met him on lots of occasions when she had visited me at the pub, and although I didn't speak to him except to say hello, I was aware that he was watching me. I was a little confused by this; he was young and had plenty of girls hanging around him. What could he possibly see in me?

But after that evening he continued to come to the pub most nights, and a few weeks later Alan proved what a friend he had become to me and to Martine when she became ill. She needed to be looked after, so I asked her to come and stay at the pub, and I was relieved when she agreed. As soon as she arrived I took her to a doctor. I was worried – I had never seen her so unwell. Alan offered to drive us so that I could look after her on the journey.

The doctor diagnosed glandular fever and ordered complete rest for several weeks. Martine couldn't lift her head off the pillow and needed to be helped in every way. Her body was swollen and sore and I was fearful for her. She would often sob; she felt she was letting everyone down at work, and she was devastated by being unable to do simple things like making her own breakfast.

It went on for weeks, and at one point I was afraid she would never recover. I took her to see several specialists, but there was little they could do, other than to advise rest. Throughout this time Alan was a real friend to us. He helped me take Martine to see the doctors, even carrying her to and from the car when she was too weak to walk. I was grateful for his help and aware that he and I were growing closer, but I still thought of him as no more than a good friend.

Gradually Martine improved, spending a little more time out of bed each day. The worst was over, but there was a nightmare of a different kind to come. When Martine appeared in public again, pictures of her were published alongside stories saying she had gained weight and was eating too much. When she saw this she broke down and cried. She had hardly eaten at all, and the truth was that the illness had left her bloated and feeling as if her skin had been stretched to the limit.

I was furious about these unkind and pointless stories, but all I could do was to cuddle her and reassure her that she would soon recover completely. And she did.

As soon as she was well enough she went back to work. The writing team at *EastEnders* had found a way to write her out of the show during her illness, and now they re-wrote the scripts to bring her back in.

Then something happened that lifted all our spirits sky-high. Despite her absence from the screen for a couple of months, Martine was nominated in the Best Actress in a TV Drama category of the National Television Awards for 1997. Knowing that she had been nominated did her a world of good, and in the weeks leading up to the ceremony she seemed almost her old self again, full of life and very happy.

One Saturday, after Martine had moved back home, a beautiful bunch of flowers arrived for me. They were from Alan, with a card asking me out on a date. I was touched and wanted to accept, but I was still very cautious about getting involved. We liked one another a lot, and I missed him when he wasn't around. Almost without my realising it, he'd become part of my life. But there were real drawbacks. Alan was recently separated, with two young children. And I was ten years older than he was. I knew people would talk and I wondered if we'd be up to dealing with the gossip and criticism. But in the end I knew I couldn't let that stop me, and I agreed to go out with him.

We had a wonderful evening – it felt so right, and I was happier than I'd been in a long time. We began seeing a lot of each other, and the closer we became the less the age gap mattered. Martine was thrilled for us; she liked Alan a lot and knew he would be good for me. Kim was happy for me too, and so was Elaine. But almost everyone else said the relationship was doomed, almost before it had started, and some people were really nasty. There was one person who would ring in the middle of the night and tell me I was a cradle-snatcher, among other insults. We never knew who it was, and I couldn't understand why they would do it. All we could think of was that some young girl wanted Alan for herself and was jealous. We refused to let it matter to us, though, because we were in love, and being together felt completely right.

With the night of the National TV Awards approaching, I was thrilled that Martine had invited me and treated myself to a new ball gown. It was the first opportunity I'd had to buy something new and glamorous in a long time. For Martine's outfit she and I had gone shopping together, and after looking all over the place we finally found it. A black dress with a gorgeous tight velvet bodice and a flowing skirt with tons of taffeta netting underneath, and a taffeta shawl to finish it off. With diamonds in her ears, she looked every inch the star.

On the night I was still worried about Martine. I knew that the illness could kick in again at any time if she overdid things, and although she said she was fine, I was concerned that she might get too tired.

So I was relieved when Martine's escort, a lovely man called Paul Fitzgerald, who'd been a friend for many years, reassured me that he would look after her.

As we sat in the packed auditorium, Martine rested her hand on mine. 'I'm not going to win, Mum, the other actresses are so talented, but I'm honoured to be nominated,' she said. I gave her a smile. Of course I wanted her to win, but it was just like her to be generous to the others. It was a wonderful evening, full of glamour and glitz. Everywhere I looked there were TV stars, and it was amazing to think that my little girl was now one of them. When it came to her category, Best Actress in a TV Drama, I could see that Martine was right: the competition was highly talented, and it was a tough contest. Then the compère opened the envelope, and we all held our breath.

'And the winner is . . . Martine McCutcheon.' The applause was deafening and there were screams of delight from Martine's friends and fellow cast members. Martine glided to the stage as if she was walking on air. Despite her excitement and surprise, she managed a speech in which she left no one out. Right at the end, she looked straight at the camera and said, 'This is for my mum.' That was it. As a storm of applause swept the theatre and Martine made her way back to me, I cried.

16

Love, actually

Jenny

Martine and I had always known that Keith would re-surface at some point, once she became a well-known face. It was almost inevitable that he would want to claim a connection with her. So it didn't come as a surprise when we saw that he'd sold a story to a national paper, claiming that he loved Martine and wanted to be reunited with her. Martine had absolutely no interest in having contact with Keith, so she ignored the story and we didn't hear from him again.

By this time Martine was getting stronger each day, although there were times when she became extremely tired and I still worried about her. She was back on the set of *EastEnders* full-time and had been asked to sing on the annual Children in Need fund-raising TV marathon. She was delighted, and she chose a difficult song, 'Don't Rain on My Parade', which had originally been performed by Barbra Streisand, one of Martine's idols.

When the night came, Martine surprised everyone. Her voice was simply stunning – powerful and moving – and she sang the song brilliantly. Record companies began to chase her and she was asked to perform at the Royal Albert Hall with the Royal Philharmonic Orchestra in a one-off concert to help celebrate the Oscars. Darren Day co-hosted the event with Martine and it was a lovely night which was covered by *OK* magazine. I went with Alan, and Laurence brought his daughter Danielle and her mum Jan as a treat.

With both my children doing well, I decided it was time to make decisions about my own life. Running the pub was very hard work and I'd had enough of the long hours and heavy responsibility. But where would I go and what would I do? My relationship with Alan was wonderful, but was it strong enough for us to plan a future together?

Martine told me to follow my heart and I'm glad I did. Alan and I decided to make a new life together. I gave up the pub and first of all we bought a house in Harold Hill, to be near LJ, but when that proved a bit too expensive, a small flat in Hornchurch.

The next few months weren't easy. The flat wasn't ideal, as it was too small, and we were struggling to pay the mortgage. Alan had been made redundant, after nine years at the same firm, and could only find temporary work with the local council as a dustman. He liked the job, but we never knew how long it would last. Martine protested when we refused offers of help from her, but we wanted to stand on our own feet and be responsible for ourselves.

It wasn't just financial problems that dogged us. Two years earlier I had been diagnosed as a diabetic, and for the last few months I had become really unwell. For days on end I would lie in bed, unable to do the simplest of things and feeling upset and frustrated at being sick. I often had to let Alan, Martine and LJ down because I felt too unwell to do anything or go anywhere.

If I'm totally honest, I had never accepted that I was ill. I therefore hadn't followed the medical advice to watch my diet or taken the medication I'd been prescribed. Horrified at the idea of a lifelong health condition, I'd simply ignored it and hoped it would go away. Now I was paying the price: slowly going downhill, lying in bed wallowing in self-pity, unable to come to terms with my illness and unable to be there when my children needed me.

It was Martine who decided that enough was enough. She booked me an appointment with a specialist in Harley Street, and I can still remember getting out of the taxi and trying to find the number on the door. I felt so unwell I could hardly see where I was going. To make matters worse, I was on my own. Alan had followed Martine's advice and started security work. Having done all the necessary courses and qualified, he had now landed a temporary job in Amsterdam.

I made it into the doctor's consulting room, where I was given a thorough examination and various tests. My sugar levels were through the roof, and the medication I was taking was no longer working. The doctor explained that I had no alternative now but to take insulin, which had to be injected. He taught me how to inject myself, and as I sat there watching I thought how stupid I had been to allow it to come to this.

Back outside, feeling better after just one injection, but shocked by the prospect of injecting myself daily, I called Martine at the studio. She sent her driver to collect me, and he took me to her house. She arrived soon after, and I sobbed when I saw her. A year of exhaustion, worry and illness just caught up with me, and the floodgates opened. That night we went out and had dinner and I spent the night at Martine's home. As she tucked me into bed and kissed me goodnight, I finally realised how worried she had been, and I vowed to take better care of myself from then on.

Recovering fully and getting into a proper routine took time. I loved to drink and smoke and eat my favourite foods, and it wasn't easy learning to do all these things in moderation. But I knew I never wanted to be that sick again, so it was worth the effort.

Alan was relieved that we had found the cure, and when he returned home from working abroad, he watched and monitored me closely, ensuring that I didn't stray too far or fall ill again. He still watches now, and knows my sugar levels better than I do.

That first year after we got together had brought us so many hardships, and yet we'd made it through. I knew then that Alan and I were meant to be together.

Kim

A couple of weeks after moving in with Laurence and Pat I started my new job, but being on my own I found that after work I had a lot of time on my hands. So when Laurence gave me a diving course for my birthday I decided to try it.

I got on really well with one of the instructors there, and she told me there was a room I could rent in her father's house. They were also happy to accept Shaggy as one of the family, which was wonderful. I moved in soon afterwards and my friend and I got on really well, going out together nearly every night and scuba-diving at weekends. The only downside was the long journey to work every day: I had to travel from Southend to Tooting.

Working in London was very different from Chester. The staff's attitude seemed much more casual; they would ring in sick at the drop of a hat and didn't appear to have the same commitment to the residents that I was used to. They also bickered amongst themselves a lot. I soon began to feel that the staff were more demanding than the residents, so I decided to look for another job, closer to where I was living.

The highlight of my week was the scuba-diving. From my first dive I loved it, and it turned out to be my saving grace in dark times after my break-up with Stuart. Through diving I made good friends and we went on some wonderful holidays together to dive in other parts of the world. I even achieved the PADI (Professional Association of Diving Instructors) dive master qualification, which meant that I could become an instructor with just one more course.

While I was still on my own and cautious about starting another relationship, Jenny had met Alan and I was so pleased for her. After her health scare it was great to see her happy and on the road to recovery. The first time I met Alan I knew they were made for each other. He was a typical London lad, but with a heart of gold, and I could see he adored Jenny – his gaze never left her and nothing was ever too much trouble for him. The age gap between them made me stop and think, simply because it was similar to the gap between Stuart and me. But I knew Alan already had children, so the likelihood was that it wouldn't be such an issue for them.

While I was still wondering what the future held for me, I was glad that both the children were doing well. Carrine and Howard had got engaged, and Daniel had settled in with Graham and his wife and even found a job and a girlfriend. Then, less than a year after moving to Switzerland, Daniel phoned to say his girlfriend was pregnant. Although he was pleased, I wondered whether he would be able to cope with the responsibility. In my heart I knew the answer. Daniel's son Michael was born a few months later, in 1998, and Daniel was enormously proud, but despite support and encouragement from Graham his relationship with Michael's mum didn't last.

Thankfully Graham made sure that he and Daniel kept in touch with Michael and his mum, and I was able to meet my grandson on a visit to Switzerland when he was two months old. He was the image of Daniel when he was born, and I too could now see the resemblance to Chief Sitting Bull that Jenny had spotted all those years ago. Although Daniel wasn't able to be a real father to Michael, Graham became a devoted grandfather, having Michael over for regular weekends and taking him on holiday. Michael grew into a beautiful, bright little boy, and I still go to visit him and Daniel whenever I can.

I had thought that I would never find happiness again. But through my diving I met and began a relationship with someone I truly felt was a decent, honest person. Gary was extremely popular with my family and very witty, intelligent and caring. After surviving a kidney transplant operation, he believed in living life to the full and trying to achieve as much as he could in his life. We became close and his enthusiasm for life was lovely to be around. We got on so well that over the next three months I gradually moved in with him. I had got myself a new job closer to home and felt that things couldn't be better. Everything had fallen into place: Jenny and I were both happy and our children were doing well. Life really had turned the corner for the smelly Pontings!

One day, late in 1999, I heard the most fantastic news. I was packing to go on a diving holiday to Mexico when a letter fell on to my doormat. I didn't recognise the handwriting, but when I opened the letter and looked at the signature it was from my sister, Carole. I hadn't heard from her in almost twenty years, so it was a shock.

Carole's letter said that our father had died in hospital, after suffering a stroke.

It was hard to take in. At last, at long last, the man who had tormented and tortured us through-out our childhood was gone. And despite the fact that he was my father, I felt no sadness at all. In fact, as relief flooded through my body, I punched the air and yelled 'YES!'

I hadn't realised the impact that his death would have on me. It was as if a black cloud had been lifted from over me, yet I hadn't even known until then that it had been there. I felt elated. The only one around to share the news with was Shaggy, and he sensed my joy – his tail was wagging as he bounced around the room with me.

When I'd calmed down I went to phone Jenny.

'What's the best news I could tell you?' I asked her.

'You've won the lottery.'

'No, better than that,' I replied.

'What could be better than that?'

'The old man's dead.'

We both screamed, and before she hung up we made a pact to dance on his grave.

Jenny

Alan and I finally managed to move from the little flat in Hornchurch to a new house in Harlow, where we settled in and made it a real family home. LJ was a regular visitor and he formed a great relationship with Alan, while Alan's son Jonathan, who was a couple of years older than LJ, came over from Northern Ireland to live with us and the two boys became like brothers.

At the end of 1998 Martine decided to move on from *EastEnders* and try other things. We were surprised when the producers decided to kill off her character, as she was so popular. It seemed drastic, and we felt sad when poor Tiffany was run over outside the Queen Vic in a big Christmas Day special. But for Martine, leaving the show opened the door to all kinds of other opportunities.

Her first single, 'Perfect Moment', came out as she left *EastEnders* and went straight to number one, followed by another single, 'I've Got You', which made number three, and a bestselling album. She also won the lead role in a West End production of *My Fair Lady*, which earned her rave reviews and an Olivier award and led to all kinds of other film and TV work. Martine's work kept her happy and very busy – so much so that I agreed to leave my job with Laurence's company to work for her, keeping her fans happy and organising her charity work and engagements.

As for Laurence, for a long time we had been so close, but people grow apart and we'd both changed. I missed him for a long time. I know he has since married and still lives in Essex.

One day I received two phone calls. The first was from Martine, who phoned to say she was off to Barbados again. Alan and I had been there before with her, when she went out for a photo shoot and we'd fallen in love with the place. This time there was no photo shoot – but once again we were invited. Martine was offering to take us there to get married.

Before I had time to take in Martine's amazing offer the phone went again. This time it was Kim, with the news about Dad.

I looked at Alan and jumped up from the sofa. 'The old bastard's dead!' I screamed. Alan looked at me in total disbelief. It was hard for him to understand my excitement – his father had died a few years before and he'd been devastated. I had never told Alan the details of what Dad had put us through, so I had to sit him down and explain why my reaction was so unlike that of most other people. I told him everything.

There was no way Kim or I intended to go to the funeral. I had no interest whatsoever in when he was being buried or what the arrangements were, or even in seeing Mum. I just carried on as usual. And besides, I had a wedding to prepare for.

Martine had got together with my friend Jaine Brent, who later became my manager, and between them they had arranged everything. We flew to Barbados with Martine and her boyfriend at the time, Jonathan. We were originally supposed to get married on the beach, but unfortunately the press found out that Martine was with us, and photographers were everywhere. Martine took over, renting an amazing villa and, with the help of the staff, decorating the garden as well as organising the flowers and food. Then she took me off to have a wedding outfit made by a lovely local lady. Decked out in a cream chiffon trouser suit and with flowers in my hair, I felt every inch the bride. Alan went for his boys' night out with Martine's boyfriend Jonathan, and Martine and I went to an incredible restaurant called The Cliffs, where we had a lovely evening together.

The following day, 12 January 2000, Alan and I took our vows, with Jonathan, Martine and a few other witnesses we had met out there. We also had a photographer friend with us. He had offered to do our wedding album as a gift and we were delighted.

We stayed on in Barbados for seven more days after the wedding, enjoying an idyllic honeymoon. It had all been so lovely, and the press had been kept out. So I was devastated when we came home to see our wedding photos, plus some of Martine sunbathing topless, splashed all over a newspaper and a magazine. Our photographer 'friend' had sold them, behind our backs. It hurt to realise that we'd been let down by someone we'd trusted.

Kim

Jenny was quite clear that she wouldn't be visiting Mum again. But for me it wasn't as straightforward. Gary, who knew nothing of my past, insisted that I should visit her, to the point where I felt guilty that I didn't see her that often. He said that I would regret it if she passed away and I hadn't made an effort.

I lay awake thinking about it all night and eventually my conscience got the better of me. I telephoned her the next day and arranged to go over at the weekend. I had decided to take her out, knowing I wouldn't be able to stand it for long in the flat.

It was pointless mentioning to Jenny that I was going over to Mum's. She had closed the door on that chapter of her life, but for me the journey didn't feel complete until I had attempted to tell Mum why she had missed out on so much of our lives, and on her grandchildren and great-grand-children.

When I arrived she had on a dirty jumper with stains all down the front and an old pair of slacks. I said encouragingly, 'Let's put something nice on and I'll take you out for lunch.' I went to her wardrobe and selected a nice blouse and trousers and she obediently got changed. I realised then that her sight was so bad, after years of abuse and beatings from our father, that she didn't even realise her jumper was stained.

I had brought some photos with me and before we went out I went through them with her. She told me she would love a picture of Auntie and I showed her one I had brought. There were other people in the photo, and when Mum peered at it she exclaimed that it included her and an old boyfriend. I promised I'd get a copy made for her.

I felt a great sense of empathy for this woman sitting next to me. She had lost most of her children's love for the sake of a bullying, violent, evil man and she didn't even realise it.

I drove all over London that day, from Dalston to Highgate and back over to Beckton, just to give her the opportunity to be out of the flat. During the journey she spoke at great length about Laurence, Jenny, Carole and me. But she had re-written history. She had said to Jenny on our previous visit that she only remembered the bad times, but the truth was that Mum only remembered the good – and most of those were invented.

I asked her why she thought we – meaning Laurence, Jenny and I – didn't stay in touch and why we hadn't wanted her and Dad to have anything to do with our children. She went quiet and said, 'I know it's because of yer father, but that doesn't mean you should treat me the same way.' I tried to explain to her that he really had done some terrible damage to all of us, and she had stood by while it went on.

But it was pointless. She couldn't, or wouldn't, understand the depth of our pain and despair as children, or the effects on us as adults. I looked into her aged face and all I could see was the years of neglect, abuse, pain and poverty that she herself had experienced. She was coming to the end of her life and she hadn't really learned anything, she had just existed.

I took her back to her little flat with a promise that I'd take her out again, though I didn't know when. She explained that she might eventually move in with Carole, and I agreed that this would be a good thing for her. She thanked me when I left and gave me a hug and a kiss on the cheek. I put a twenty-pound note into her hand and told her to treat herself, and it pleased me to know that this time she wouldn't have to hand it over to Dad; she really could spend it on whatever she wanted.

In the summer of 2000 Carrine and Howard were married. It was a very proud moment for me, seeing my daughter walk down the aisle on her father's arm, glowing with happiness. She looked absolutely stunning. I liked Howard enormously and I truly believed, and still do, that she had found someone she could be happy with for the rest of her life. Gary was asked to read a poem during the wedding and he felt really honoured and proud.

Unfortunately my relationship with Gary ended a few months later, although we remain close friends and keep in touch regularly. And soon after our relationship ended I had the traumatic task of having Shaggy put to sleep. I lost my closest friend of fifteen years and even now, six years on, his name tag is still on my key ring and I get choked up remembering him and his daft ways.

In 2003 I became a grandmother again, when Carrine gave birth to a son, Lewis, another lovely little boy, weighing a whopping nine pounds twelve ounces. The day he was born I was skiing in France, but I cut short my trip and rushed up to Chester to meet him and to look after Carrine, who was quite ill after the birth. She soon recovered and she and Howard both dote on their gorgeous son.

I had wanted to keep in contact with my mother, but when I called round at her flat a few months after I had last seen her there was no reply. I rang the warden's bell and she explained that Mum often went to Carole's for the weekend. I left her my business card and asked her to get Mum to phone me. When she didn't I telephoned the warden again, and she explained that she thought Mum had actually moved in with Carole. She gave me a number for Carole but when I rang it I got a dead line. No one else had any idea where Carole lived. I tried the information base at work, with no result, and that seemed to be the end of the line. I still have no idea where Mum is and I still have the copy of the photograph she wanted so badly, framed and wrapped in Christmas paper, ready to give to her.

Friends who have read Jenny's first book, *Behind Closed Doors*, have asked why I wanted to keep in touch with Mum, but I don't have a simple answer. I suppose I felt that, in the end, her loss was greater than ours. Jenny and I have travelled a tough journey, but along the way we've grown stronger and wiser. We've shared laughter and dreams, hopes and heartaches and we've made good lives for ourselves. We have loving relationships with our children, good friends and so much to look forward to. And we've had each other. So perhaps, after all, we're the lucky ones.

Jenny

In 2004 Alan and I took the decision to move to France. We bought a run-down farmhouse in a rural area of the Dordogne, dreaming of doing it up and making ourselves a lovely home. It was a big step, especially for a real East End couple like us, who were townies and loved London and England. I was excited at the thought of starting somewhere new again and looked forward to the move with slight trepidation and much joy as well. It brought up a mixture of emotions for both of us, as we were leaving all that was familiar as well as our children and families.

We arrived in France on 14 February 2005 to a snow blizzard, no water or heating, and no furniture, as the removals van was delayed by the bad weather. Jonathan and LJ were with us, and we all huddled together to keep warm on the first night, but what I think about most is the laughter. It got us through some tough times.

Kim joined us in May and we all crammed into a little one-bedroom house, but we made it work. Gradually, as the months have passed, we have done things we never thought we would do. We go to French lessons with our ever patient teacher Virgine; I cook all my own food, as well as grow some of it; I walk for miles, and I can drive a tractor!

I still can't give up old Blighty completely, though, and come over on a regular basis to catch up with friends and of course Martine and LJ, who still lives with his dad. They visit me often in France, and by Christmas 2005 we actually had bedrooms for them, built in the old barn attached to the farmhouse. We spent our first Christmas all together in France and it was wonderful.

If ever you feel your life is not going to change for the better, then trust me, it can. A few years back I would never have believed that I would be living a whole new life, in a beautiful place, with the man I love, and doing so many things for the first time. But here I am. I look back and I feel humble, but also strong, for I was able to change my life and truly live it!

Final Word

Jenny

Life is a series of roller-coaster rides. We never know where we'll get off or what will happen to our hearts. But no matter what bumps and bruises we encounter on the way, we carry on with life in the best way we can.

I don't think anyone can write an autobiography without being honest and without trying to give some kind of message of hope, love or lessons learned in life. I have tried, through my story, to give hope to all those who have been victims, and to let them see that there is life after abuse.

It's odd how a word, a smell or a song can trigger off memories that have lain in the back of your mind for years. They're not always pleasant or easy memories either, and we have to find a way to cope with them. Mine was to write them down, the good and the bad. I have regrets, as I'm sure most people do, but they are also experiences and lessons I have learned from. I've never pretended to be someone

The story of continuing abuse is an important one. Keith entered my life and I let myself fall into a trap, just as my mother had. Despite all that he put me through, I had loved him once, and the proof is my wonderful daughter Martine who continues to astound me with her unconditional love and support in everything I do. I have chosen to remain quiet for many years, and I haven't written this book now to put the record straight with Keith, but to recognise that a victim in childhood often goes on to become a victim in adulthood too. And to show other victims that, despite years of abuse, it really is possible to change the course of your life, to walk away and to make new choices. For many years, Martine and I faced life alone and there were times that were very hard, but our love for each other helped us through. We laugh when we remember the sofa with no legs, the television that had a green picture and the old car that broke down on every trip. Martine has always been there for me, and when success came into her life she never missed an opportunity to spoil me or the rest of the family. It is hard living in the public eye, but Martine has coped well and I thank her from the bottom of my heart for supporting me in telling my story.

Her love for LJ is enormous, and she has watched with pride and delight as he's grown into the fine young man he is today. He's doing well at school and, with the love and support from all the family, has achieved so much. I can't thank John McCutcheon enough for all his dedication to LJ: we have a son to be proud of.

Thoughts of Auntie and Chris are never far. Recently, while visiting a French abbey, I lit a candle for each of them. When I returned home, I told Kim, and she said that only a week earlier she had done the same.

As I creep towards my half-century, I look back on my life and reflect on many things. Despite everything, Kim and I have remained close, and I love her dearly. It doesn't always work that way in families, but I feel lucky to have a sister who was there through everything with me, and knows the truth.

As for children, it's a funny thing. We protect them with the ferocity of a lioness, and then the tables turn, and they want to protect us. Martine and Carrine are true cousins, and they often talk about Kim and me, and the things we've experienced. They've never made any judgements; they're our girls and we're their mums, and that's what we will always be. People come in and out of your life, and some stay for a short while, while others stay for ever. I feel Alan will be with me for ever. He knows my moods, my ups and downs, and my bad temper, and he remains at my side always. Alan knows the complete Jenny, warts and all, and still loves me. I can't believe my luck.

As for looking ahead, who knows? If I could

have anything, it would be to see a world without abuse. A world where we protect the future, by protecting our children, now that would be a dream come true. If I could continue writing too, that would be the icing on the cake.

I feel very lucky to be able to share my life and experiences, and I wish everyone happiness, health and hope. Most of all I am happy that Kim and I are no longer the silent sisters we used to be. Writing and living together, as we do now, has given us the opportunity to unite our memories and lay our ghosts to rest. The fight against abuse will go on, and I'm sure Kim and I will shout for justice from the rooftops, now that we are free of the past and no longer united by silence, but by a joint voice.

Kim

The first thing I want to say is that I have truly enjoyed working for the first time with Jenny. It went amazingly well, we grew together through the book and for the first time ever we talked about the nightmares we had both been through. We truly were silent sisters, never discussing the details of what went on as children or our fears for one another in adulthood. Writing this book has opened up the doors we hid behind for years. I'm no longer ashamed of what our father did, because I have learned that it really wasn't our fault.

I must also say that the hardest thing for me, in writing my story, was referring to my father as Dad. He was nothing of the sort and I feel it's an insult to the dads of this world that he should be referred to by the same name. I have always referred to him as 'the old man'. I hate him and always have; never have I hated anyone with so much passion. So to all the good dads of this world I apologise.

For years I truly believed that my nightmares as a child didn't affect me at all. I brushed them aside and locked them away deep in my memory somewhere, only remembering the funny, amusing and some-times loving times I experienced, most of them with Auntie. But of course they did affect me, although I'm not one to wallow in past miseries. I try to remain positive about most things in life and am proud of what both Jenny and I have achieved.

The list of moments of joy and pride we have shared with one another and with our children is endless. I was the person who screamed with joy and danced in the courtyard when Jenny's first book, *Behind Closed Doors*, went straight to num-ber one the week it came out. We were the rowdy family cheering and jumping over the seats when Martine won her Olivier award for *My Fair Lady*. And it was me who shouted from the top of the French ski slopes that I was a new grandma.

Like any mother I am very proud of both my children, and I would do anything for either of them. Daniel still lives near Graham and his wife in Switzerland, and Graham continues to support Daniel and to see his grandson Michael on a regular basis. Now that's what I call a good dad. Carrine is still happily married to Howard and they are blissfully happy, with their three-year-old son Lewis. Carrine is still working in childcare and is planning to become a teacher.

As for me, after 23 years I left the caring profession. I felt I needed to do something different, more challenging. And after gaining a degree in business management I took a managerial post within the police force. The work was totally different and I enjoyed it immensely. I made lots of friends and few enemies and remained there for four years until I recently left to join Jenny and Alan in France.

When they fulfilled their dream by moving to a smallholding in southwest France they invited me to come too. It was a big step for all of us and since the day we set about renovating the main farmhouse for Jenny and Alan and the little cottage for me, we have all shed tears of frustration. But the laughter and the joy have always overridden the moments of crisis we've had to weather, and as the dream takes shape we've known, without a doubt, that it was the right thing to do.

At nearly fifty Jenny and I are back in school, learning French every week. Each time we leave, our French teacher, Virgine, shouts with immense confidence *Au revoir*, and Jenny and I laugh all the way home because neither of us had a clue what most of the class was about.

Gone are the days of rushing round to Jenny's to show her my new Prada bag, or to look at the Jimmy Choo shoes that Martine had just bought her. Now she rushes home to tell me the local shop has drill bits and cement on special offer, and Alan's new set of wheels is a forty-year-old bright red tractor called Adam! Then, of course, there are the two boys, Frankie and Louie, our rescue puppies. If they steal another shoe or paste brush, I'm going to threaten them with the vet!

Jenny is happy and fulfilled with Alan, and although I still haven't found that someone special in my life, I remain confident and optimistic and feel that if it's to be, it will be. On the other hand, if I'm meant to be single for the rest of my days, at least I'll never suffer a broken heart again!

Jenny and I often sit out late and gaze up at the thousand upon thousand of stars we can see on a clear night. We rarely talk, each of us has her own private thoughts, but we both know that those are the same stars we gazed at as children, from the window-sill at Monteagle Court, wishing for a better life. And it's only now, looking back from where we have arrived, that we are able to say thank you.

Fin x

Don't Ignore Domestic Violence

For women and children.
Against domestic violence.

**Sandra Horley, OBE, chief executive of Refuge,
national domestic violence charity**

Domestic violence is a crime. It takes lives and it shatters lives. Every day in this country thousands of women like Jenny are living with the terror of domestic violence – two women a week are killed in England and Wales by a current or former partner. And thousands of children are witnessing domestic violence. In 90% of domestic violence incidents children are in the same or next room – and like Jenny – in 50% of known domestic violence cases, children are abused directly.

I would like to congratulate both Jenny and Kim for their courage in speaking out about domestic violence. Their stories will help thousands of women by encouraging them to seek help from organisations like Refuge. I have no doubt that *Silent Sisters* will show many abused women that they are not alone – there are thousands of women experiencing domestic violence every day of their lives. Like Jenny, all women have the right to live a life free from violence.

Many women reading this book, and who are experiencing domestic violence, may feel responsible and ashamed of the violence. Jenny and Kim are both right when they say that they were not responsible for the violence that they experienced. Let me be absolutely clear, no one is to blame for another person's behaviour. Violence is a choice and men who abuse women *and children* must take responsibility for their actions.

Growing up in a violent home can make a misery of a childhood. It creates confusion, fear and anxiety. However, as Martine has shown, with the right love and support, children can overcome their experiences and realise their potential.

Refuge is committed to creating a world where abuse does not exist and where children are safe. Refuge provides emergency, life-saving domestic violence services and campaigns to challenge negative attitudes to bring about positive and enduring change.

I have no doubt that *Silent Sisters* will give a message of great hope to the thousands of women who will read this book. Together, Jenny and Kim have helped Refuge break the isolation of so many abused women and children and in so doing are saving lives.

I would urge any woman experiencing domestic violence to get in touch with Refuge – it is a brave and positive first step to receiving the support and protection she needs and deserves. Or, if you are reading this and think that someone you know is being abused – a friend, a daughter, a sister or a workmate – contact Refuge. It could save a life.

Domestic violence is a crime. Don't ignore it – everyone has a responsibility to challenge violence. And from all at Refuge, a big thank you to Jenny and Kim for sharing your stories and for helping us to bring domestic violence from behind closed doors.

Freephone 24-hour National Domestic Violence Helpline, 0808 2000 247
run in partnership between Refuge and Women's Aid
www.refuge.org.uk

2006 marks Refuge's 35th birthday – 35 years since we opened the world's first refuge in 1971. In celebration of this milestone year we are launching a £3.5 million birthday appeal to help us sustain existing services and develop new services to reach out to women and children, like Jenny and Kim, who are in need of our services. If you would like to find out more about Refuge's work, or how you can help, or how you can make a donation, please visit *www.refuge.org.uk* or text REFUGE to 80172*

* The cost of the donation is £1.50 plus the standard network rate. Refuge will receive 92.5 pence

Refuge charity number: 277424